This book is dedicated to the malcontents and the unruly, the unwashed and the scruffy, the ones who drink strong lager at 9 am in the morning at shitty cold train stations waiting to travel to some shithole to watch their team play football.

Not all who wander are lost
J.R.R Tolkien

VIVA NUNO II

NUNOISM

Introduction (of sorts)

What is Nunoism? Is it a worshipping of a divine entity? A religion or a faith? No, it is none of these things. Nuno Espirito Santo is but a man however much we venerate him and Nunoism isn't about Nuno but really about all of us. How we go about our matchday experience is a many faceted act, in many ways there are as many ways of experiencing a football match as there are people there. This book is just one of those experiences, spoken truthfully and in the best way I can describe. There are parts you may disagree with and even some you may be angry about. That is the way it should be. This book contains not one negative word about our team or our Coach. This is a book about love and positivity, not hate and denigration. Who am I to judge these players? This Coach? Our owners FOSUN International? Sometimes I put Fosun in capital letters and I don't know why.

   Nunoism is about us, the supporters, and how this crazy journey has affected me and those around me. Apart from the joy of promotion last season it has affected me in many different ways. It has made me realise that the things I am scared of are numerous. There are loads of things that chill me to the bone. But even though these fears are many I have come to the conclusion that the dangerous things, the things that can really hurt you are few. We grow and we develop, we make new choices and moves within our lives. Nuno has made us all look at the world a little differently since he came. But is it him? Or is he just part of a combination of things that just seemed to materialise at the same time? I suspect the latter to be honest, that's why I have called this book 'Nunoism' instead of 'Nuno is fucking great volume two'. I think we have all played our part in the success of the team over the time Nuno has been here. Things have clicked bery smoothly into place for me and I know I am at the soft end of the whole endevour. I don't have to lie awake worrying about whether the frame of mind of an important player is stable and OK. I don't have to worry about players full stop, even if I do a bit. At times.

Nunoism is everything connected with the current time period since Nuno came. The way the fans have been, the fireworks during the night matches...sorry, before the match, it would be weird if they went off during the game. Nunoism is people making stickers and tshirts, songs and flags, it's the wrestling masks and the ponchos, the sombreros, it's Nuno running down the wing to celebrate with his players, it's Conor Coady telling the famous WWE wrestler 'Sin Cara' that 'You look well pal' at this hulking Mexican...with a mask on. Nunoism is the realisation that yes, we are on the path to Europe maybe but we must never forget where we have come from, and Nuno reminds us of this every week. I don't know man I get confused easily by what others think and do but here is another book about our season. It's a bit crazy in parts...a bit like Wolves.

Chapter 1

Modern Art Sculptures and a Broken Nose

Awake for the new season! With a face like a parking space, like a lock in at the local Chippy, like a feral coat, in the distance Nuno is looking at the sky wondering if it will ever be sunny....

Molineux Stadium is home in many respects. A home we always try to get back to and make a happy return. But we never really get there, we never do have that triumphant return. Molineux is being redeveloped and we never get back to pieces of the Southbank roof falling in on you. The chipped paint, the smell of piss and beer everywhere and we never see our players jog onto the pitch during warm up grimacing from a pair of shit knees, a bad hip or a cack ankle. No, we never get back to it even if our memories now are still crystal clear and we still expect to see the young faces we knew which have now turned into old cracked ones. I'm up here on the subway looking down Molineux street and it's warm and Juney. Summer at last, when you try to forget football for a few weeks but it's always there in the back of your mind wheedling around like some kids merry go round full of screaming children. Football. Fucking hell.

The movement itself was beautiful and graceful. Not football, no. It was 1977 and we were ensconced on the hill right in front of the University Art block. There are white concrete structures. Two great modern art sculptures, triangles and numerous columns or tubes. They are great...I mean not in an artistic sense of course. Although I could wax a bit about how they 'did' something for the area although I don't know what. There were footprints all over the bleedin' thing from us muddy footed youth. When we were bored at these times we would throw each other down the hill in front of it for a laugh. Sometimes there would be dog shit and the pissheads on their way to the match would laugh at us and we didn't care. We just tumbled laughing. We didn't give a shit.

Now, these great weird monoliths are quite high compared to Molineux and in those days it was a great place to watch a third of the pitch (The North Bank end). In those days as a kid (who didn't get pocket money) it was a great place to watch a bit of the game. That is until your feet which were trying to grip the smooth concrete started to ache a bit. But what 'movement'? My mate had just jumped up to stick the nut on a loud and reprehensible psuedo punk Tottenham fan who having been chucked out of the ground sought to watch our agreeable football from said artistic monument, shoving my mate off in the process.

Of course this act couldn't go unpunished but we were little kids really. But the need to watch the match overcame all our fear and anger so we all dived in then and gave him a little shoeing for his sins. But what is this? Violence and anger? This is how our team galvanises us, provokes us and we love every minute. How many times did this happen? Loads. But it's the first time I saw a pair of Flourescent socks and I was amazed even if the drops of blood from his conk were freaking me out against the bright white monoliths. The art none of us understood of course, but those drops of blood, well I knew that art well enough for sure. In those days there was a lot of drops of blood around the ground. I'm not having some teary eyed moment about how great those days were...they were a bit crap to be honest but the theatre of it? Crazy fist fights between grown men and us watching and cheering, already we had been hardened off in the fire of growing up in Wolverhampton in the 1970s. The drops would splatter the slabs around the subway right by the ground. It was art I suppose, a kind of gritty post modern thing for sure.

So he hobbles off into the town center in his home made Sex Pistols shirt and weird hair and we (all three of us) scramble up and perch ourselves right at the apex of the biggest triangle trying to see the game. We jostle each other and sometimes someone falls off and scrabbles up again gripping onto the smooth concrete in our 'Redhouse' trainers with a sole so fucking devoid of tread they are like silk slippers. You feel everything through your feet. I grab hold of a shapeless jumper to pull myself up. Or a leg. Or a bit of barbed wire.

You see there was another vantage point right at the back of the Southbank just above the toilets that away fans used. This was great, all you missed here was the Southbank end left corner bit. It used to be a small factory or something now demolished but leaving this part of the wall which was crumbling away slowly. Crumbling away that badly that often while we were up there watching the game the odd brick would fall off onto the poor sods underneath trying to have a slash. Shame. Often some giant angry Copper would run up to the wall and drag you off, you would get an occasional slap too. What was more fantastic was come November we would be throwing fireworks over there and running off laughing down the subway, voices bouncing off the walls and our feet slapping the slabs. Amazing. Later on this season I will be watching an FA Cup match from up there by the sculpture again and remembering those days even if it was colder and the bones ached a bit more.

Now everything is shining and new. Our team have navigated the blasted and scorched madness of the Championship. The Great Demon Warnock has been banished for a while at least. He will find other things to moan about in this division rather than just us. He will be seething at the player prices, the beautiful stadiums, the media bollocks. I watch him this morning on Sky Sports News while I eat some scrambled egg on toast and he seems....angry already. I laugh and choke at the same time. Nunoism eh? It's like dipping a hot chip covered in salt and vinegar into a runny egg yolk. Now what? Bread and butter mate.

What is this Nunoism? There are commandments for sure. Work hard, train, it's a holistic experience now and light years away from Dean Saunders turning up on a Monday morning to meet his new team, do some training...and forgetting his football boots and having to scrounge some off the kitman. What days they were and I think they couldn't be described better than Saunders knocking doors at Compton on the rob with his furtive little rat perm bobbing. Now this Nuno embarks on stage two of the plan and this? This book? Another mental joyride on the crazy train. I get up, let the dogs out, make a cup of tea, drink tea, smoke roll up, catch up on Wolves news, have some oats, take dogs for a walk, come back, make a cup of tea, have a roll up, catch up on Wolves news, fire up this laptop, write about Wolves and Nuno for an hour. So I can write a book before Crimbo and get it out for then too so you don't have to sit and watch Finding Nemo again while your inlaws do inlaw stuff and the kids are annoying you and the dogs been sick again from yamming the Quality Street. It might die but you don't care at this moment. Let's get drunk instead and get through the season so far, see what's been going on. It might be good to try out your new headphones too, put some music on while you read. I'll listen to a bit of Led Zeppelin and some solo Rob Planty stuff just for added Wolvoness.

Somebody told me a mad story about meeting Nuno when he first came to the Molineux. My mate was outside and saw him pull up outside the Sir Billy Wright stand. He went over to say hello to this Nuno bloke. They chatted for a few minutes before Nuno got spirited into the interiors of Molineux. My mate was impressed with him straight away and said to him, 'You might have all these new fangled ways of playing football but men like him (he pointed to the statue of Sir Billy) he was here before you and you walk in his footsteps'. It went something like that. When he told me I was getting roll up rage at the back of the South Bank while it was pissing down...and we were a bit drunk to be honest. So yeah a bit of artistic licence but you know what I'm getting at. Sir Billy was an original. He with others built this great edifice of Molineux and this idea of Wolves. But where Nuno and the Heroes of old differ is the way in which they have decided to hoist the gold flag even higher. But where do these new heroes fit into the Wolves narrative? We hardly know them, they don't really say anything to us, it's just plush polished media slices and interviews. The players all look like they are on Take number 34 and want to go home. But there are smiles, there are moments when we can see that they are human beings and maybe a bit like us.

What is Nunoism? I think for a start you can't quite seperate Nuno Espirito Santo from his Philosophy. I suspect that within the mind of Nuno is four seperate entities. I think you have a King in there. A proud and noble King like character. He has suffered some pain in Portugal. Some madness as a player and as a Coach. Maybe growing up too. This pain he has gathered into himself and it now makes his football and his ideas about football more than just a sport. Perhaps it has become a philosophy? This King in waiting aspect of his football is displayed in how he looks after his subjects and players. He knows them intimately. They are his troops and he is using them to seize the crown I suppose. The other three I will wax about later on in this book and see what the fuck drives him, try to ascertain what the hell is going on in this mans head. What the other three are I'm not quite sure of yet...talk to me at the end of this book when I have some idea.

We have to watch Wolves of course. In those days we would walk around the stadium constantly trying to find a way to scale the walls and watch the game. If we couldn't sneak in then it was off up the Art block. Scrambling up the art, holding on for grim death. If it was raining then tough tit. We would gather on top of the subway where you could see maybe 20 square yards of pitch and every ten minutes there would be action there and we would all go quiet...if there was a goal there (I think we could see half the goal) then we would go as crazy as the people inside the ground.

I know I'm getting nostalgic but the thing is dear reader...the more this club of ours progresses, the more I keep thinking back to those days. Perhaps it's getting old, or perhaps everything is that new and positive we don't quite understand what the fuck is going on. The past is treasured of course. The past is comfortable and warm sometimes...if you forget the early eighties. But what happened last season? I spent most of it half pissed watching our team smash opponents week after week with a squad of players that seemed to understand the job given to them by Nuno our Coach...sorry not our Coach, the players Coach. Or perhaps Nuno is our Coach too maybe? Do his sublime media appearances delight us? Inspire us? I think they do even if I think that there is a barely hidden aura of violence in the man. You see I thought last season he was a Wizard but now I think I am a bit scared of him.

It's all going to be crazy isn't it? The Summer spent fiddling with that fence panel that blew off, cutting the lawn...or the bits of grass and ruderal weed you call a lawn. I found myself cutting around the dog eggs on a few occasions. My leg busting all these pain tunes when I stepped in a hole or eight. God help us in close season. It's an abyss of football things. I know the World Cup was on but it doesn't give you the love that comes from watching your local team and don't hassle me about that. I will be honest of course, the close season has been a much needed break for me. I needed the close season, my head was everywhere and my body was broken. I watched us get dicked by a Sunderland team who hadn't scored in their stadium for months. I didn't care, we had done it, thank fuck. I nearly started crying but I knew if I started I wouldn't stop, even when they put me in the ambulance for a foggy trip to the asylum. Football. Fucking hell.

Our Coach Nuno Espirito Santo is probably in his garden right now, standing in the Summer twilight, smoking a Cigar and contemplating whatever strange things enter his mind. But are we any closer to what he actually is? I s there a possibility we may even come to know this character through his team rather than through the man himself. Could we even contemplate his mind through the trials of last season. We know he is passionate and that is all possibly. He was a Hero last season and I suspect he is again. I want to meet him, I want to talk to him and share a cigar, maybe a glass of wine but who am I? Who are any of us really. I know we become one when we are crammed into Molineux to watch our team. We share the madness as Nuno does himself. Am I in search of Nuno? I think I am...

Chapter 2

Linda Lease-Audi and some Summer Heat

Awake. With a face like a well fingered pocket, like a drunken mons nod, like a packet of fish heads...in the distance Nuno is looking at a teamsheet.

But it's a long hot Summer for sure. Global warming, global this and global that. Global bloody football as well. But it's hard to get that global groove on when you live in a small part of Wolverhampton and the heat is beating down on the top of your vehicle, the Tshirt sticking to your back, the dogs panting...the engine of the van is going 'tick-tick-tick' from an errant camchain and as I sit here I see Jota and Costa, Cavaleiro and Coady knocking the ball around the pitch with the same rythym as the overcooked engine and I close my eyes and I can see it, it is beautiful. But who are you Nuno?

On the Lichfield road sat in the van. There is traffic. Pull up to the bumper ba-bay in ya...long wheelbase battered Ford Transit. The dogs are hot. I'm hot. Everybody is hot. But not Linda Lease-Audi in her white Audi 4×4 who is aggressively dinking around inches off my back bumper in some hurry to do whatever Linda does in her 40k white fat arse carrier. I bet she has her Air-Con on full blast and fuck the Globe and the environment, she doesnt want her pancake make up to start sliding off into her double chin. I find myself staring at her in my rear view mirror. Her eyebrows look like angry slashes of a marker pen. Like Spocks Mom.

Of course in another world I would have gently tapped my brakes and annoyed her a bit but Linda isn't important today. She can wiggle her eyebrows all she wants. Now she's shouting something but my exhaust has fallen off months ago and it's noisy and the van is full of fumes. She has got purple hair. Nuno has signed a contract extension. I'm asking the woman in Tesco for a pouch of tobacco..they have photos on them now showing the various deaths you will suffer from smoking the odd roll up.

'Have you got the dead mans leg?'

'No only Hole in throat, tongue Cancer and open lung surgery'

'What about the baby that looks like a young Putin smoking?'

'No'

'Ok can I have a 30g packet of Hole in throat please'

There is a dichotomy here, I can feel it in my balls. It was sunny last year when our team buggered off to the Australian mountain land to do some of that sexy stuff we watched on a shitty GoPro somebody had wired up. Connection problems and Memories eh? They did double team sessions and then went out to dink the ball around some other Euro knobhead team we'd never heard of. It's happening again. I watched Jota skilling up wearing a pair of flip flops. I saw Costa looking like he had found a magic crystal of henchness and was waxing around with his new muscles. He's had the Coady trim. Short, business like. A fighting trim. They all look new and fresh like they have been dry cleaned or jet washed. I feel battered...I don't quite think I have got over the madness of last season yet, I don't know whether I am ready for another one to be honest, not yet.

But I'm awake at last. With a face like Grandmas elbow, like a tired cake, like a smashed arsehole...in the distance Nuno is crossing the T's and dotting the I's...

Coady looks cored up to fuck, looks like he has taken on some advice to ditch the muscle and concentrate on the mobility angle. But you wont move him off the ball. We will see Coady making attacking runs into midfield this season. Trust me. Mobile? He was quite nifty any way but now? Has Nuno given him the green light to impose himself on the upcoming seasons fixtures? I think he has. What does that mean for the team? We may see him chasing down potential attacks from faster opposition players. I see this. Linda Lease-Audis driving reminds me of a Moth booping a lightbulb. What's the matter with her. Fucking Star Trek eyebrows, Jesus Christ.

Rui Patricio has come to our club. I'd never heard of him before but he is a goalkeeper and Portuguese so of course I wouldn't have. He's very handsome and debonair of course. We have a great looking team apart from Doherty who constantly looks like he just remembered he's left the cooker on. Patricio eh? I see him at a pre season thing and he walks off the coach like a beautiful lithe beast. His hair is perfect, his strides are tight and on point, his trainers look like expensive Wizard slippers, he has a D&G Tshirt on and a man bag. He is tall, dark and incredibly handsome and instantly I move back in time...'Kendal show us yer arse' and there you have it. A gap of massive proportions. But I loved Mark Kendal and I don't love Rui...yet.

I watched some YouTube videos which is the extent of my 'research'. So automatically I get gigabytes of these graceful, beautiful swallow dives to all areas of his goal. Brave and creative movements where he saves the day again and again for his team. I like him straight away of course. Whatever incentives Uncle Jorge and Uncle Jeff have given him it worked. At least he wont get attacked at Molineux by foaming mouthed Ultras and masked thugs waving belt buckles around. It will be Brian and Gary with a protest bed sheet waving it around shouting incoherently about… something. The biggest injury will be sheet burn. Welcome Rui.

I hear a scream of expensive alloys on the kerb as Linda tries to take a corner in her expensive tractor...amazing work Linda. Your husband or partner will be pleased. Hundred quid a wheel to get that sorted?

The other addition that thine hand of Nuno the wisest one rested upon is Raul Jiminez. Back to YouTube. Whoah. He can bang them in. But he does other things too. Sexy things with his feet. This lad looks up as well. Gareth Southgate. Shit. I'm struck by that hollow feeling in me belly remembering last nights match against Croatia. God almighty. Croatia Modric is spouting his propaganda on the TV. We 'underestimated' Croatia. Fuck off. England beat themselves, we always do. You lot are just bystanders to the greatest tragedy drama in the world. That of the 'English Footballer'. It's a dramatic live production of many acts and characters. In some of the most beautiful parts of the world and on the grandest occasions. Jimmy Jimenez is from Mexico.

Alas my friends, the beauty of it all. Who would fucking swap being a participant in one of these displays? Who would give up the chance to feel this way? We lost but fucking hell we lived. I read the joy of Scottish and Irish fans, the Welsh too. How they bray and celebrate the loss of this team of men who at least kissed the sweet lips of that most troublesome, coy and shyest of Championships. The denizens of those countries may laugh and carouse. But at least we loved and hoped, just for a second. While you distil your bitter thoughts under cloud filled skies and in the greyest of lives.

The close season was filled with this madness. I mean those dull rumblings from last season are still echoing off the houses around here for me. The ghosts of those Championship teams still wail around. I'm sure that when our season kicks off that the wails will be silent for a while. I mean, Cardiff excepted. I don't see them adopting any philosophy beyond the snap, crackle and pop of last season. I wonder whether I may like to see Cardiff play us again. I have a strange affinity to them I think. Their ugliness makes my team more beautiful. We play a team in Switzerland. Basle. They are a nice team and nice players. Their supporters are nice and everything is still sunny I suppose. We beat them 2-1. Willy Boly clearance at one point. That man knows football. I see Boly, after football studying in some beautiful European University, sipping coffee outside a Café. But our team are having fun. They are laughing. They look chilled out. Nuno looks pensive. But Nuno? We have your back. How could we not after last season? What you did for us. How you made us feel.

Why did Pickford keep booting the ball upfield? Was it a collapse of our midfield? Would you have taken Kane off? Stirling? Post Mortem football. I was very proud of the team and Southgate. Losing in the semi final is the most English of things. The world cup is a brilliant thing. But why would you need a Cup made of gold to underline that you played some teams and won against all of them. Who were the best team? Belgium? Spain implosions. Argentina. The cup doesn't represent anything but a very abstract idea I suppose, that through some variable route the team managed to win most of its matches and lose none or one. I'm starting to warm back up now. Soon it will be the opening day. The end of the tabula rasa of everybody on nil points. What stories will it have for us this season? It fucking terrifies me to be honest. I'm not scared of the other teams. Not a bit. I'm scared at what amazing or terrifying things will happen as we traverse the country watching Wolves. Last season was fucking crazy. Now? In the Premier? The volume of insanity will be cacophonous. OK I'm warming up.

Chapter 3

Ajax and CS Gas Traffic Fumes in Walsall

Awake. With a face like a Lithuanian Chip shop, like a Welly on fire, like a day out in Wednesbury Ikea, in the distance Nunos eyes are stinging...

The sky was the colour of brass. Hot brass. I've worked in a foundry, I know what it's like. That factory was in Walsall too. Outside the Bescot 'Stadium' I waited for people and just wandered around in four square yards of space smoking roll ups. The team coaches turn up nearly squashing your humble scribe. Wolves coach is a funky chrome and black air conditioned thing all tinted windows and curvy love. Ajax coach turns up and it's a Happy Days coach. Poor bastards. I feel a bit shit smoking a roll up close to these gorgeous looking athletes. Windmill Gollums eh?

All these Ajax players look fit and veiny, tanned...and miserbale as sin itself. Avoiding the Ajax supporters waiting to see them. All four supporters. A couple of them shout 'Ejjionkkedahzzuurt' which I think is a name of one of their players. It sounds like they are having some kind of seizure. 'Aya Hunkadinka'. Horace say's that one is 'Der Lig' or something, and he's brilliant, but he looks sad and I don't think the sunny climes of Walsall are doing a lot for his happiness.

I feel like a gonk waiting so close to the players entrance. They might think I want some sort of interaction with them. But what do you say to Cavaleiro or Jota? 'Orite mate' and that's it. Hey Diogo, here's my 50 squid new shirt. Here's a permanent marker please scribble your unintelligible signature all over it please. There's Marc Overmars signing stuff. He looks fit and well. I suck my belly in and wonder about my man tits. These Dutch players trims look like they've been moulded on with clay. I haven't seen one smile yet. Walsall. Happy Days. Burning plastic smells. One of the Stewards has got a woolly hat on. Mate. Walsall.

"It's fucking hot ay it?".

Somebody mumbles as they walk past me trying to get near the players. This fan doesn't smell too fresh in their new Wolves shirt. It's those man made fibres. It's like wearing a carrier bag or something. They make me itch. I don't buy shirts because of this and I look like a blobby fat twat in them too. Let athletes wear these tight lycra things.

Helder gets off the Coach. Fucking hell he looks hench. What has he been doing over the summer? Boinging those protein drinks down his neck, eating power foods? Found a Dragon Ball? I wonder if his extra muscle will slow him down. The sun is baking my head. Walsall. I don't want to say too much about it but fucking hell. What a place that is. I'm feeling inclined to forgive Barnsley on a cold winters day. The whole ethos of Walsall is one lost on me. Their stadium makes me think of terrorising those old 4th division grounds in the 80's. Funny. Lost in thought for a moment. Bonatini walks past. He doesn't look happy for some reason. Somebody tells me they left two tickets for tonights Ajax v Walsall match on their dashboard in the car. Some bastard smashed the window and left two more. Bloody hell. Walsall could do with some Ajax and not the footballing variety

Let's talk about the football. A friendly against Ajax. They have some history although I'm not interested what it is. They have brought about thirty fans over and they are dotted around me. I keep thinking they are being sick but it is them shouting a players name again. They are a loud bunch. A few are drunk too. A few very quiet. Why are they quiet? Ryan Giles is running down the wing again and I can feel his thunder though the ground. He jinks a ball off the edge of his foot and knows where the thing will end up. Away from the presence of the Dutch fella marking him. Dink. He's off again our Gilesy. It's the first time I've seen him play I think. But he's a lovely player. The occasional fumble and loss of possession he has is purely initial 'meshing' with the team. We flick the ball around with aplomb. Cavaleiro making those diagonals into the box. The sure presence of Doherty. Jota thunders a header in. Our front three are still in first gear. Fair enough they sweat and they puff but it's early and the subtle Nuno riffs are there right under the brassy sky twirling around the Ajax defence, muted perhaps. Waiting. We look bloody dangerous to be honest and that rythym is there again lurking under the odd misplaced rusty pass.

Rafa Mir our new striker thing looks well handy. Physical. A bit mad looking. I like him. He powers about and is shrugging off players left right and center. One minute playing deep as a kind of a false nine as Jota and Helder move in like a pincer and crush a few half chances here and there.

Mir moves ably and into good space looking for that lay off from Neves to get some movement going. Ajax are aware and they squeeze in somebody to hold onto Rafa, keep an eye on him.

Horace has noticed a 'civilian' in front of us holding a stack of programmes and merchadise for signing obviously. Horace is staring at him and I wonder what he has done to raise the ire of the Horace so early into the match. Then I see it on the blokes neck, under the layers of dirt a tattoo...The Lord is my shepherd. Jesus Christ one of the North Birmingham Albion fans has sneaked into the ground to grab some autographs. He's in disguise, I think he has a Real Madrid shirt on so he looks like a football fanboy.

Horace has sniffed him out. This lads trim is home made for sure. Definitely a council haircut. He looks like a fucking chewed dog toy. His fingers look like canal condoms and he's biting his lip. He's a cuddly lad, he's probably hungry. Rafa comes close and I forget about our little Albion friend for a moment. The voice of our Captrain Conor Coady rises above the stinging tear gas air of this place. He's ordering people about.

Coady is 'dealing with shit' again. For ages I have been waxing about Coady. Every time I watch him my heart leaps. It's not a man crush, it's a footballing crush. When he negates an Ajax attack he does it by stealth and it's all academic. He is doing what Nuno has told him to do. Keep the line active and concentrated. Keep everybody in line. Coady shouts and demands that shapes be kept, that everybody is reminded of their business. I shout his name often and people are starting to look at me. Ajax fans close to me just smile. I am in my element. Walsall means that you are close and can hear nearly every time the boot hits a ball. We hear emotion and agility, intent and drive in every movement. Coady is bollocking Willy Boly.

Gilesy thunders past again, hooks a leg around an Ajax tanned limb. The player shouts 'Zrrty uurky zzzt' at Giles and our young bloke hooks the ball out. 19 years old he is. He looks mature and assured. He doesn't give a shit. I like that. He's off again down the wing. He spurns the affectations of an Ajax player with a shrug and maybe a dazzle of a smile too, his efforts are in vain, Ajax have a terrific defence but Giles knows that there is a way through. The Ajax defence is stolid and brusk, maybe even impassable? Physically Ryan Giles is a match for any of them, his impressions on the pitch remind me of Andy Keogh a little. But it's hot as I mentioned before and the heat is radiating off the top of this horrible place. The roof is sheet metal and it sucks in the sun and spits it out upon my head watching this display.

Coady is shouting at Gilesy about some defensive duty but our Giles doesn't really listen too much. He can't be a body in defence all the time. There is a point when he unleashes the combative, running into space with the ball element. That's good, that's positive. Nuno is shouting too. Everybody is shouting. These Dutch lads are playing a Champions league game next week. Giles turns his man again and is off. I like him. I think we will see more of his madness this season and I am looking forward to it.

They have attacks. Their bloke has five minutes in our box and bungs a header in. 1-0 to them. Yay! 'Guurgazzrt oplong zrt' the Dutch fans shout. Horace tells me this scorer is off to Barcelona. That's nice. Bye. Don't let the door bang your arse on the way out. The kid looks like a member of the Hitler Youth. He's got one of those Euro fringes and a razor cut that looks half done, he looks like he should be sobbing in a trench at Stalingrad.

I'm fixing into this fan friendly thing. I want to throw them down the stairs these Dutch fellas. But no. It's a friendly. Stop it Mikey. Nuno is not fucking happy. He is grooving a tracksuit today and his beard has grown. His pointing finger isn't waved around like a limp dick, this finger is fucking aimed. He aims it at players he would like to move into danger areas, to negate Ajax attacks, to define what happens on the pitch. The players are tools, everything has it's place and it's job. Yes, Nuno aims that finger like a magic wand and the team shift and move under his will. That is the way it has to be now. Total discipline but with a chaotic positive angle too.

Boly blocks another foray into our box. Mr Boly is a poetic beautiful thing in defence. Bravery and vision. His foot will appear in mid morning lucid dreams for those Dutch blokes tomorrow. I don't think he is too bothered about Dutch passy the bally quick and easy stuff. Ajax play some sexy balls around. Neves understands it totally and pings the ball to feet. Poetic like Boly just poems about different things I suppose. Boly has milliseconds to decide. Ruben has two or three. It's a different quality to one we watched last season in the hellhole of the Championship…Fulham aside of course. It's enjoyable and artisanal football played by craftsmen who respect each others trade. So there are moments of brilliance. Oh God Boly again. What a bloke, he just sent an Ajax player into limbo with a neat twist. My eyes water from some fumes blown in by a weak breeze. I can smell kebab too, and sweat. This Albion doughnut in front of us isn't very clean. I wonder to myself what sort of evil chemicals are being lashed around this atmosphere. My eyes are sore and there is a definite smell of Sulphur in the air and it can't be this half washed Albionite in front of me.

Coady delivering that beautiful pass from the edge of his own box to the feet of a Wolves player 30 yards away. Bonk. Right on the foot. I may offer Coady as an Acolyte of Nuno. He understands fully the academic and philosophical ideas Nuno puts forward through the medium of his coaching staff. Coady understands because Coady is highly intelligent. The ball delivered to the feet of a Wolves player. We stand up in anticipation. We are alive again in this desert of industry. The whole team looks like they have stepped up a couple of gears since last season. There is more twang to them and more zing. They do not look like a team that have been on Holiday. A Wolves player flashes past us...

Who is it? Giles again. Boom down the wing he goes again. Neves wants it. A pass here and there between our Gibbs White experience and Neves. Curling between the Ajax midfield threatening. Jota prevalent and alive to any ball. Cavaleiro wanting it. Cav isn't vocal but his intent is sure and real. Into the box he goes, he shoots. Blocked. The Ajax player grimaces. Flesh slapped Cavaleiro love. Pure and simple. But coming into the ground earlier we pay for parking and give the money to a dude in a reflective coat who looks the fucking spit of Cavaleiro. Helder fends off a lunk of Dutch funk. Physical Helder. He is away and yes. There is a push and Helder lets that push become a deliberate shove and he tumbles to the ground in the penalty area. Peno to us. Ruben steps up and scores. 1-1. We've got Neves. Ruben Neves. And I've never completely understood how.

It's still early days of course. There are new bodies to assimilate. Patricio in the stands wondering what's going on. He was in Russia the other week getting his World Cup gimp on. Now he's at Bescot and the hot sun, the eyes stinging from the fumes that roll off the M6 yards away. Nuno demanding action from the touchline. I don't think the environment even bothers Nuno. It could be an all singing all dancing European super stadium for him, or a gentle park kick about. But his idea is paramount. To play his way. To play the way he wishes. And among the pretty players and the super quick touches of the ball Wolves press. Always pressing. And in defence, poised. Ready again to move, pass, to delight and probe. Still. It's a friendly and the groove is refined and passion restrained.

There are that many subs I forget who's come on and gone off. There are players in our new shirts I've never seen before. Strange names. It's all preliminary this stuff. The season is a long way away really and already we look highly dangerous. This momentum from last season shows no real signs of abating. The team still looks hungry. They look focused too. You could see the hunger on Leos face as he sits and watches the game. He wants to be on there, playing, fighting. Rafa Mir makes a run into the final third and for a minute I am seeing Steve Bull running. Fucking hell Mir is fast. He thunders a header too. That Steve Bull-Rafa Mir dichotomy is strong for me. I like him, not because he reminds me of Bully in the way he plays and runs but his intent. This lad will explode this season I think, if Nuno can get him more angry of course. You see Mir has also put on some muscle. I see some close season stochastic fiddling, some long hours in a dark room poring over possible teams we will face. I suspect Nuno and his staff have built up some idea of how we will play against every team already.

Everything is tanned and hot summer happy. Your eyes gently get back to normal away from Walsall and the M6. Your new shirts look beautiful, the football looks beautiful, our players handsome and debonair, confident and eager. Are we confident? Ar. Warming up ay we. As we drove around the back of the stand to get away I saw a bloke having a shit in a corner. Fucking hell.

Nuno walks back to the Team Coach like a stalking Tiger, but his eyes seem relaxed and chilled and he smiles at the fans surrounding the Coach. He signs some autographs and I am a few metres away, close enough to maybe push aside the little snot noses with their sticky hands clutching things to be signed, adults wanting shirts done, maybe a sideshow to actually talking to Nuno. But I stand back. I am in search of Nuno but Nuno is not really here, not yet, his mind is swirling with ideas about the game his team just played, how they performed, the new signings, everything in detail. But I do se the Nuno in other things. The way Coady walks back to the Coach, the way Patricio stands and smiles, the urgency of the staff in depositing large sports bags full of kit into the chasm of the compartments at the side of the Coach. Nuno is there. But not here, not yet. I awake the next day to the news that Barry Douglas has been sold to Leeds United. I don't know quite how I feel about it yet...I sit down and write something...

Chapter 4

Ikeme, Chasing Horses and a Farewell to Duggo

Awake...with a face like a spaghetti breakfast, like a glass of fizzy tea, like a Giraffes armpit...in the distance Nuno is selling Barry Douglas...

God bless you Barry Douglas. Bristol. I was in tears. We have flogged him to Leeds. Somebody tells me he was pissed off because we are seriously looking at someone called Jonny Otto. Duggo threw caution to the wind and approached Nuno The High Priest with protestations and was quickly excommunicated from the squad. Don't try and hassle the 'man' who Nuno Santo is turning out to be. Bit of hardness from Nunnyman, I like it.

My van is fucked. It has a dodgy wheel bearing, suspension issues, a crack in the windscreen, one of the dogs puked in it years ago and the smell never really went. But fucking hell what a vehicle. It has took me to the tops of mountains, it has been filled with half naked models snorting cocaine while I talked about chalk from a geological perspective. They found it hilarious. They spilled out of my van the next morning and all my friends saw them. My reputation is enhanced, if only they knew I had just sat there reading and smoking my pipe before I dropped off to sleep in that tangle of tanned legs.

But my van is not what I need any more. It is still brilliant, but now I want an auto gearbox, a faster responding throttle, petrol, an estate. You see the vehicle I have now hasn't changed, it's still my favourite van I've ever owned…but I've changed. It's me who isn't the psychopath any more who does wild things in the mountains. I've chilled out. I don't like driving any more. I want to feel like I am sitting in a comfy chair and I only have to move one foot.

Thing is about Barry is that he hasn't changed. He's still the consummate athlete, the dead ball expert, yes, he had much more to his game than that but…fucking hell Leeds are getting a bargain. Barry hasn't changed but we as a club have. Douglas was a tool we needed for part one, the Championship. Now there is a different problem, an obstacle in the way. That is the pits and pratfalls of the posh end up there. Premier league shit. Things are different up there. Last season we were playing Ron Argoscatalogue and Jemail Jermallionz-Brown or whatever their names were. Now it's going to be games against Runnio Fastio and Jesus Lukatimgo. Could we expect Barry to face these denizens of the Premier? We will never know. That particular problem must be played out in an alternate universe. But never in this one.

This next stage of the grand plan maybe calls for a nexus if you like of highly talented, skilful, artistic players, around them constantly revolving satellite team who are utilised ruthlessly but with great reward by the subtle management of Nuno and the Fosun entity. We of course will love them and then have to wave goodbye as our club makes a profit on each one which we then utilise in the transfer market buying depressed young Mediterranean men who lack direction. Bringing them under the tutelage of the coach that will be one of the greatest football coaches in the world in the next ten years. They join the team, they learn the philosophy and then they are sent out like Missionaries into the league that has been lacking any viable philosophy for a long time. We will grow. Witness the propaganda already. They are the drums of war being beaten by people that do not like us, and do not like our owners. Dark times ahead of course.

Just a thought. Farewell Barry, but not goodbye. Come and see us soon with Leeds and don't forget to lose the knowledge you learned (if you play us again).

I suppose your life changes a little when you have dangled your feet over the edge of the abyss, then have a little sneaky look over the edge to see what's going on down there. What is down there? Not a lot my friends.

Carl Ikeme isn't going to play in goal for us any more. Something else has captured his attention. His life. That thing we take for granted most of the time, you never really take any notice of it while you are busy living it. Life is a wild horse you know. When we are young we can spend most of our hours running after it, trying to tame the fucking thing as it runs over the green grass of our existence. We grab it's mane and hang on as it stampedes across the meadows hanging on for grim death, trying to get on top of it and always getting thrown off. At these times we feel tired and settle ourselves down in the sweet grass looking up at the blue sky until we have the energy to get up and start chasing it again. We do that all the time.

For ever in fact. Get up, shake the dust off and again we are running after that beautiful pony all sleek and muscled. It tosses his head and neighs so loud it shakes the ground. Again we chase it, try to get on, get a leg over and fucking hell, see stars as we are dumped back onto the ground. That horse gallops a short distance away, it neighs to the sky, but it's not laughing at you, it's encouragement. To sit on it? No.

When I finished my chemotherapy I went for a skate, tried to catch that pony, tried to catch it good. Off it went. Dumped at the bottom of the quarter pipe in Wednesfield skate park. Lying in the dust and the piss, the litter and the crap, holding my ribs trying to catch my breath so I could get back on. Carry on fighting and chasing as the fucking thing has me back on the ground spitting blood out. A bit angry.

Carl is at that point where he is the proverbial would be rider. He's watched that pony for a year now as he has been too tired to chase it. Sometimes it comes close and sometimes it is far away running over the hills. He glimpsed it you see. When his kids smiled at him. When people showed him some love, when he looked out of his window and saw the wind moving the trees outside, the blue sky. All of this, all of it. But some times it's dark and you can hardly see the pony running. Sometimes all you hear is it's hoof steps, a thunder low and bass like. You struggle to see it but just glimpses. Flashes behind the trees, the crashing of the undergrowth.

Carl has decided to retire. I knew he would when I heard about his diagnosis. Sometimes as you sit back resting from chasing that Pony you get a little tired and it's good to feel the sun on your face and the wind on your skin. You have taken your shoes and socks off and are feeling that cool dew covered meadow grass between your aching feet. You feel like maybe it's too much trouble chasing that horse around. Sometimes it's good to just relax.

These thoughts havent even got a football angle. He will not play for us any more. I am sad about that. Ikeme trotting towards the Southbank always filled me with pride in my team. I trusted him. I knew what kind of a player he was but…the abyss, that's a thing. I knew he would beat it of course. Inside Carls head is the Warrior but also the lover I suppose. Ikeme isn't daft, he is a Philosopher also, a Wizard between the posts. Long hours having that shit pumped into your veins gives you ample time to think even if the chemical makes you sick, foggy headed and forgetful. Football is now not really important. He will still love it of course and at times he will feel sad that he is not out there fighting and clawing at a fast shot at his goal or wrestling away snothead big centre forwards. Oh fuck yeah he will remember those battles but this fella has just had the hardest battle ever. For his life. Did he catch the Pony? Nah.

You see…there comes a time when the beauty of the horse running free over the grass kind of captivates you. As you sit tired and sweaty, hands peeling from battle, but feeling also the warm sun on your face. You start to appreciate the Horse running. All of a sudden you don't want to chase it any more, instead you want to admire it. The energy and the delight, happiness as it flicks its mane as it gallops and jumps. This is the point where our Carl is now. Admiration for life and what life is. The courage that the Horse has as it escapes you again and again. But still stays close. Of course as you sit there admiring this Horse it will come closer and closer to you and eventually it will let you stroke it's flanks, ruffle it's mane, it will let you give it an apple maybe too. The Horse is quiet and tame not because you chased the thing all your life but because you realise that it's beauty and it's freedom should be your life. You will never possess your life but you can admire it and learn to live with it as equals I suppose.

Enjoy these days Carl, they are precious and beautiful. Fulfil your dreams and enjoy your family. Cast your mind forwards and make great plans my Brother. Warriors we are mate, we know both love and war so let those wild horses run where they will. Carl is deep in my mind as I walk down the cut. The Lily pads have flowered, lovely white petals. I have one eye on them and one eye on the dog eggs.

Chapter 5

Down the Canal with Gaz Mastic, Superfans and Villa Real

Awake...with a face like a shit trim, like a beer monsters hug, like a parasitic laugh...in the distance Nuno isn't thinking about canal walks...

I was sheltering under Perry Hall bridge yesterday with the dogs as it has started to fucking pelt it down. Me and Gaz Mastic who has appeared out of no where his little legs flapping and his little Staffy 'Mucky' dragging him along in a rush for shelter. Where has the sun gone? It's a bit cold. I came out in a t-shirt which is now sticking to my back. I scrounge a roll up off Gaz. He smokes 'Drum' loves it. His baccy is dry unlike us. His rizlas are a bit damp as I try to take out one and pull twenty out. Bollocks.

I have just given my first 'live' poetry reading. I wrote about Derek Dougan, indeed I waxed quite lyrical even if the rain had dampened my bit of paper I had scrawled on. Even if the dogs were pulling me this way and that to sniff a piss wet leaf or three, even if my audience were half pissed on the deathly blue cider they drank. They laughed and cried but to be honest they could have been emotional over anything. One of them didn't have a tooth in his head. He threw his head back to laugh and he looked like a crying infant.

'Shouldn't have sold him Mikey…he did us a great job last season' Gaz says. I like listening to him. He's got that Willenhall Black Country twang going on. Of course I think that perhaps Gaz might have a point or not, I don't know. It's hard to roll a fag with two Staffys trying to pull you in half so then can lick a piss covered nettle fragment. Barry Douglas. You would think he would buy some new jeans with the money he earns. Look. His fucking knees are hanging out of them!

Opinions are great, I love them. I love it when people talk to me about my team and discuss the whys and wherefores of the tactics, team sheet, management. Everything. I disagree with most of what I hear but that is also good. You see it's all information, all data. I have lost count of the times people have said something to me about the team that has made me re-evaluate what my thoughts were. A prime example is Dave Edwards. I was a total fan boy. I loved singing his song at Molineux. I loved everything about Dave…until somebody sat down next to me and disassembled his method of playing football. This dude took Dave Edwards apart succinctly and academically. This fella knew more about football than me and it was great to listen to him. I took all of what he said on-board and watched the next weeks match with everything he had told me 'on-board'.

Fuck. He was right. Dave Edwards did point a lot. Then Dave went to Reading. Bye Dave. Gaz is muttering about beer, then a Midfielder, then a Striker, then a left back or something. He wants all these positions filled in our team. I just nod and try to keep the roll up from curling up like a forest fire. This baccy is dry and stengy. On social media the fume is real.

Threats and counter threats, madness and crazy shit. People losing their shit. People saying shit. It's shit. Not fun and not informative. But it is what it is. It is pure 2017 shizz. Same stuff as what we read last year. We lose at Derby in a friendly. Jesus Christ we are doomed. The tendrils of fear that roll through our stomachs when a bit of a bobbly road comes up. We are assembling a team that can challenge for the top half of the Premier league. We are two weeks away from our peak. Physically at least. Mentally who knows?

Superfans. 'Am I a Superfan Gaz?' I ask Gaz who chuckles...'I wish ya was I'd stand you in the corner of the bedroom'. I laugh but I don't get it for a few seconds. A shoal of Roach swim past us as the dogs smell patches of historical piss under the bridge. A dude runs past in full running gear, he's running fast like he's trying to escape something. He doesn't look like he's enjoying himself. His face is red and bloated, then I notice he's got an Aston Villa training top on. I dont wish a heart attack on him but I hope he trips up and his hand squashes in some dog cack...and maybe he gets some in his mouth too. Or falls in the canal...maybe gets tangled in a bike frame...and drowns.

Sometimes I don't enjoy Social Media. It can be full of Vampires you see. Especially when you interact with any of them. They can suck all the joy out of your day in seconds with a few choice words. Sheila from Wordsley or Liam from Penkridge, a dichotomy if ever there was one. Two sides of the same coin really. One laments as he gobbles can after can of Monster while he plays Football Manager or twiddles with his fantasy football team. The other tweeting as she drives herself or the kids around swerving in and out of traffic. One peels off the pepperoni stuck on his tshirt which is stretched over his fat gut. The other channels her menopause angst at slights on Barry Douglas's character…she will never forget that time she flicked her bean over Baz in his Stoney as she digested a bottle of Lambrini. Our Monster drinker checks Sheilas entire social media history for an angle he can get at her. Vampires mate. But maybe I'm being too loud about it. Social Media is the new Coliseum. Peoples denigration and bullying of other accounts is the new entertainment. Somebody calls me a 'Superfan' again. I am a little sad.

This two weeks before the season starts is No-Mans-Land mate. What is a Superfan? It's somebody who has nothing in their lives apart from Wolves. So everything is amplified, everything is LOUD, every subtle twitch of a finger on a screen is a fucking declaration of war. We lose our minds over a rumour of Douglas and Nuno falling out with each other. We extrapolate our bitter and twisted simple existence onto those we support and look to for support. We lose our minds that we haven't got anybody in the club in the positions we want filled.

We want, and we are often disappointed. They don't have his size of shirt in the club shop and for fucks sake he's going on holiday Monday. It's a 'fallacy' and a 'fucking disgrace' that he can't get his kids the new fucking shirt. I haven't been able to spunk fifty quid on a shirt for years mate. I signed a few books behind the North Bank a few weeks ago. A fella came out of the club shop with five carrier bags worth of Wolves stuff. 'I've just blown £600 in there' he says to his kid who was a bit slow catching up as they walked to their car. The kid looks bored. Dad gets in the car and I watch him fingering his buys as his kid looks out of the window at me signing books. Best Wishes. Petalengro. My match day expenditure will be a Coffee somewhere before the match…in fact I know the place well. A coffee machine. A mug of Latte something. £2.10p. I used to teach the girl who owns the place. She will put me a chewy cookie on my plate for free as I used to give her the odd roll-up at break time because 'Mikey if I dow have a fag at break I'm gonna fucking lose it'. How many roll ups did I make the kids I taught? Loads probably. I got into trouble at school constantly...as a kid and as a Teacher. I wonder if Nuno would be a good Teacher? I could see him teaching Science. Like me.

Trust in Nuno? Fuck off. Nuno is a giant among us, philosophically and footballing wise but does that leave him untouchable? Of course it doesn't. Fosun are the same, a great business that dwarfs anything we have seen before. Must we bow down and tug our forelocks to our Chinese Overseers? Nah mate, not a chance. When you stop debate and exchanging ideas then the force that the whole crazy train has just grinds to a halt. Do I trust Nuno? Fuck yes. Who am I to challenge his thoughts? I am untangling dog leads and trying to peel a Rizla off a stuck together mass of skins. I'm fucking useless, I don't know why anybody listens to me at all. Do I trust Fosun? Of course I do…there isn't any intellectual basis for me to challenge their ideas…yet. It's the Chinese Revolution and sometimes I feel like everybody is having fun but the revolution is all smoke bombs and people walking fast and I cant quite keep up with my dodgy leg. I limp after it waving my flag with a big picture of Nuno on it.

Monster gobbling Liam on social media says that Douglas doesn't defend as well as most Premier league players in similar positions. He posts a graph. It's interesting and correct. Douglas lack the ability to attack a player running towards him. His covering play isn't brilliant. Sheila says that she feels that John Ruddy has been unfairly treated what with the Ikeme news and Patricio coming in under a cacophonous thunder of bean flicking joy. I tend to agree Sheila. So the whole pantomime grinds on like some incredibly fucked up Punch and Judy show. Yes he did! No he didn't! Yes he did! This lack of football has made a vacuum of information. People fill it with their own shit.

But we can we subtly point out some areas that are concern to us? Of course we can. As a club and as supporters we can discuss what's going on up at Molineux towers whether it's negative worry-wort bollocks, angry ranting or sublime dismantling of the whole train ride. Because that's how we make our ideas stronger. By talking and debating things that may seem uncomfortable to our cosy existence at the present time. I remember reading one of those quote sites where some doughnut said 'Tea women and Busboys always have the greatest ideas'. Who ever said it was right of course. So Liam from Penkridge who jerks off over Brazilian fart porn might have a bloody good point. Sheila from Wordsley might also have one tucked among the Donald Trump memes and the big black dildo she keeps under the bed covered in fluff.

Gaz is talking about his love of fishing as we watch the Roach swim past. I wax a little about the woodcarving I'm doing and we spend ten minutes waxing while the rain blows over and then we part. His little legs flapping, my weird limp. I think maybe these fractured online personalities may have some point in all their invective but I don't know what it is yet. I'm not looking at them. I'm watching those bastards we are going to play this season. I'm watching their fans closely for propaganda. I'm watching the Media Giants mate, waiting. It's pointless arguing with those around you when there is a bigger enemy waiting for us.

Football is the craziest fucking thing isn't it? Drives you mental, makes you write books in the dim light of an environmentally friendly lightbulb, makes you cry in front of other men, makes you rage too.

Being smart is a strange thing…I don't mean 'smart' as in clever, I've never been that…but smart in terms of appearance. I wonder as I bump shoulders with Jeff Shi and Laurie Garglypimple in the catacoombs of the Billy Wright stand whether that particular zeitgeist is a thing. I've got my hands on a corporate ticket. It's all very nice and Tettenhall like. Ladies here walk around with their norks out which is not displeasing to me as I enjoy fleshy delights. Am I not a man? I try to stay focused and aware. Try not to say 'fuck' or bollocks' or 'bastard' too much. There is carpet and curtains and many servants on minimum wage doing the servant thing. I make conversation with all the workers doing their shizz. You see I have been there too. I have waited tables. I know this stuff. So I am chatty and friendly with all the staff I meet asking them about their day and all the happy small talk I can muster. The staff like our little table so now we get our dinner first, our drinks magically appear from nowhere...I look around and the snotty gits who didn't unleash this love of the minimum wage staff are devoid of love. Their dinner takes ages and their drinks plod to their tables. A lot of people don't look happy to be here and that's a shame. Maybe they should have a day in the Southbank to make them appreciate this a bit better. Everybody is polte here and it's as weird as fuck. There are no Cops giving you the hairy eyeball, we aren't being recorded by video or having our photographs taken. I feel like I'm in a strange film or something. One of my teeth has come loose and I'm wondering whether it will come out as I'm talking to somebody. That would be hilarious. I guess if it comes out I will tuck it into a napkin and try not to smile.

The team look very smart and so do I. The new infrastructure in the Billy Quiet stand is also smart. The glasses in the Executive thing where we ate Corporate food is crystal. It 'tings' beautifully as we clink glasses like Kings drinking 30 squid bottles of wine. Can I extrapolate my penchant for Motorhead T-shirts with holes in I was wearing most of the week with our fortunes? I'm not even going to try. But there is a bloke dressed as a Gas Boiler walking around the Hawthorns and I'm watching Mouthino warming up. Patricio looking all shades of awesome. What is a Villa Real? A team. A bloke is walking around West Birminghams ground dressed as a fucking Gas Boiler…I will let that sink in. Somebody mentions us playing European Football soon and I agree but I pretend not to hear that observation. Never look too far into the future mate. Take things easy, let things slide into place. Let the plan unfold. I guess that Nunos plan is a many tentacled thing and complicated too. But it's all based on hard work and improvement. Nuno has set his stall out now let's see who wants to buy.

Sitting in the Billy I was struck by the amount of kids in there with their new Wolves Tops, also the amount of people in there who didn't really have an idea of what they were actually watching. The zeitgeist in here is a bit moany to be honest. Several of our new men are shit apparently. This is the most virulent word I hear in the Billy. Most of the chatter is non football related. A lot of old men in here just sit and scowl at the pitch like it's all some kind of effort. A woman walks past with her boobs hanging out. Amazing.

The kids gave me a glow of happiness, the future mate. I also notice a lot of bald men too. Does success make your hair fall out? I watch Nuno for a bit. He's shouting something at Moutinho and motioning with his hand. Moutinho moves position, immediately he collects the ball and is in space. Nuno is conducting this symphony mate, Nuno is doing his Wizard shit already. That's why he stands on the touchline. He's smelling the football, analysing it, he's a player himself, he is coaching but fighting for every ball, making decisions, a shout here, a word of warning there, a slap on the back for a player, soft words and hard words. Beautiful to watch and to be a part of.

Of course itching in these clothes was offset by the spectacle itself, and it was a spectacle in spite of the whole thing being a Pre-Season Friendly.

Villa Real not Villa Fake. Beautiful footballing team absolutely oodles away from those Witton bastards and Duffel bag head Steve Bruce we had to contend with last season. Nuno I suspect had put out his inked in squad and how he expected them to play when Everton pour down from the North next week. So we see Neves and Joe Moutinho in midfield. What's Joe like? Well he was deffo quality. Minor teething problems for sure as Ruben and Joe hassled for the same space a few times and there was a bit of Ying Yang going on as they found each others bumpy bits a few times. But the quality of Joe Moutinho was apparent. Some of his area management was gorgeous to watch as he tracked players and moved the ball around. Was it an upgrade on Saiss and Big 'Olf? Ar it was for sure. Big Alf got a nice hand when he came on. Have we upgraded on him yet? I'm not sure. Maybe an Alf type player will be coming in. Monday/Tuesday/Wednesday and Thursday are going to be mad. Shopping possibly, I dunno. I like Jonny Otto. He looks like he should be driving a cab and doing drug deals. He looks a bit mental.

Saiss in defence? Ah well theres a problem at the moment and of course you can't lump a player like Saiss into that hotbed of madness without some lubrication. Villa Real started putting some slicing balls across the back three. Those balls had a slight clockwise spin on them which automatically lead Boly, Conor and Saiss to hesitate a little, they are split and the Villa Real pacey bloke who's name I forget dinks one over Patricio and boom. 1-0 down ahk. Teething aggravations. First half madness. But it was all there. Jota doing his Wolf thing. Tenacious and aggravating movements that plucked the ball out of no-chance periods into all of a sudden a movement and a chance. Everything of course was defined by that 'friendly' aspect and fair enough the contact between the two sides was muted for sure. Legs being pulled out of tackles and contact minimal and soft.

But our shape was lovely. Our position high up the pitch unleashed pressure. This Spanish team were put on the back foot a few times. Lovely to see and better with a four course meal inside you…have I mentioned I was in corporate? Suits man, everywhere. Decent shoes, clean collars, moist handshakes with the lizards of the Billy. Crazy. I watch Coady for a bit. That makes me happy always. People have been giving him neck… that's … just like…your opinion man. So Coady positions a beautiful cross field pass to Jota forty yards away. I clap and shout. People look at me. Billy Quiet. I'm not sorry. I look great in my new Burton sales outfit but I've got odd socks on and my pant holes could strangulate a bollock if I'm not careful. Shape is good. Saiss isn't understanding the Coady and Boly thing. Apparently there is a Cheeseboard and wine at halftime. Instead of a roll up by the Grit Bin. I fancy a roll up to be fair. A chat with some lunatics. Some dude is shaking my hand and he thinks I am someone else called Darren. I laugh. Cheese at halftime. Darren for fucks sake.

Wolves have done a good job of the executive groove inside the Billy. Air conditioning. Staff running around everywhere. Jeff Shi pops up every five minutes and he's running around like a blue arsed fly with his Joey right by his elbow. We are given excellent service as the waiting staff rapidly suss out that we are normal. Of course we get great service as we are laughing and yamming. It was A'La Carte? Something like that? Big plates and the food scrunched into the middle all sexy looking. Not enough mash….sorry fondued potato or something. Not two ladles of mashed tayta with a chunk of butter and a splosh of milk. No Sir. I asked the Waitress if some of the food had fell off. She laughed. Some tables didn't eat their cheeseboard so we nicked it and ate it as ours was all gone. I probably wont be in there again this season. It was a Spring onion that confused me. And a little weedy carrot on the plate. I know this is fancy food because I've only just started eating and it's gone. I nicked two lemon tarts nobody ate at the last Wolves dinner and shoved them in my suit pocket for later. I eat everything here. Nothing left. There was a little mini Shepherds pie the size of a fifty pence piece. Mad mate. But there is nothing left to cram into suit pockets today. I am hungry and it is all gone.

Second half, on comes Ryan Bennett. OK we knew that was going to happen. Strange how he was denigrated by Norwich fans and yet five minutes on the pitch and Coady-Boly look a much happier unit. Those slicey dicey balls are cut out by Ryan. He is assured and solid. Weird thing is that I never wrote much about him last season but now…yeah Ryan Bennett. I see you, I see your presence mate. Shape in defence is now stoic and solid. Perhaps Coady can now take his eye off the ball and watchdog what's happening in front of him. That's what happens. He's confident in Bennett to his right and can channel his thoughts elsewhere, which he does filtering out attacks on the box. That sliced cross box ball for their rapid nine to chase onto? Gone now. Coady is out of his head shutting off the route. Closing shit down. Trusting Bennett. Coady does nothing wrong for me, ever, we are lucky to have him.

Jimmy Jimenez I liked. He looked hungry as fuck to be honest but still needs a bit of that communication love between him and Jota-Costa. But he was physical and fast. His movements were lovely, he got a beautiful tap in for our second goal that was moistened by the temerity and full metal jacket lunacy of Costa on the touchline goofing his feet everywhere in order to pop that ball out of the melee he was involved in to get the ball onto the feet of Jota who was pegging into a crossing position for the cross Jimmy would tap in. Helder bloody Costa you marvel. That's what I want to see. It's our ball, and no, you can't have a fucking kick of it. Piss off. He looks stronger and I like it a lot. He got some shite at the start of last season. Jota and Jimmy seem to have some understanding going on. I like the idea of that.

Strange thing…watching our potential subs warm up. Fucking hell. Quality subs. Blokes you would actually play from the start in your first team. Three blokes with the physics and the ability to change a game. Quality. First the cheese selection at halftime and now the insanity of these beautiful players warming up right below us. They flick a leg out in some strange way that makes me wince. My hip would dislocate if I tried that. I'm getting that age where stuff is crumbling away. Teeth, bones, muscle, thought processes.

Everything looks good and I sit in the Billy quite happy with the way things are going. We press high, play the ball from the back. Press and consolidate our shape onto the game. Watch the opposition try to ameliorate the passion and speed of our football. They counter with some excellent football of our own and for a moment I'm transported to Barnsley or Preston last season. The cold and the rain. The awful quasi-football of lacklustre shameful teams we faced. It's getting hotter but I think we can impinge some idea on this season to come. We look good, we don't change shape over the game, we force change on the opposition, we make our ideas much stronger than theirs. Nuno is shouting. Substitutions. Morgan Gibbs White who I keep calling Mowgli. Cavaleiro, how I love watching him play. I keep looking over to the South Bank to see who is in my seat. One of the Wolves staff recognises me and says 'Not like the Southbank is it?'. I laugh and the dodgy tooth nearly comes out. It's hanging by a slim thread. Just hold on until I get back home please.

Is it like the Southbank? Nah it's not, but it's the same really. Somebody is castigating Neves as 'useless' behind me. I laugh. Maybe it is different being in another stand maybe it isn't maybe it's just me struggling to keep pace with everything that's going on and trying to form some sort of consensus in my own mind as to what's happening. The last fifteen minutes are post coital. Light a cigarette football full of endorphins and lazy cocktails. I can't wait to get back into my own stand. The cheeseboard is nice. The Cheesecake was powey and nom. I could eat another one mate. It's all funky and gorgeous, beautiful and sexy, same as the football. Everton next. What is an Everton?

I love Fosun and Jeff Shi. He's a ruthless player of the game, part diplomat, part salesman. I've often wondered about writing a Biography of Nuno but I think that a biography of Jeff may make better reading. Maybe.

The Express and Star have been summoned to Molineux towers and been sat down in front of Jeff. 'Of course moving the new development away is an option we have considered'.

Wow

Of course if you were that way inclined you could either join the torch wielding mob the large part (of which I would be among) The Sacred Order of Saint Derek Dougan. Or I would vent my injured angst on Social Media. Crazy times. We should make stickers and flags and demonstrate.

Or we could sit back and digest the zeitgeistyness. Jeff Shi is a fucking Jedi Master. There have bound to have been tentative below the radar pokes into the world of Wolverhampton land acquisition in the past 18 months. Maybe Jeff just had a look on Google for a minute see what was going on. Maybe he has a small crowd of degreed up to fuck Land Law specialists drawing up plan A-B-C-D-E and F for the tactics they are going to use. One of my mates is Chinese and he worked in the family Take Away after emigrating from China. He was a Lawyer for the local Land Registry a fine job. He left because he was given a case to arbitrate a land dispute that had been going on for 185 YEARS! Is Jeff Shi hardcore about this? I fucking bet he is. I bet you something else too. He knows how to deal with shit. You see I've met Jeff twice now. He hasn't got a clue who I am. So when I looked at him past his PR face there is a bloke behind the smile who would hammer six inch nails into your head if it brought him honour and success within his company. He knows these battles to come.

At this stage all the redevelopment madness is in its initial birth phase. Ideas have been thrown out to consultancy teams to look at traffic flow and facilities, health and safety plans, evacuations, ways in and out, costs. Maybe they will love the idea of an environmentally sustainable stadium system. Hotels, shops, bars (not pubs)….it's all exciting. The consultants would have found a group of Architects they like, maybe these Architects are commissioned to produce stadium A-B-C-D-E-F and to extrapolate all the information to potential sites 1-2-3-4-5-6. But Jeff probably has his hands behind his back and he's looking out over the dingy car park and the top of Molineux alley. He knows Molineux is Wolves because he understands the magic of geography. He understands 'Territory'.

Robert Anton Wilson once said that 'The Map is not the territory'. He was right of course. but there are exceptions. Jeff and Laurie know that the real enemy they have to deal with isn't the owners of the land. It's the Council. Not the Councillors of course. They will get their snout in the trough at some point. You could move the Molineux to Telford for all they fucking care. But the politicians of the civic center do worry about votes. Voters wont be happy that the one jewel in Wolverhamptons Crown is about to be pawned off for a car park or fucking student apartments called 'The MoliMews' or some crazy fucked up shit. So the enemy Jeff is thinking about are Council Officers. These are the grey fucking suits of the

Wolverhampton Kremlin mate. They wield great power behind the scenes and they are the ones Jeff has spoken to over the medium of our local newspaper. That fucking news was just for them wasn't it Jeff. You wanted to have a little chat before the big files start to fly around the murky world of local politics and services. What a fucked up place. Would you put 'Little' Jeff Shi at war with these reptiles and lizards? Am I being too hard on the Council? I don't know, they have been decimated by Government cut backs. There probably isn't anybody there to answer the phone when Jeff calls.

But Jeff isn't daft. The name 'Jeff' belies what lies beneath my friends. Remember the six inch nails. Jeff has said...Hey guys, this is how it is and this is step 1 of the whole discussion. You give us a slice of the big city cake. We will build beautiful infra structure. Invest in jobs, build huge projects, change the face of Wolverhampton into a vibrant tourist attraction where people will watch great football and have great times looking at the things we have built…or we can fuck it off somewhere else. Your Councillors will face the abyss of disinterest in anything to do with Wolverhampton center. The couple of million squid Europe threw at us will dry up. Investment will be at an all time low. Social problems, the negative list is endless. What will the Wolves be without Molineux? Another Milton Keynes Dons. A manufactured entity for an easily beguiled audience across the world? How long before some billionaire then decides to start a new Wolverhampton team, call it Saint Lukes, Steve Bull would be on the board probably, maybe Planty as well.

Jeff ain't going anywhere. I bet, thinking about it. Maybe Jeff has got plans B-C-D-E-F tucked away on his hard drive somewhere or the FOSUNCLOUD a great fucking satellite computer in space. Who knows. But Jeff aint opening them. They are just the back up plan to show the Gonks at Fosun China that he has his head screwed on. What Jeff has read is Plan A at Location 1. The redevelopment of Molineux. This place fucking drips emotional history. It has soaked into the stadium and the surrounding areas, blood and soil I suppose. Or blood and tarmac. Jeff knows the power that idea of territory actually is. Because Robert Anton Wilson was right. The map is just a system of lines and angles on a piece of paper or a computer. Territory is something much deeper. It is a relationship to the land no matter how dysfunctional it seems. It is love and respect for that territory, because the territory holds all the fucking history. Does Jeff know this? Of course he does. The Chinese revere history, they learn from it constantly, history and the study of the past is reflected deeply within that culture. It is academic and metaphysical at the same time. It is a most successful model. Molineux is Wolves and Wolves is Molineux. We are rare that we still inhabit the same place we began all those years ago. Most of the other clubs in the Premier league do not have that. These grand renamed monobrand stadiums a spectacle but not spectacular.

I'm sure the whole tangled propaganda machine will keep spurting out claim and counter claim. Subterfuge on an industrial scale. Threats and counter threats. We will watch from afar like cowering humans as the giants hurl mountains at each other. Ah fuck knows. I do know we ay going anywhere. Tomorrow I will wax about the land around Molineux and all that shit.

Steve McNanamoon is in his shed at the bottom of his Cheshire garden. Outside only the bats are moving, all is quiet, just the gentle purr of another footballers 100k Audi R666 rumbling across the misted fields. His garden is littered with expensive LED lights and abandoned kids toys. Within the shed there is an unholy ethereal light. McNotherloons face is lit by a phone screen. His face is excited as he tries to get blood to flow to his withered member within his pummelling sweaty hand. He is watching something on the phone…on the screen is an old bent man in his garden. There is a smouldering fire in front of him. He pokes it with a stick. He is wearing a blue tracksuit. A Cardiff FC Tracksuit. Around the old man the landscape is dim and dark. In the distance it looks like a body is hanging from a tree. But the phone screen is small, it's too grainy to tell. The old man is saying something, his face is twisted and surreal. Vincent Price like maybe... snarling and guttural…

'You have to get the Mother Hedgehogs Steve…they will have babies, about five of them'. McNattercack leans closer, his jeans puddled around his ankles as he watches the old man flick another baby Hedgehog onto the fire. The hedgehog screams as the flames take hold. The face of the old man comes closer to the camera…

'You see Steve…hear them scream, hear them suffer' McGnadsacka sighs as he pummels away at his balls. The old man on the screen smiles…'We don't like Wolves do we Steve?' and we see it is the snarling face of Colin Wanker. The Hedgehogs carry on screaming…'No Uncle Colin..' McNackajacker says, 'We don't'.

Chapter 6

Toffee Gollums and the first day at school

Everton are a strange one aren't they? They have spent 200 Billion dollars on their team. That's a lot of money. They enter the stadium to a roar of Molineux madness, fire, smoke, somebody leans over bodies in the Southbank and screams into my ear. 'I love your podcast you cunt' I laugh as the ghosts of the many beers he has killed that day vapourise from his gob into my face. I am sure he has spit a bit of crisp into my hair. I don't care. I'm back in the Southbank. Thank God.

Somebody stinks of sweat. There is a fight going on a few rows down. It's the same bloke I had a scrap with when we were back in League One. He loves it, fair play. I'm glad I'm not involved as the punch he gave me made my head spin.

The bloke in front of me says he's having a heart attack. Some doughnut violently jabs a flag in my ear. It might have been on purpose. Horace pretends to look at the pitch. Wolves. Premiership football. Fucking hell. Everton. Freemasons. Where is the town of Everton? Is it near Liverpool? Big team anyway but the fans look like us for sure. Same clothes, same shoes, same groove but there is a difference and you can see it on their faces. They are not looking forward to today for some reason. They look sad and depressed. Their songs flutter like an old mans fart. Intent to bellow and all they manage is a half hearted squeek occasionally.

In the pub I am looking at the bar staffs tits...not the women, its a dude with massive man boobs and they are joggling around in his polo shirt with (I think) the Royal London on it, I'm not sure. He has just asked me if I wanted serving and he has the voice of a seven year old boy. I'm nearly dying with laughter. Inside my head I am on the floor rolling around and not breathing with laughter and hilarity. But outside I am calm and I order another one of thoise IPA things at 5.2% or something. I am not a real ale twat I am just reading the chalkboard beer menu so I dont start losing control in front of the twenty stone man with a 6lb voice. I am talking to people I dont know but want to know and people I know do but don't want to know. Sweat is starting to break out on my head. The only deodorant in our bathroom was some pink whiffy womans one. I will smell great when my armpits start to kick in. It's a bit clammy in here, they could do with some air conditioning.

It's the new school isn't it? We have a new sports bag with a new pencil case, a protractor, ruler, pens. We look like dickheads in our new uniforms, the sleeves hanging down because there's no way Moms going to spunk 50 quid on another one for a couple of years. Everton are the kids that have been there a few years. Their blazer sleeves are stiff with snot and have shrunk halfway up their arms. They have a sneeky and hardened look to them this Everton. They look like they are resigned in some way…to re-enact their existence on a football pitch time and time again like Groundhog day. They are dispassionate about their football. As slick and as sexual as it looks it lacks anything to define it. Evertons football looks like it should spend a few years in an isolated hermitage to 'discover' itself. I mean you can have all the sexy players you want but if they don't have an idea to fight for then it's just work isn't it? Everton are at work today and they would rather being doing something else.

As we walk down the proverbial new school corridor, our team are a little wide eyed I suppose. Jostling and the speed of which these Evertons run around is confusing. We get an elbow in the neck but it isn't the Cardiffian Warnockian elbow. It's more like 'get out of my way while I do my job' kind of elbow. They score. It's a lovely cross they put in. As the scorer celebrates two of his team members kind of tut because they have to run twenty yards to celebrate too. It looks like they can't be arsed. Everton fans go wild, but the jollity seems a little forced, a little too loud. It smells of pantomime. Is this the Promised Land? Or just another stepping stone to Europe? Who fucking knows. It's a statement not a question.

I am enjoying Boly and Coady getting to grips with this whole school corridor thing. They did seem a little confused at times. Boly wont get bullied here. He's a massive man striding around, bumping, shifting and pulling Everton attacks apart. But sometimes Mr Bolys attention is caught by a colourful school poster or a window to the outside. Coady is content to wait to see what Boly does and sticks close to him. Bennett is doing what he knows best, blend in, look like you have been there years. But don't make too much noise. Considering we were faced with a 50 million quid striker they did bloody OK thanks very much. But this 50 million quid bloke Richarlison is doing stuff for sure. He's getting his timing spot on but players around him are not. There is a rythmic stutter in their play. A fly in the ointment.

Little Jonny Otto wasn't taking any shit at all. He's got that gnarly carved out of granite look to him. Low COG and a wiry thing. He had a few chops at Everton attacks, dealt with most of them, got up a few times to bung a few crosses or passes in. There wont be any trouble from Jonny but don't pull his fucking string or he will be chewing your throat out probably. Jonny is the kid you leave alone to do what he has to do. He still has to get onto the wavelength of the team. That will come. Moutinho too, listening and learning. Starting to get the telepathy going with Neves. Starting to see in his minds eye where people are without looking. Getting the sixth sense on. He throws a few beautiful shapes while trying to keep a lid on this Everton thing. Crisp passes from them and they are running into spaces like we did last year. Spooning sexy passes here and there. Waiting for opportunities.

Raul Jimenez is a thunder. Darting here and there like a predator. He is moving people out of the way with his presence. Pulling Everton defenders out of position. Jota sees a gap, moves, awful Evertonian tackle and boom. Red card. Phil JaggedElka. Free kick right on the edge of the area for Wolves. I turn to Horace. This is going to be 1-1. Smack. Ruben. He is everything to me. Despite having a little less spark he has positioned the ball beautifully. Back of the net. Crowd erupts. Flag smashed off my head. Glasses are off. My bad leg is booted. Pain and ecstasy. Fucking hell. 1-1.

Ah, The Premier League. Everybody looks smart in their new Wolves tops. I hope nobody notices I am wearing a Primark pyjama tshirt. It starts to rain. Pickford is running towards the Southbank. People applaud him. I tell him to 'fuck off'. Somebody tuts at me and I try to grab hold of them but they are gone into the crowd. Pickford may be our heroic England goalkeeper but today he is the enemy. Today he must be castigated by the South Bank so that he may fluff his concentration for a minute. Years ago he would have got a few coins bouncing off his head. Today...'Well done Jordan!' like people know him. Some wave to him as he jogs nearer towards the noisy madness of our stand. I flick the V's. Have that you weirdo. Fancy clapping the opposition. Jesus.

A few people around me are cussing Boly. I am not listening. There will be attacks that split us apart, there will be goals scored by 'them' whoever they are. These opposition aren't the mucus addled senseless kick the shit out of it football from last season. Everton are dynamic, they are skilled and they are not averse to falling over dramatically, with much groaning and moaning after a Wolves tackle that wouldn't have broke the skin of a rice pudding. Richarlison you absolute doughnut. Shame on you. But they play, of course they do. We in response learn. Everton sit deep and Jota-Jimenez axis revolves constantly looking for spaces to play people in, to move them, to score maybe? There are half chances I suppose. We never break tactic or idea. Our movement is constant and dynamic as Evertons. It is perhaps more beautiful because it has an inner glow. Our shirts are shining under the new floodlights. It looks like a sexy Instagram photo filter. We shine and press. We look like we belong here and we do.

Patricio is a Godsend. He's a good looking sod for sure and tall too. Stretching here and there around his goal. I like it when he comes out for a cross. He is assured and solid. He needs to find his voice within the team and to learn who Boly and Coady are. We move upwards always, it's always learning and teaching as Nuno and his staff cajole and inform their players of 'the way'. Richarlison gets his foot on a good shot. 2-1 to them. Bollocks. Fuck off. Everton fans are voicing their joy. I had forgot about them to be honest. Quiet bunch. Let's sing the signing on song. Throw a few ironic xenophobic slurs about Scousers in the hope that they see it in the spirit it's meant….no? Oh. 'With a pen, in your hand, and you'll never work again'. I'm laughing but they are not. One of them waves a five pound note at the Southbank…we laugh. Toffee Gollums.

But…yes we continue to press the game. The ten man thing, well, I dunno. It does make it tough to move when all they want to do is obliterate our movements and wait for a chance to break. We posses the ball a lot. But movement down the wings is lacking. I think Doherty and Jonny had Everton deeply on their minds instead of Wolves. Doherty stand on the touchline to receive a ball dipped from a long way away by Neves. He collects superbly. Runs into two defenders then the ball is back. None of that physical Doherty who runs at people. Not today. He has one eye on getting back.

But we are getting the ball into the box. Jimenez waits. Stumbles, physical madness and yes. Neves floats a Neves ball in. The fucking thing is singing in the air. Jimmy peels himself from a sticky Evertonian defender. He gets a head on it. 2-2 Jesus Christ. Leveller. Jimmy Jimenez you fucking beauty you. He is massive. He celebrates and is loved already. He reminds me of Bully. Brave and angry to score. There is a hunger in this man I like. He seems happy too and I love that. It's always better to see a big happy face rather than a scowling miserable git.

Morgan Gibbs White and Bonatini come on. I love Bonna. His new hair looks scary. I wonder if he has been looking at the whippy trims around him. Morgan of course starts to throw some beautiful shapes. I would love to see him start a game but what do I know. Vinagre comes on for Jonny. There is all of a sudden movement down that side. More pressing down the touchline. It all looks balanced all of a sudden. Perhaps that youthful excuberence was exactly what we needed. Ruben V wanted to wax some important lyrics for sure and he was jinking shapes here and there to get past his man and make a cross or a chance. I like him too. But it's all shiny and new, it alls smells fresh and clean, turn the plug on and stand back to see what all these flashing funky lights do...at least it fucking works even if we don't quite understand it yet.

I liked everything I will be honest. I got wet through walking back to the car. But there was happiness. Yes, I know it's a new school and we need to learn where everywhere is but we must remember where we have come from. Last season. Barnsley, Bolton, Cardiff and now this. Teams who at least attempt to play some football. We deserve to be here and test our ideas against these teams. When we next play Everton they will stand back amazed at what we have learned and found out about this strange Premier League thing. We will learn under Nuno everything this division has to offer us. Learning curve mate and we nearly aced the first exam. Nuno in his own inimintable way waxes over the match in his post match press conference. He is surly somewhat...I think he has really taken on his experience of the Portuguese and Spanish press when he managed over there. Guarded maybe? For sure. What the hell is a Nuno?

...on the video screen Steve MunMunnon watches his Uncle Colin stir the ashes of the Hedgehog massacre. Inside the chasm of his existence our Steve mulls over the sad dichotomy of his hatred for Wolves and the perverted wiles of his Uncle Colin. Uncle Colin was right about those Wolves of course. Coming here, playing nice football, with a fantastic Coach, vibrant dynamic ownership. Yes, Steve doesn't like it...but he knows other people that don't like the Wolves too. Steve fastens his trousers back up and stares at his reflection in the shed window. He looks ghoulish and wrong especially when he smiles. 'Don't worry Uncle Colin', he thinks. Now down the garden, in last years brown and dried leaves there is bound to be a few Hedgehogs all snug and warm, I will make them a bit warmer...he picks up a can of petrol. There is maybe half a gallon. It was for the Lawnmower. There are a few cobwebs on which he brushes off with distaste.

'Don't worry Uncle Colin.' Maccamanbun sobs again.

Chapter 7

Cripstown and a weird defeat

Awake with a face like a burning clown, like a feral carrier bag, like a Fishermans cough...in the distance someone offers Nuno a Crisp...'I only eat Pringles' he remarks with a look of disgust on his face as someone waves a bag of Walkers crisps under his beard.

This Premier league madness. Have I said anything about it yet? I must have loads of angst about it but I can't read through my notes yet. My club Wolverhampton Wanderers are a woman I have stood by for years uncounted. I watched her hair tangled in rucks because she couldn't be bothered to brush or comb it. Her breath was none too sweet. Sex was a bump and grind of machine like tenderness. Love...but the varicose veins were like the colour of these Leicester shirts running around in the sun. The wrinkles on her arse were a testament by Christ, of the shit we have had to endure over the years. Yet I was always there for you baby. Even when things seemed so dull that I felt like making effigies of Glen Hoddle and burning them on the pitch. I have always loved you...and now of course my love has had some things done to her. She no longer smells of stale roll up cigarettes. Her hair is beautiful and waves around like some tart in a hairspray commercial. It's all hard body Yoga time now and those legs, those new teeth. Dear Lord she looks good. I however am the same…except I have a limp now and look like more of a tramp than I ever did.

At the K-Po stadium yesterday we are only ten yards away from the Crisptown fans. There is one Crisp fan who is jumping up and down next to his son and going full Monkey Bollocks at the joy of his sides second goal. His hair looks like its been trimmed by a bloke with a club foot and a dodgy hard drive. He is a meme of the gesticulating barm pot. His arms are going up and down that fast he looks like he's on a desert island somewhere in the middle of the Pacific and he's just a heard a plane fly overhead. He looks he is a Block paver or a Tarmac Gyppo. It's cool, I love that shit. All the other Leicester fans look like Central heating engineers. They have just come back from Spain or Cyprus whatever. They are the colour of a decent cup of tea. They are ranting like mad. What's wrong with them? I suspect they rant because they lack something here… the stadium is weird Lego, the area around the ground is the same, it's that Reading Identi-kit stadium thing. The decaying cheap infrastructure that surrounds it. It was their first home game of the season. They looked pissed off before they went in. I put my hands in my pockets and stare at the pitch for a while and then at the Leicester fans, back at the pitch, back at their fans...

'Wanky Wolves hahahahah fucking wankers'

'Mate your flies are undone' I shout to him.

'Hahahaha fucking wankers'

'Dude your flies are undone zip yourself up'

'Hahahaha wankers wanderers hahahahah' He shouted over. His son sat with his chin in his hands looking glum. Why does Dad do this? He wants to be back at home fucking about on his PS4 playing some shoot em up, eating munchies...not here with Dad and this pointless shit. He doesn't even look over at us he's just existing. Of course his Dad will grab his hand after the match as they walk away through the greyness of that place...

'Enjoy that son? Fucking brilliant, here hold my clapper' The Dad says with his weird shaped head bobbing as he walks. The son doesn't say anything because the Dad isn't really listening.

At one point Mr Blockpavers dong falls out of his Primark shorts and I shake my head and wonder where those pound coins went that flew over my head occasionally. Obviously Crisptown. Must have been four quid at least. I remember in the 70s at Molineux. As soon as people started to file out us scruff bags would be running up the terrace back and forth trying to find the coins that had fell out of pockets, the badges that had been torn out in the limbs. There would be maybe twenty of us searching. All scruffy bastards.

These Leicester fans man. They are all angry too. They splutter and moan, shout things, hurtful things probably but I'm not listening, not today. It's the first away day of the season and there is madness in the air, you can smell it. Underneath the beer and cheap aftershave smells is that tribal horribleness. I think one Leicester fan is trying to invite me for a fight outside. How rude. I wish I had a foam hand to wave at him, or a clapper.

Reading about how Adama Traore is fit after his shoulder injury fills me with a happiness I find hard to fathom. I'm not that aware of what Traore is. I don't even think he does. What ideas he found under Tony Pulis would probably beggar belief. These ideas probably involved 'putting a shift in' maybe 'getting stuck in' and 'get the fucking ball up to big neck'. Stuff like that. Stuff probably that went down well at West Birmingham Albion. To be fair both Boro and Albion sucked long on the strange wormlike philosophies of Mr Pulis. We see those ideas now playing Barnsley and Preston on cold days as we did. So Adama. What have you got for us mate? Lets have a look at the Crisptown lot first.

Jamie Vardy, striker, handful, fast. Harry Maguire, massive head, like to put his head on things. Silva, Maddison, Gray…it's a feast of course. Players with undoubted ability. I can't mention them in a negative light only to say they are the enemy today. Of course my confidence yesterday, my happiness was tempered. I read about Adama being available as I went to take the dogs out. This made me happy.

I was smiling as I walked down to the canalside. There were some baby ducks getting rid of their fluffy feathers and putting on proper size. There was a Dragonfly hovering and doing whatever Dragonflies do. There was a Heron further down fishing. I turned the corner…a pisshead having a shit under the bridge. I caught him in mid bite obviously…I didn't want to disturb him. I am polite like that. His face in shock, me trying not to look at him but wanting to be polite, 'Orite mate' I said. He nodded. As he squeezed. Then I wanted to kick him in the head for being an animal. Me dog growled at him. The stories down this canal wouldn't be believed I swear it.

Last week against Everton was a thing. I didn't feel like it was a wake up call about anything. Didn't we expect this football? Are we not entertained? Did a draw really 'expose' any weak links or underfunded positions? Are certain parts of our team a bit under the weather when faced with such football. All fluff and thunder I think. I suspect we have performed admirably in our one game and I am loathe to start making any predictions about anything. Only that we will smash every team in some certain way every game we play until we are sat on top of the Premier league…I keep saying it I know. I'm not going to apologise for it. What's the point in having a scrap if you think you aren't going to win?

This Leicester team are just that, another scrap. Albeit with all the fanfare of the telly there and maybe some pyro or dancing girls. It's still the same shit. At Barnsley last season we had to dig deep and face the abyss of Championship games with all the attractiveness of a canal side shite. We had to dig deep. My writing about that game denigrated the town and their team. I offer no apologies for it, my head was stuck in a lovely land of Portuguese football, fast paced and often beautiful. We had to dig like fuck didn't we? All those games wrapped into one drink fuelled freezing day in Nowhere land. I remember how cold it was but inside a warmth for sure. We knew we were going somewhere else…here mate. Premier land filled with gooning vehement insults and the rich miasma of the oft repeated gesture and the wordless exaltation about how they hate us. Brilliant. Leicester City are a fake team with fake fans.

The Premier league will be just like that, fake, but sparkly. Like the Wizard of Oz tinkling away at his magical contraptions before the curtain is swept aside and we see Jamie Vardy working the pedals and pumps until he notices we are watching him. Yes, this game will be like that. Dig in Wolves but dig with beauty. Play our game and this Leicester team will take notice quickly. Let the nerves flutter away lads, it's really day two of the campaign. Still early, but at least we know a little about the place. It can be very tough and scary. But if you pretend you have been there a while you can get from place to place quite easily.

Will Traore play? I hope so. I wish to see him doing his 'thing'. Physical yes and fast, but I suspect there is something, some space in his head that wants to be filled with an idea or two. That he wishes to become his own man with his own ideas I suppose. I watched his football on YouTube for an hour last night, where he liked to move and run, how he made use of space, how he twisted and turned. It was beautiful and at times scary too. So in my minds eye I substituted his team mates on those videos for our players. I try to see in my own mind something of Nunos mind, why Traore was bought, how he would fit.

Traore can shield that ball. He has that Low Centre of Gravity that Nuno likes, the ability to protect and nurture the ball until players have arrived in his wake…now will Traore have players already there? We move fast, unlike Adamas Boro. We will have heads going mad for that ball Adama holds up, keeping the JAMS at bay. I don't want to hear about how his 'final product' is lacking. I don't want to hear how 'physical' he is or how he is a 'beast'. I don't like it. If being overly developed muscle wise is some sort of memetic pre-requisite for how a footballer performs then I'm not interested. I want to know how he reacts to Nuno. I think that big hole in his heart that Pulis and Villa have ripped out will be filled up with understanding and love maybe. Probably some great ideas too. You can't tell me that Nuno hasn't watched Adama with that forensic eye. I see Nuno and his team sitting watching him in a dark room, discussing his movements, how they can squeeze a little more out of that move, this idea or that pass. In Portuguese of course…fast paced chat with plenty of hand movements and drama, arguments. Can they add to his game? He wouldn't be here otherwise. Will this be your day Adama Traore? Are you going to be our new talisman like er…… Sako? Maybe?

Of course all these quasi philosophical bollocks are OK in the scheme of great wins away. We should have been three goals up in the first half. We should have been more clinical, we should have had more aggression. Blah. I wasn't even pissed off I will be honest. Even the bloke with his little dong flopping around while he denigrated our Town didn't bother me too much. We were still happy I think. Pissed off yeah but happy. What a great load of football that was really. We scored a lovely header. Doherty, bloody hell. Skimmed off the top of his head. I bet Patricio is thinking what the fuck is happening all his players having a bang at the wrong goal. Second one for them is a deflection off Conor. Shit happens when you are faced with attacks like that from a lively but weird team like Leicester. That boy Maddison eh? I said in the close season we should have a look at him but what do I know again?

I didn't like Bennet being targeted straight away but little incisive attacks where his pace or lack of it was EXPOSED? I dunno, maybe he was a bit off the pace when he has some ten stone whippy young player throwing shapes you could never hope to deal with. But I think he did do OK of course. This was another day of learning for our team. Another day in School maybe. Learning and assimilating. But learning what? We hit the post that many times we should have uprooted the fucking thing. I bet their groundsman this morning is shovelling some Compo down the holes as I type this. Thundercunt shots from Moutinho and Jimmy. Chances squandered. We were at times fucking lovely on the ball.

It looked bloody effortless at times, like we wanted to be there. I looked to my left at all our fans, we were two nil down mate but there they were singing their hearts out, shouting, getting involved. I look to my right at the Crisptown fans. They looked sad. But they were winning. What the hell was their problem? They should be ecstatic. There is an illness within Leicester I don't understand. Something is up. Someone throws a Clapper at us. Oooh you're hard. Bennett goes in again and magics the ball away from a threatening Crisptown foot.

You know two years ago we would have hoofed that ball into the air and away. The opposition would have collected it and they would be straight back at us for another attack. Now, Bennett pings the ball to Coady who dinks it straight onto the foot of Neves who takes a single look up and the ball is moving again. We are moving too and everything is slowly coming to fruition. I see these Nuno ideas redolent here on this pitch. We are losing but we will never lose.

Of course it's always a thing when their chances and half chances are converted and ours are not. This was a game where the cogs and gears of the Wolves Looniverse have decided to get a bit of grit in them. We were maybe half a second away from full on domination in terms of winning the second ball. Maybe an inch or two away from a three goal lead in the first half. I watch Nuno for a few minutes pacing the technical area. Looking at him is like staring at a three bar electric fire. Premier League eh, fucking hell. But is it that whole Premier League experience? We looked like we deserved to be there, we looked like we weren't really the new boys, the fresh meat. We did not look out of place, we did not look like strangers in this landscape.

We were just as good as these doughnuts. Maguire, England International, fresh from the world cup looked decidedly average as our attacks cut him up again and again. Reg Vardy, England Striker. Average. Gray, average. Crisptown was full of average shit. But two goals up. They ride their luck these teams. It is a symptom of Premier quality games where chances have to be taken, have to be smashed into nets. We are learning that for sure. I see our team still being too beautiful. We are far too smart for our own good sometimes.

Far too pretty too. I suspect that our philosophy was laid bare for

Leicester when they decided on 51 minutes and two goals up that they had to start time wasting. Wasting time? You are a Premier league side for fucks sake. Have you no self respect? The ball rattles out of play and one of their players goes to collect, he drops the ball and kicks it further away from himself, he dawdles, he slinks to collect and moves twenty yards up the touchline away from the original position where the ball left the field of play. Jesus Christ. Crisptown.

Traore comes on and immediately I see spacetime warped around him as his presence if one of intense gravity. Jesus Christ he's massive isn't he? Even the air sweats when he is around and I enjoy his cameo where he throws Leicester players around like the free t-shirts the ground staff were throwing into the crowd at halftime. He was beautiful, I love his kind of football, in your face stoical shapes, shrugging off the JAMS. But what was this game crying out for? Ryan Giles.

Can I maybe throw that suggestion forward with my lack of knowledge? Maybe. I could see Giles throwing some of those shapes down the side for sure. I think Matt Doherty is ready for a rest…I see Giles playing these funky rhythms with Traore. This is what I see in the future. Vardy has been sent off for a tackle on Doherty. I wave to Jamie as he leaves the field of play. He walks off slowly. Jesus Christ what are these Gonks? Doherty is on the floor for a long time getting love off the Physios. There is much spraying of magic spray and much sponging of offened limb. He shuffles back up and hobbles off the field for a moment. He is off but the team adjusts instantly covering the hole he leaves until he comes back on.

Again we were not disgraced but the chances we shook off are just tweaks. Just little bits of fine tuning and maybe Lady luck has to smile on us a little bit. A Crisptown fan says 'Wolves are the best team we have seen down here for a while'. That's good to know. We always need that critical non Wolves view to put everything in focus to give an unemotional view of the day. But I am quiet. Theres something amiss here and I don't know what it is. It pokes around my subconcious like a knock in your engine and you tell everybody to shut up a minute so you can listen. Can you hear it? Everybody shakes their head no. Fuck.

I always say we played brilliant even if we played crap. But that's the way I look at things. Always positive, always looking for that sliver of light in the blackness of the Looniverse. This whole Fosun-Nuno-Wolves thing is still a baby of sorts. It's still finding it's feet and clicking into place. Some of these players are still finding their feet, sussing out what the whole thing is. We have to be very patient with this particular seedling of ideas, be gentle and look softly at what is going on. I mean, when it does finally click then we are going to start to shithouse results too. Maybe the ball will fall more kindly to us and that second ball will be easier to get to. Maybe our toe poked shots towards goal will go in like theirs, the lucky bastards.

Me and Horace are waxing lyrical going back to the car. We are Yam Yamming like fuck talking about the game and every now and then he shouts at the Old Bill about something or other. But we are talking, sharing ideas and views of the game excitedly and with passion. I look around us and we are surrounded by Leicester fans who are quiet and sombre and I don't really understand it until this morning. You see their chances to grow and develop as a team have gone, they tread water here in the Premier league. We on the other hand are finding the whole thing vastly more interesting than them I think. We have a young beautiful team who are learning the ropes fast, who are starting to rumble into life too. When we do start to mesh and to get our groove on. You'd better fucking watch out mate.

Chapter 9

Doog and other things

Awake. With a face like an argument over next doors fence, like Harry Kane on a bouncy castle, like a shattered crisp packet...in the distance Nuno is not thinking about Derek Dougan...

I wrote this a fortnight ago when I had five minutes. It's not brilliant I know but I put in down in biro on a piece of paper and put it in me pocket and forgot it Until I walked the dogs and met my crackhead and pisshead mates down the canal. They asked me what I had done that day so I showed them my poem and recited it. They were confused until I read it again. One of them cried a bit. Not because of Derek but because I stood there and did it. It was my first live poetry gig. Among the dog eggs and blue bottles of Cider that ay never seen an apple.

Derek Dougan groovin' with the Moog on His eyes like Tangerines, your moustache thick and black lost in the middle of Whitmore Reans, the heart break Red Roofs Hotel Lost in the North Bank we were mate, feet stamping and shouting I used to see you when I was a kid as I delivered the paper Getting out of your swanky car with your funky flares and mad tie Lost in the early seventies the sixties just gone Shot like a big arsed IRA bomb, glass everywhere Cortinas and Granadas and Vauxhall Vivas,

Hillman Imps. You always waved and said hello, I gave you a free Express and Star but you were stuck in the strings of the maudlin Cello half the time that played as it did during most of our games. I am not going to name names But you Derek, what did you mean? What did you listen to? Strike fast and keel showing keen throwing shapes You might have been a Wolves player, a maestro a magician but I knew what you really were, I sensed it.

Derek Dougan could have been the first Rock Star footballer Playing guitar for the Grateful Dead or Jefferson Airplane with the songs from the North Bank stuck in your head the buzz of the bass just kicking in you plinking blues riffs football as life without and within. I loved you more than George Best You were always a hero to me and to them. I look at your old photos As you moved you flashed colours unseen, pink purple, red and violet of gold and black and luminous green a wizard you were mate and we all agree fucked up on 250mg of LSD looking at the birds flying up above Psychedelic Derek scores makes it three, face crushed up the barrier, streams of piss we sing and shout and scream aloud, looking for the odd fifty pence piece underneath your suede fringed jacket and hair long and proud you looked like you should have been in Black Sabbath I think, a rock star not a footballer avoiding another errant truncheon dink, another shove off a Coppers angst I keep thinking about you Doog, lately Especially when the sun sets and I'm listening to Pink Floyd Wish you were here or Shine On you crazy diamond" Mad as fuck isn't it?

The more shiny this club becomes the more I tend to look back to those black and white days when everything seemed a little more truthful and moral...ah I'm pissed off. We should have done Crisptown for sure. The script was wrong of course. It was like the edited highlights on Match of the Day when everything we did good was edited out and made Crisptown look like Real Madrid...which they weren't. Disinformation again and I don't know whether I have the strength to rail against it.

Ah Leo Bonatini. Our striker, our point of entry. The amazing things I have in mind to wax lyrical at the idea of everything you do. I grab my roll ups and a steaming cup of tea. I am enraged and full of ideas on what I want to say to you. I slosh the tea on the dining table, I roll a fag ready to wax. Turn on the lap top. It's fucking updating Windows. I sit and wait. It's endless as I suspect next door has turned his WiFi off. I'm not that pissed off about Crisptown any more. I am slightly more positive. I am doing what Nuno says. Heads down, next match, forget this one, always the next match, always the next battle and whenever I listen to him I feel better straight away. It's like I trust him or something. But Leo...man, what are you doing?

Of course who knows the myriad of variables that has suddenly (well, last Christmas) turned up to facilitate your lack of goals scored. Who knows? Who am I to try and work out why you have hit a dry point in the moisture inducing landscape of your football? I am at a loss to try and explain it. My mind wanders when I do.

You came from some strange Egyptian team and burst into life within a Wolves team that was just starting to get their groove on. You had power and intent, started smashing goals in left, right, centre. I may unload all the memes and tropes to explain how physical you are and how intelligent. I could wax lyrical about Nuno teaching you to play a different game now. A holding one maybe, darting around the box pulling defenders here and there as you splash your colours all over the pitch. But now as I watch the Apples fall off the tree outside in the back garden I am thoughtful and I am still in awe of your football. My watching of your highlights reel on Youtube is punctuated by the odd apple clonking onto the glass topped patio table in the garden. Bonk. I wonder as I sit here whether or not one will bust through shattering it.

There have been new faces appearing within the team. Jimmy Jimenez, Benik, Rafa, last season, but on top of that you are faced with other minor aggravations. The crowd are rumbling their discontent. They don't see what I see, they don't look upon you with my eyes. What do I see? A man that is finding it hard to impress his personality within the swirling madness of the new additions, the new strategies and the new ethos within the team. That is cool. That is life. Trying to fit in and do what everybody else wants you to do. To have that kind of a herd mentality. To sacrifice the Warrior within for the good of the team. To find yourself learning…but not doing.

Football Leo, is the craziest of things. I watched you last week at Leicester with your new trim and your intent raw and dripping. I see your movement and runs, I see exactly what you see on the pitch with the only difference being the angle of our viewpoints. I watch and I observe what you are trying to say and I see this…Raul Jimenez is here, he's after your stash mate, he is here with something to say.

You are thinking too much Leo. Whatever madness you have in your mind as you train and think about another barren goalless appearance is weighing you down. These days without a goal probably plague your thoughts when you are sitting resting. Maybe you think and analyse every pass and every movement until the whole thing becomes a cacophonous swirling noise of lights and sound until you just feel like throwing yourself on the floor and smashing your head off it a few times. That's cool. That is what we want. At least you 'feel' everything we do. At least you have some emotion.

When we played Ajax in our pre season friendly I watched you drive off the car park at Bescot with things on your mind. I didn't see a powerful striker in that car. I saw a man deep in his own mind. In thought, an internal dialogue about the game and the team. Yourself as well. You are in dialogue with a part of your shadow self. That is the darkness within you. That darkness asks 'Why am I not scoring goals' or 'Maybe it's because I am not good enough for this team' or 'Maybe I should have done this or that'. Soon the dialogue with the shadow Bonatini becomes long conversations when you are sitting alone or driving your car and this aspect of the shadow talk is always negative and always dark. On the one hand I want you to explode into this whole Premier League madness, grab it with both hands and wrestle with it, destroy it. In the end you can hold your head up and say this is who I am, this is what I can do...but alas.

You see Leo, if we maintain the dialogue with the darker aspect of ourselves we soon start to see that dark personality become more and more dominant. It's a self feeding system where the shadow Leo starts to become self critical and morose. Because this is the result of Shadow Bonatini. Criticism from outside becomes less of a hindrance and more of a crutch. We wallow in negative criticism because we start to agree with it, to nurture it, because at the end of the day we love it, because we always hate ourselves more than others ever will. In fact I bet, as you find yourself in a goal scoring opportunity, that voice starts to shout and to denigrate, you may become a little confused and unsure. Pass the ball instead? Lay it off for Jimmy? Move the ball back to Ruben? All these thoughts transfer to your physical self. The one standing on the edge of the box. It revels in torturing you with it's shadowy faint but wilful voice. It affects you physically, it ruins your day, it adds ammunition to those 4 am philosophies we entertain ourselves with when every body else is asleep. How can we expect you to win these matches, to win our wars, when you are at war with yourself?

But there is light at the end of this tunnel Leo. There is always hope. Shadow Leo is at the moment relentless in his warfare. The ball never falls for you, maybe that shot flies off into the crowd. Somebody boos or moans and you hear it, and you agree, you are crap, you shouldn't be here. But Leo fuck that voice, and fuck that shadow self. The way to beat that voice is to enfold and encompass it. We have a light and a dark to us Leo. It is in everybody. The Shadow has a shadow in many aspects too. Within that darkness in us we have another powerful entity. Warrior Leo. That part of us that has to win, that has to destroy our opponent, that has to score that one important goal. It makes us shrug off the physicality of a defender. It gives us adrenalin when we need it most. It makes our thoughts fast and more agile. It is the nitrous oxide of our survival. This is part of the Shadow us, that when we were primeval, surviving in dark caves in cold winters, that would fight back against the powerful sabre tooth tiger, bear or killer hedgehogs. It is the part of us that bites and scratches, gouges and kicks even though we know we are fighting a much more powerful adversary. It is the Shadow part of us that has made us truly what we are.

Utilising this Warrior aspect is simple. Look into yourself Leo and look at all the nasty and wicked aspects of your personality. The one that finds himself watching gore videos sometimes, maybe finding people who trip up a funny and amusing thing. It's the part of us that wants to punch the person who has denigrated us. It is the dark violence of survival Leo. It is the dark Leo and you have to stretch out your hands and grab hold of it.

These shadow parts of us are an integral part of what makes us what we are. But it must always be subservient to our needs and our activity. In essence light truly does come from darkness here. We utilise the shadow for the greater good of the whole. So what should you do? Be a bastard Leo. Start to revel in your opponents demise and loss. Enjoy looking at their sad fucking faces as they walk off the pitch in tears. Look at the crowd Leo. Enjoy and bathe in the adulation you receive from the crowd. Fucking feed off it Leo. See our faces twisted in joy, see us tumble over the seats, see us sing our songs, feed off us Leo. For surely there is nothing better than scoring a goal and running up to the South bank, your fist punches badge, you are shouting something lost in the volume of our joy, your team mates surround you. You are the King at that moment Leo. You have grabbed the Tigers balls and ripped them off, you hold them up to the sun and let out a piercing razor sharp animal, primal, scream, you are triumphant and you are a God…for a moment.

How does that feel Leo? How is that moment when you feel the world has stopped? It is beautiful isn't it? Leo, I think you are a beautiful player, you are an artist. But put down the brush and pick up the sword.

Chapter 10

Into The Mystic

"Together we will go into the mystic'

Van Morrison

It's hard when you meet a few other people through a friend. These people are unknown to you and you don't quite know how to deal with them socially. Everything is a little awkward and strange. It's basically dogs sniffing each others arses. We don't circle each other we just regurgitate memes to each other defining social status. Finding out if they are 'worth' knowing. Do they make us laugh? Are they great to be with, a night out, are they trustworthy...?

'Manchester City are fucking great to watch…I'm looking forward to watching Aguero to be honest. I don't go to the Molineux normally…today I've grabbed a mates ticket…he cant go…not often you see good football up there…of course I'm a Wolves fan…I always look out for their results'

I just stand there in Wednesfield village centre and gaze at the 10 am drinkers in the Wetherspoons over the road kind of lost in my own world for a moment. I have to go into the bank and wax lyrical over the £1,629 I owe them. Yesterday I found a Berghaus jacket stuffed in a bush by the side of the canal. No rips. It fits. It's fucking getting recycled mate. Cheers Blue Cider Youth whoever you are. Manchester fucking City. Jesus Christ.

Am I bothered? I read that I shouldn't upset Wolves fans in case I upset the cash cow that is Wolves. Brilliant. I didn't eat yesterday. Cheers Wolves cash cow thing…the milk of glorious cash does not flow freely from thine udders. You love Man City? You're a twat mate. Buy a book from me and have a cup of tea and a chat? I eat that day…maybe two days depending on the 'whoopsie' shelf, the stale scones, the dented tin of pop, the strange rice thing nobody around here wants to eat, but I will, I can't taste it any way. Cash Cows? Fuck off. I see Gaz Mastic and his trouser turn ups have fell down and he's stapled them back up but one of the staples has worn a hole in his ankle and there is a trickle of blood on his trainers, his sock is soaked. He seemes not to notice. He's wearing a 'Chaucer' Wolves shirt and his omnipresent Wolves bucket hat from Sherpa Van Trophy days. His one tooth is moving around like it's dodging sniper fire. I take him into the pub and buy him a pint but he's already had two cans of Kestrel Super Strength and he's moaning about his dog and his Missus. I give him a tenner.

I'm going on about money again and everything is dull and boring when I think about that. I suppose you can have a mental austerity as well as a financial one...but I digress...

Nah. We used to do Man City most weeks back in the day and they were really just another team we demolished occasionally. Nothing scary. Nothings changed. I'm still not scared of them. Yes they have a team full of sexy players. I watched them train this week just for a laugh and yeah. Jesus Christ they can move that ball about can't they?

City have some cash don't they? Oil cash isn't it? Sheikh money or something. I remember them well, knocking around the Championship/Division 1 before they got a few quid in their pockets and started buying all these funky players who could move a ball around a bit. Same as our business plan really, investment, long term planning, loyal fanbase, local roots. I don't want to big them up too much of course but this is the model we need to have in place. Growth, dynamic change, vision maybe, a global outlook. It's mad that I'm using all these keywords, I suppose one day we will see what they mean when we are playing City twice a year and nicking their Euro spot. I'm not angry about not going tonight, I've been to loads of great matches. I'm not greedy. I'm saving for the European matches in a few years. Pound in the jar.

'The Rightful Place – Southbank Resistance October 24th 2017

I am not bothered about this doughnut that's looking forward to watching Man City instead of his team. I'm kicking my heels wondering what I'm going to tell my 'Client Adviser' in the Bank. Gaz wants me to stop in the Wetherspoons but I can't hack that, not today any way.

I've just seen (on Twitter) the O.L.D.G.O.L.D banner Fosun have made. I wanted to weep. It's all changing, all in flux and emotions truly are everywhere. On social media all I read is how brilliant Man City are and it's all Wolves fans doing it and I wonder. Perhaps it is time at least till Christmas to peg back my addiction to Social Media. Too many humans on there. We resist of course, but now the resistance is under attack I suppose.

The voices of the unholy are loud and noisy. Manchester City will be that today. Peps idea at Molineux, against the ideas of Nuno. A battle if you like of Philosophies not football…kind of. Football is simply beautiful or ugly.

The time I spent wanting this and now having it seems weird. I want points not denigration. I can't say anything negative about Peps team. But although I have respect for an opponent I am loathe to say anything nice about them. FOSUN look upon Toaster Wolves as a better model of 'fan' art and 'feeling' than us. Southbank Resistance this thing, will never sell out I will just delete it.

We are not glamourous in spite of me waxing on Midlands Today or some stinky Premier League channel. Southbank Resistance is seen in jackets we found, waiting to tell the bank lies, feeling the hunger that comes from not eating for a day. Southbank Resistance is laughing at Art Project banners by London hipsters. It's glamorous this whole art thing, this Fosun project…but we are not. We are about attacking people who harm our dogs. We are about putting an end to others teams plans.

I watch Gaz Mastic beat the shit out of somebody who nearly ran his dog over in Wednesfield High street. This dude was big and sleeved up with curly blue tattoos. Gaz dropped him with one punch. Gym muscles versus a life of manual labour. Gaz shoes the dude in while I stand there holding his dog. I give her a gravy bone. She's a Staffy named 'Mucky'. She licks her arse while Gaz does his stuff. Gaz is 60 years old and he's doing ok thanks very much. The dude in the car is trying to say something to Gaz but a few straight lefts and curly hooks shut him up. Gaz is now tiring but the speeding dickhead is done and sorted. I feel a bit sick. I hate banks and I like being in the fresh air

Gaz tells me a few minutes after he leaves the dude hanging out of his car half unconscious…'Wolves ay we'. I laugh and give him his dog back. He hasn't been to a game so far this year. We walk back to my yard chatting and laughing. We both look like crackheads but I'm a 'famous author', he finds this funny. He watched me on Midlands today and asked if he could borrow my sexy jacket for a wedding he has to go to. Of course you can Gaz. I put him another tenner in the inside pocket and I will send him a WhatsApp about 10 tonight tell him it's there and to get himself a beer. He got made redundant last week.

I predicted the score at full time. 0-0. I was confident we would display the same resolute and solid underpinnings that have been exposed to us for the last few weeks. It was a pure delight from start to finish. The stream of course went blah a few times but it was all there for me to see. This wasn't a 'second string' team by any means. This was another subtle materialisation of the will of Nuno and his coaching staff. A manifestation of the same idea but in different form. And yet I suppose I at least fell into the trap of thinking it was the second stringers, at least until they started to play and it became apparent that this wasn't a gathering of the dysfunctional and the forgotten. They were the weapon Nuno and his staff chose to select to counter the threat of one of the top teams in Europe.

Were we not entertained? Fucking hell, no joke there were a few times when I kind of locked into the rhythm of the whole spectacle and I saw a team that were vibrant, steadfast, agile and attack minded. A team in their rightful place.

'The Rightful Place – Southbank Resistance October 24th 2017

Today is what it is. I always expect us to beat whatever team, and here they are today. This Manchester City thing, after halftime today they put on over a hundred million quid wrapped up in two subs. Mahrez and 'Bacon' Sane. This Sane bloke could move about even if he did look like a novelty make up brush. Of course by the time Aguero had fucking rolled on the floor for the fourth time I was laughing…who the fucking hell were these doughnuts? Welcome to the Jungle. Welcome to Nunoland.

'Its a very controversial goal'

HAND OF BOLY

Kompany has got a head like a Ford Capri bonnet. It looks like a clay head made by Stevie Wonder, he looks like a cheap Chinese rip off of an ET doll, he looks like his head was on fire and somebody put it out with a stick…that was on fire. Kompanys head looks like a homeless mans sleeping bag to be honest. I'm watching him huff and puff. His brilliant footballing mind is making up for the lack of pace he now has. He cuts out bristling Jota a few times, Kompany is popping up everywhere but he is slowing for sure.

We were one nil up. Before that of course I'm fucking dumbfounded by the whole spectacle. Here we have a team who are going to smash this… not not Man City! Us! Jesus!…No not him on the pitch…the whole thing is like some fucked up acid trip where you sit down and play FIFA or Football Manager ay it?

These blokes for Man City are bloody names mate, heads, personalities, men about town mate. Yes…Boly skills up Aguero again. Costa is taking these fools on for sure. He slides shapes all over the place making the City defence stop and think about things in a deep and meaningful way. Jota bunging more shapes around the place. Bennett…Bennett? Yes bloody Bennett, a bloke we suspected we would slap on the back and thank him for being around the place for a while…the Bennett who Norwich fans vilified as being hyper shit. Watch Bennett smash another vital foot in the way, look at him close down this class on display. Look at Bennett truly shit on the party table. Jesus…no not him. Bloody hell. Neves lays off to Moutinho who drags the play from side to side always looking for a pass. City and their movement is sublime and passionate don't get me wrong. But now heres a whole plethora of Wolves madness and Nuno grooves to put the whole lot on some sort of back foot for large periods of the game. Moutinho is a nibbler isn't he? He wont let the City defence rest at all. Even when they have possession. I was a bit wrong about him. I saw shades of Dennis Irwin and Paul Ince, last pay packets, a club in need of some 'experience', you know the score of course. But this man is a revelation. He's playing on that Molineux pitch like he grew there mate.

Amazing. 5 Million squid we paid for him. He's got to be on some bonus money I'm sure of it. His beard looks well trimmed in fact his whole footballing ability looks trimmed so it doesn't have that airy infallibilty that other expensive players might have. I like him.

I'm finding it hard to make sense of any of it because they have large spells holding the ball, we chase and shut down and it's effortless proper football. Neil Warnock is on the radio on the way back from the game and he say's Cardiff are just enjoying themselves in the Premier League and loving the experience. I juxtapose this with what I was watching in front of me. Jesus…no not him again…Aguero falls over quite early into the match and it's a symptom of the Looniverse again. They fall over and play act because they don't know what else to do. Pep is sitting in the dugout hugging himself and rocking backwards and forwards while Nuno paces the technical area like the fucking warrior he is. Pep looks ragged and confused. It has to have a nervous breakdown at some point for sure.

They score a goal. Header. Their dude who's name I forget is unmarked and basically strolls straight onto the ball with no hassle. He does it another three or four times and we aren't picking him up. The Groundsman will be putting compo in the goal post holes tonight too. They give them a right fair whacking these City blokes bunging in the odd distance shot that comes close. Pep is rocking backwards and forwards in his chair and City play this absolutely seriously surrealistic series of moves. It's sexual. I hate them but I love them…I shake my head. Look at the City fans, One of them has a mint coloured Stoney on and an angry face. He reminds me of the Dad with the shit trim at Crisptown, in fact for a few seconds I'm sure it's him and I feel weird. It's as if the faces of all these other fans at the bottom of the Steve Bull stand are blending into one amorphous blob of shit haircuts and way to expensive shit coats. Stone Island is great but it's not going to keep you warm mate. Better a Primark parker that will at least keep you warm and if you do want to roll around outside the ground with other like minded freaks you won't waste your 500 squid coat. I'm so old and moany, it makes me laugh.

Patricio…a word about him. I watched John Ruddy and Norris warming up with Rui. I feel a bit sorry for Ruddy, I think he would have done a thing here but Patricio. This bloke is a class act, he ay going to be shifted I'm afraid. City place a beautiful ball towards the top bin and Patricio is nowhere near it mate. It's delayed action angst. I had started to turn away in horror but the sense of 'That Neves Goal' started to creep in. A special moment was happening and the lithe vision of this goal mouth magician pulled the magic out of everything and all of a sudden he was there, a hand to it, palmed away over the bar I think, he saved it, he protected his goal superbly. It was like a goal for us. A victory. But his kicking and distribution is a bit funny. He's got a 50p foot this lad. I would have him practising that Nuno...after training maybe.

The tide is starting to shift even in these early days. I can smell it in the air, I can see it in everybody's faces. I sense that we are starting to find out where everything is and what it's for this Premier madness. When I think about the Albions eight whatever years of Premier league football I could laugh out loud. We have done more in these three games than them lot ever did in those boring lethargic, turgid bollock ball they played.

We played beautiful incisive, hard working creative fantastic football. Indeed we were on the back foot some of the time. These City dudes are European mad men. Most of them played in the World Cup. Conor Coady swept up another jingly jangly City attack…Coady was a midfielder sold by Huddersfield. He's now running the madness of defending our goal from a few hundred squillion quids worth of talent. This is the Nuno idea, this is it in spades mate. We don't really go shopping in the megastores of strange clubs in Europe or South America to buy talent up. We recognise raw talent and raw effort because that effort can be moulded to shape by practice and bloody hard work to forge a team that can take on the best in the world and of course have a fucking right to play teams such as these. Of course we can, it is our right to. We don't park the bus against these teams, we don't lose our ideas over theirs. We attack always and we defend when we have to, we fall and we pick ourselves back up. I watch Doherty moving into space and he is alive again and dynamic.

Traore has a go as well. Replacing Helder (who may puff out his chest tonight and be proud) he all of a sudden has three City defenders right in his grill. I bet he can smell their aftershave, can read their tattoos. But who cares? He doesn't he fucking runs and jinks past all of them like they are just dust in the wind mate. Traore, bloody hell. Its all madness, all of it and I expected no less of course. But each aggressive run he makes is tempered by something at this early stage. Probably a bit nervy. The sound from

Molineux is so loud I bet it's rattling the cell phone treee on top of Bushbury hill. We are loving this madness because we believe in it. I can't watch some parts and others my eyeballs are on stalks. We are moving the ball with a delicious tempo that seems controlled. We are attacking endlessly, even when are defending we are attacking...if that makes any sense? Who cares...Neves has the ball, it scalpels past an onrushing City player who seems dumbstruck. Traore falls over again. He must be dizzy.

Our players were protecting an idea today, of where we think we should be but more importantly 'How we must be when we are there'. Are we to take our seat at the high table with gratitude? Or sit and look upon the great and good of the Premier League and know that we are their equals? Today we intimated that we are not afraid any more. We have taken stock of these teams we have played so far and we see that they lack nothing except a Nuno. Someone who can galvanise a team to play with shape and discipline, to fully believe in the ideas he and his backroom staff have and it is a precious thing. It is one we are very fortunate to have.

I found myself talking about League 1 a lot today. Our games there against Brentford and MK Dons etc. Thinking about how far we have come and still the journey stretches out in front of us. But man, watching the team troop off the field at full time and looking at their faces they looked sad and disappointed. This filled me with hope…our team knew they could have had these glam football freaks, we were a hairs breadth away. The crazy train is moving.

Chapter 11

Steeltown Gollums and a Cup Game

I'm beginning to enjoy my trips to Hillsborough but sometimes during last nights match I think I enjoy (more) the descent into mediocrity of Foresteiri or whatever his name is, I can't get the Sako incident out of my head but I digress…I bump into a dude with a head like a battered traffic cone and he says something I don't understand so I just smile and carry on. The sky is low here tonight and everything is a little grey and my eyes start stinging from the traffic fumes but the feeling is friendly, the feeling is that Wednesday are going to get dicked. I eat a tray of chips outside the ground before I go in and they are tasty. I feel like I visit this ground eight or nine times a season it's that familiar now. I'm starting to not mind it and that's weird even if outside the ground is surrounded by that identikit semi industrial wasteland that typifies most football ground I have been to. Ammo and Horace eat their chips fast but I have to take it slow. I will get heartburn otherwise. But everything is fast today, everybody wants to be somewhere else I think.

Was it so long ago I watched our other first round Caraboa or whatever first round Cup match. Bristol Rovers I think it was. We sat in the Northbank and basically watched our second stringers muscle some sort of result out of it. At the time there were cameos from the first team that smelled a bit like what we had suffered the year before under Lambert. It was laboured and bitty. You could see of course that there was some sort of revolution going on in the team but there was more a sense of maybe…the revolution was just here and there. Seedlings maybe, just starting to unfurl their green leaves of the Nunolution.

Last night at Hillsborough there was a completely different zeitgeist to the whole thing. Where last season it was a rather insipid display of Caraboa or whatever football that still had the tendrils of Lambertism running through it…this was different, this was a whole new thing. You see I think Nuno now has a template not a team. I suspect although the team has a duty to play their beautiful football they do it under the auspices of the Nuno template. So we take last Saturdays match for instance. Shape. Nuno has now reached the stage where he has extrapolated the Philosophies and the training and now that 'idea' has become mobile and is able to be transplanted from line up to line up. So we see a whole new plethora of faces playing exactly the way, shape and form the stars of our side do. Am I right? I don't quite know. I want to tsalk to somebody who knows more about this but everybody is too busy, too singy and shouty, I fancy five minutes sit down and a chat.

I mean, we are playing a Championship side. Standing there in the Leppings Lane end there was a definite smell of puke as some youngblood lets go of the contents of his stomach all over the seats a few rows away. He's been on the Dark Fruits obviously. That alcopop thing. I hope he feels better this morning. Dude we have all been there. There was disgust from several of us and then stories of when they puked up somewhere odd. I felt like being sick watching the strange fucking football Wednesday were playing. In fact I had a fucking weird flashback during several parts of it as the ball flew into the air for some head ping pong. There was that 'tackling' thing where a Sheffield player clattered into one of our players. There was tugging and some elbow action. There was everything Championship football had, which was not a lot.

The first half kind of blathered away like the fans in the Chip shop before the match. The football Wednesday offered was hidden under a thick Yorkshire accent while they rolled a hot chip around their mouths making any utterance on the pitch kind of muffled and unidentifiable…and a bit painful. I'm staring at the window of the chip shop and I'm sure for a moment that Nuno walks past me, behind me, all I see is a reflection of him and I twist around to see. But there is nobody there, just bodies moving towards the ground.

Donk puts a foot in and dispossesses a Wednesday doughnut, split second and he's off into space and razor sharp he tangles a ball through two Wednesday players to Saiss who dinks the ball out of play. Saiss is rusty, he needs game time and maybe needs to chill out a bit. Donk runs up to the centre of the pitch looking for a pass again, he finds Morgan Gibbs White and an attack is on. Donk jogs back into position with Coadys voice reverberating around his head. Donk likes to get forward. I see Kortney moving forward too. The shape is everything and if Nuno is the Conductor of this mad orchestra then Coady is the lead Violinist for me. But this defence isn't really a defence sometimes, it's more of an attacking aid. Kortney or Donk move into space and the whole shape moves up a gear and forward. Lose possession and they are hunting for the ball constantly seeking to get it back. Wednesday don't have much time on the ball before there is a player in Gold chomping away at the back of their neck to get the ball back. It's our ball mate, you can't have it, you don't know what to do with it any way.

But it was kind of good natured. Wolves struggled a little due to the abstract and strange shapes Sheffield were throwing. I suppose the 'groping' stage was the first half really. Unbuttoning the bra of Sheffield was a sticky fumbly thing only really sparking to life when Morgan Gibbs White bust a shot wide on the wrong foot. We aim for a big wet tongue kiss but keep licking an eye or a chin in our frenetic pre coital football. But we had him and Saiss back in midfield. Morgan was in the Jota role I think and seemed to be pulled a little out of shape by the set up. Maybe that first half he had the directions set in stone by Nuno and couldn't dare to question it. I know a few of his positions were a bit strange and he found himself in territory unknown. So Nuno is stalking the technical area and taking everything in while the stink of puke wafts around the stand. What formation are we actually playing? At times it looks like this and other times it looks like that. There is an air of maybe 3-5-2 other times 5-4-1 ah bollocks to it. Who knows?

Ruddy was back too. He didn't really put a foot wrong to be honest, it was nice to see him back. He dealt with most of the shit thrown at him, ably protected by Kortney and Conor who were themselves busting some defensive shapes again. Conor is growing fast, sniffing out attacks before Sheffield Wednesday even knew they were attacking. His voice echoed around the ground as he directed play. He is our Captain you know and boy does he do some Captaining. The philosophy is naked and raw, play from the back and direct the attack. He splashes some beautiful passes around, diagonal and inch perfect to whatever player is in space and primed to attack. He directs shape and possession with his passes and ameliorates the directions and tactics of Nuno into the physical realms so it becomes less about airy fairy ideas of tactics and shape and more into direct aggressive movements.

So Wednesday at the end of the first half looked knackered and we looked like we were just warming up. It was looking good. It was looking beautiful. But there wasn't any real penetration, no real intent as yet. Traore one side of Bonatini and Morgan the other couldn't quite get the groove flowing. But at least Wednesday weren't throwing the Jackie Chan moves yet thank fuck.

I'm tempted to think this Sheffield team have gone backwards…but then I remember when they chopped Conor Ronan to the ground in the cold January we played there under Lambert. It's as sure as Tangos tits flopping around that some Wednesday doughnut will lose it at some point and I'm hoping we stay injury free and get out of here quickly. Elliot Watt tangles up a player by shifting the ball from side to side and he's off. I like young Elliott, I like the cut of his jib.

I go for a roll up in the break and talk to people. It's good but I don't think many people know why they are there, but I take the opportunity to gobble two 30mg Co-Codomol and a funky 50mg Tramodol as I stepped in a pothole outside the ground and twisted my leg a bit and now it's sending shooting pains up into my hip. It's a good job I didn't have a drink or I would be slumped in a chair dribbling…again, or singing technicolour love songs with the young lad behind us who is just holding his head in his hands and staring at his reflection in the abstract expressionist remains of his chips splattered all around him.

I think about Vinagre as I watch him. Twisting and turning, moving constantly, he gets a few flavours from the Wednesday backline. These flavours are dull insipid things. He's only a slight thing Vinagre but he doesn't half shrup off the attentions of the occasional Steel Town Gollum with an idea about a grab of the shirt or a stud in the ankle bone.

Vinagre is a fucking delight. In my madness I would throw him into the first team every time but what do I know? Traore wants to put his own stamp on the game. A swish of the tail and he's off again. Busting apart the obstacles Wednesday put in his way he shrugs, he dips, he is off. Who has an answer to Adama? How do you actually defend against him? It was like he had a forcefield around him, some strange Star Trek technology that repels opposition players. He is relentless when he has the ball. He gets to the touchline and arcs his body to get a cut back in. To Leo! Fucking hell, at last. Leo scores. Spiersy reports it as 23 hours and 59 minutes since he scored a goal. I don't know what Leo is doing to celebrate it but I'm just looking up at the roof of the stand and thanking the footballing Gods. Jesus Christ Leo…1-0 to us. I never said a bad word about you Leo, I always trusted you. Are you channelling Dark Leo? I hope so. Traore, dude, you are not a 'beast' you are not a 'unit', you are a fucking treasure, a true footballer and you make my heart leap. Donk looks ecstatic at the goal which also makes me feel good and Conor Coady is shouting something loud and happy. Teams eh?

Pedro and Helder come on. All of a sudden it's fucking samba time again, limbo dancing, carnival. I like Pedro a lot, in fact I think if I watch him again soon I may start to love him a little bit. He's ultimate Steez for me. Like a young Moutinho maybe, same shapes and movement but with some tweak here and there as he produces an absolutely magical move between his feet that makes the ball jiggle like some quantum particle puffing in and out of existence as a Wednesday player merely observes. Pedro is gone mate, like a flash of Magicians magic powder he pops up again somewhere else while we all dribble as the painkillers kick in and it's a bit numb. But Pedro…dude.

Helder is doing Helder type things. What's got into him? Now he's busting between players he goes past one, two, three Wednesday players. Head down, resolute. They chop him down. Their ideas lack anything beautiful these Wednesday lot. Penalty. Helder steps up and smashes it in. 2-0. Fuck off Sheffield. In the cold of Fulham they denigrated you my little Helder, but I knew you would have courage and tenacity. I wonder what words Nuno spoke to you? You came back out of the abyss my friend and are now in the light for me. Sheffield Wednesday make a substitution. It's that Serbian lanky bastard again. He's got a neck like a Telegraph pole and a head like a students rucksack. This my friends is what ideas Wednesday have…the same ideas they had two years ago. Since I mentioned Foresteiri at the start of this match I haven't thought of him again because I simply never saw him..he is fading away like Sako maybe and those battles they had a few years ago are fading too. This team Wolves team are a bright light and they are dazzling.

Walking back to the car I am concentrating on the paths and roads underneath me so I don't stumble again. So I listen to the Wednesday fans that surround me. They talk not of their own teams failings but of us. I hear words like Strong/very good/a different class/brilliant/exciting and I am proud of my team and prouder still of the way we play. Discipline and hard work training. We only see the tip of the iceberg, the product of the pain that seeps into the Compton pitches after training. The hours spent looking at tactics and shape, sculpting those ideas into verifiable results like tonight. Yes, it's the start of the Cup run, yes it's still early days and yes, I suppose it's not really important before we go to West Ham…but man I feel good about this madness.

Chapter 12

Wolves Versus the Alf Garnett Gollums

Has their ever been such an emphatic victory in such a vast and empty place? The Olympic stadium was full of course…but there was nothing in it except the well oiled hum of the machine as we took to the field, cranked up the starter motor and sat back to wait. Plus 3k Wolves fans on a day out. How beautiful we looked. Apprehension, excitement perhaps happy in the knowledge even before a ball was kicked that we would win it. Confidence? I'm not sure. Maybe we saw ourselves filling the stadium with something that really wasn't three thousand fans, maybe we would fill it with ideas, Nunos ideas. Maybe fortitude, intent, courage and adherence to pure footballing Philosophy all the traits the greatest teams hold dear. In that soulless Olympic stadium we would bring soul, maybe into that vast bowl of abstract nothingness we could bring passion and light?

As the Tube train rocked and shuffled us from strange place to strange place the rhythm of the tracks was nullified by the stoney faces of the people that live here. They were like grey faced things these Londoners. On their faces the realisation that perhaps their time has come and gone. Maybe they see the decimation of their cities once dynamic ideas reflected in the performance of this most London of teams. West Ham United slathered by cash, held hostage by the Dildo brothers and that most hated of figures Karen Brady who has the traits of a Disney Villainess, dark and brooding her present held tight under the bonds of the past. The Karen Brady blow up doll at Saint Andrews, her demanding pinched face with all the emotion of a Plasterers knee. A West Ham fan gets on the tube in a team shirt with Snodgrass and the claret and blue, the name on the back gives me an icy stab of instant Villa hate again. Claret and fucking blue. Peschisolido the little wanker, Sullivans, Alf Garnett, scouse gits, sex toys, KY Jelly, strange pies and eels, Lulus, Villa, my leg, Horace staring like a psychopath at someone, probably his own yellow reflection in the tube train window. I am talking about the dirty Veg man on Wolverhampton market and a woman opposite is smiling at our conversation. The tube is full of these Garnett Gollums and again I am struck by the unhappiness they have on their faces. What is this Premier League doing to people? Perhaps it's too early into the season. Perhaps the whole show hasn't kicked off yet and here we are Yamming to each other like day trippers, which we are I suppose.

Next to me is a twenty something West Ham fan, he has that vacuous stare that all the people in this place have, they look into spaces but not in a creative way seeing the spaces as places to manufacture ideas, conversation etc. But they tend to stare at nothing because this is where they hide. This is where they find identity, here in the nothingness or the hot tube train, here in the coffee shops and the violence. This is their identity maybe..I engage him in conversation about the game. I'm a nice bloke, I can chat shit with anybody. He answers in a hot machine gun fashion, errant half words that cook off and fire in the breach before aim has been achieved.

'Doing orite aintcha' he says. Well that's a brief examination and conclusion of the whole caboodle I suppose. But how do you explain Nuno to a lone West Ham fan on a hot tube train? How do you explain the feelings we had last season? How do you explain the Wizardry of Nuno?

'He's a Wizard and a Philosopher not a Coach' I say…but he looks at me like I'm a lunatic and he's probably right too. He is looking at Horace who is like a coiled spring ready to burst out and smash things…Tube people pick up quick, these feelings about other people and he becomes quiet and reflective watching Horace.

Leo Bonatini squares a pass to Traore who is unstoppable. From his own half Adama suddenly does have idea, intent and madness. Those sinews stretch and prime themselves as he attacks. He's like a Lion chasing an Antelope, he bounds and strides as the acids and chemicals flood his muscles with electrical messages, to stretch and leap, to contract and expand at scarily rapid crashes and smashings of electrons deep in that muscle fibre. I hold my breath and sense something and it is a hush, we watch and wonder. Adama leaves players in his wake, all they have is a memory of him, a distant foggy memory of Traore once there and now there, 3-4-5-6-7 yards away now, gone. They were defeated by Adama before they even knew it. He is the Bruce Lee of this team.

But the vision? Adamas arrival was perfectly forseen by Leo who when he came on was a delight again, probing and dragging West Ham players here and there. The smoke and Mirrors routine of the Brothers Fantastic Moutinho and Neves, a perfect interplay of delightful rapid passes and movements, it was mesmerising and I was mesmerised, but West Ham also slipped into that warm zone of absent minded football as they luxuriated in the display of the Brothers Fantastic. And verily Leo made much of this. Adama (at one point) wasn't even looking at anything, I suspect he had visualised the ball coming to him, where it would be, what power it had and probably which way it was spinning. Here is the real magic. Adama knew because Leo knew, because Moutinho knew and Ruben knew, as did little Ruben, and so did Doherty and Bennet is starting to know as Coady always knew and Patricio who knew last week against Manchester City. They know because Nuno told them. Nuno told them and they trust him so what Nuno says is 'The Truth' and that my friends is the fucking most powerful thing in the world. But what is this truth?

Hard work, courage, skill, TEAM work, never the individual ALWAYS the team, always Nunos way. West Ham probed, they spun, they threaded delightful passes, they looked like the multi million pound team that they are. As Everton and Manchester City before them I delighted to watch them. This was the Premier League and nobody is here by mistake, they have all fought long and fucking hard battles. But what is the truth of this place, this stadium they play their football? It was vast and beautiful, swooping lines, wide concourses, relatively easy access, friendly staff.

Their fans were still West Ham fans, but there was a sadness in them, a deep sadness. You saw it in their faces as they trudged up the sun baked tarmac towards the great monstrous thing this place was. Madness. They were sad because they were not in their rightful place. They were not linked in any way to the geology underneath this stadium. There have been no battles there, no great losses, no blood spilt on the steps of this place. There is no history for them here and without the memories of the past how are you supposed to look to the future? This sadness that pervades this West Ham team is a product of this removal from one dynamic, crazy and creative Upton Park to this amazing architectural swooping delightful place of absolutely nothing at all except vast empty spaces that ideas should fill. Perhaps in a few decades things would have happened in this place and those feelings and emotions would drip into the new concrete but that time is not today my friends. West Ham have given the ball away three times on the trot now. They have zest but it's dysfunctional.

But us? Shape and movement, here and there a snubbed chance. Less defensive frailty at times than a team learning, a team playing against a multi million pound attack from West Hams frontline. Coady has a voice that at times I heard even though he was eight miles away from the pitch but 'HEY…HEY…HEY…HEY' he shouted. One simple word that hid an avalanche of information about positioning, control and luxurious movement. He swept up attacks, he instigated counter attack, his communications were short and brusk, demands of movement and of adjustment. He pulled players wide for Boly to collect and to neutralise.

Coady moved players to Bennet who would deal with the threat with a delightful dig at the loose ball to 'player' or to hustle the threat to safety away from goal. Coady strains at the bit to move forward to instigate attacks but his discipline pulls him back every time. This is the truth of Nuno, he needs Conor back there, in 'that place' and no other. Otherwise nothing would work and the whole Gold and Black machine would grind to a halt. The simplest disobedience to 'THE PLAN' will result in the whole edifice crashing down.

So from West Ham in the second half great passes that split Wolves and resulted in half chances, crosses were pin point and dangerous. Patricio hustled and controlled. Is he going to pull these world class saves out of the bag at every match? These Patricio moments are sublime and fast, his hands are safe and movement into a ruck of players courageous and here is some other word we may insert into this idea…trust. Our defence are becoming a true unit where the chain of understanding is starting to grow and grow. At the other end Costa, my little big Helder was menacing. Jimmy Jimenez was thinking too much. Such is his tenacity and belief, his need to do his job and repay the confidence Nuno has in him…there is too much strength in him. It is over powerful and intense, too intense. It is time for Jimmy to start playing with the Nuno 'Hive mind' that permeates this team and to utilise it fully, to embrace it.

Adama has that bass thing going on so of course the shot, when he meets it, is low and fast. His journey across the pitch has ended with him smashing the ball beyond the goalkeeper and hits the net which performs a sensual ripple across the rear of the goal. I see no more of this, there are limbs. I smash against the seat in front, my shin, my bad knee. My back cracks, somebody punches me in the ear, I hug and I am crazy, we all fucking are, my head is aching, the lagers, the dark fruit cider, the cocaine, I haven't eaten all day, I feel sick and all of a sudden tired. 93rd fucking minute mate. First Premier League win. Three fucking points. Are we being daft thinking we belong here? Nah. The stress of thinking about this game dissipates out of me and I feel like going to sleep for a few hours, folding up my coat and putting my big fat head on it to sleep.

Outside the vast ground we engage in small talk. My head is pounding now. The cocaine, the lager, the singing and the emotion all swinging back and forth and I delight in seeing various people, in communicating within a smaller more nooky form of talking and celebrating. Wolves fans mill around animated and tactile. We are ascendent are we not? This win, at the moment absolutely everything at this moment. I think I see Nuno in the crowd, moving. I see him as a Security man, I see him as a Cop bored motionless and scanning. I see Nuno everywhere.

At Moor street station in Birmingham we walk back to the car and there right in the middle of the near empty car park is a lone pair of shoes placed side by side like some Mom had tidied them up. There is nobody around so I quietly put my foot against them. Pick them up, have a look. Size 10's, I can cram my foot in these bad boys. They have loads of life and I am chuckling to myself and pick them up, put them in the car with me. Horace is disgusted.

'I will buy you some shoes' he says, bless him. But it's never been about that. It's all about recycling, all about using forgotten things, lost things, making them alive and viable again.

On match of the day later I watch Shearer say some nice things, I always mute Lineker and I'm laughing at Keowns monkey head too much to hear what he says. The edited match is all West Ham. Fucking standard. I only watch it so I can see Nuno, what he thought and what his analysis of the game was. He talks about the TEAM a lot. But my eyes are heavy and in my mind I was in dark deep City of London pubs, drinking lager, with people I love. I am thinking about Matt Doherty, our ever present right back.

This little story about Matt Doherty of course begins in a strange place, an unforgiving wilderness of ideas and intent under various managers. But I think Matts story isn't really about how he overcame the lack of ideas and policy under Lambert and Jackett to an extent but about how he found meaning within the atmosphere of dogged and brutal football he found himself within. Matt possibly struggled with the 'Hows' when he didn't really understand the 'Whys'. I say struggled but this is maybe the wrong word…possibly a better one would be something like 'fought'. There were times in the past few seasons when among the acid commentary from others I too struggled with coming to any semblance of conclusion about how Matt fought his matches down that side of the pitch.

The foundation of his match and his play I suspect was always trying to find some kind of meaning to his football, how it made the environment around him change, how it affected him personally. At the end of Lamberts brief tenure I remember watching Matt stalk the pitch on the last day and looking at him closely…you see I alluded to him having a face like he was wondering whether he had left the cooker on at home. I was mistaken of course, as I suspect now, at this time, he was struggling to understand what role he had to play within this team, his ideas, his physicality, his team mates, the changing face of Wolverhampton Wanderers and what role he had to play within it. All meanings and all explanations like trying to grab smoke.

Matt Doherty stands out for me as a man trying to find meaning in the most torrid of circumstances during that time. I suspect that when Matt struggled with his environment in that time he wasn't trying to seek meaning in the wider view we hold. Of life and why we exist, why we struggle…but it was more localised and close. A sense that the meaning he had to grasp was immediate and lasted 90 minutes or so. It was a struggle with the way we played our football.

Did he question the football being played by Lambert and to a lesser extent Jackett? What did he make of the heart on sleeve madness of Zenga? With the arrival of Nuno I suspect that the beautiful ideas of this new Coach were presented thoughtfully and with skill but perhaps this presentation of exciting football didn't particular impress Matt Doherty. Perhaps Nuno in his wisdom didn't present ideas to Matt but made him question not the football he was playing and the form and function of it but possibly Nuno made Matt question his own ideas about football and so the answers he came up with became a mantra of sorts or an interface between what Nuno required and what Matt could deliver.

What job did Matt have? Simply to run that channel, to defend when required, disable attacks, and when attacking to support, to get the ball in the box, to collect the ball, to win challenges and occasionally to score. A simple explanation I know, but one that will suffice for now. But Nuno I think required different answers and one which fitted within the ethos of the team he was about to inspire.

So Matt was given a job as I wrote above. To create (for himself) a set of tasks that he had to fulfil, to achieve the required fitness levels, to tick all the boxes that his position required. But within that empirical framework there was another just as important task…to enjoy, to create and more than anything to experience his football and to revel within it. This experience of creative football is what will elevate the mediocre player into the realms of the hero, this ability to experience and create within that experience. The motivation this gives a player is the aspect of the battle, they after all are Gladiators to some degree, this football is just stylised combat in its many forms.

Doherty at the start of Nunos arrival would have instantly identified this Warrior aspect in the endless tactical team talks and the bullshit of working within a team framework. Nuno would have identified in Matt the rawness of the Warrior aspect I suppose. Doherty is Irish and they are a Warrior race. I think Matt maybe started to play football not within the moment but looking externally outside the bubble of Molineux and used this external

Nunoist philosophy as the platform on which he could build his own ideas. Of course when you struggle to find meaning externally then you tend to look inward and the great internal monologue begins. Am I good enough? Can I be arsed? Should I do this, or that. It is a memetic and coarse dialogue and one we have seen Helder Costa, Ivan Cavaleiro, Leo Bonatini have recently. I think our 'Little Wolf' Diogo Jota is about to suffer the same feelings that plagues Matt at the moment. They are struggling to find meaning in these great empty impersonal spaces that the Premier League is presenting to us. I don't mean the stadiums and the razzamatazz of a game but the struggle to understand the roles they have to play in what seems like an 'industry' solely devoted to financial concerns, money, cash, the cars, the houses, the deals and the schmoozing around signing shirts for corporate guests, glad handing and smiling. Maybe I don't know. It's a fucking strange place jiving with the player lounge lizards.

You have to have a purpose to keep fighting and it has to be a firm and concrete purpose otherwise the realisation that the bullshit that surrounds the life of a modern footballer is bigger than the 'purpose' results in another fight. This fight is the battle motivate yourself and to dredge every last iota of strength and power out of your body at every match and every moment of the game. To inspire yourself to greater and greater heights. This is what amazes me about Conor Coady, a man that in every match he squeezes out every last effort to allow his team to win, to revel in victory and battle, you see it in his face every match nearly. We draw, he is stoical, in victory he is transcendental in his joy, in defeat not sad, not angry but wiser and more learned. Coady is a footballer who finds this Philosophy of Nunos much to his taste, not only understanding the physical aspects of Nunos requirements but also the Philosophical. Who has a will to fight when there is nothing to fight for?

Matts fight of course is the realisation that an errant tackle or a mistake, a lost ball, a moment of distraction could cause the existence he has at the moment, a player in a Premier League team with all the trappings of success, to be ethereal and transparent. A time out of the first team maybe a relegation to the outcasts like Zyro and Graham, maybe eventually a loan to Scunthorpe or Plymouth maybe. So this realisation of course makes Matt look at the world he plays his football in to be transitory and everchanging, so is it worth the struggle and the pain?

Of course it is Matt. For we can find meaning even within the hopeless and the pain? Of course we can. Matt is at an important juncture in his playing career now, and he is in an enviable position too. I don't mean his success and his football, his position etc.

I mean he is at the point when he has a choice to maximise his potential and to battle the greatest of battles we Humans can ever take part in. To transform the negative aspects of this whole footballing life into positive ones, to exchange your existential tragedies into total triumph and to achieve something at last. I think Matt Doherty is on the cusp of realising that although he cannot change the situation and the existence of himself as a Premier League footballer there is one thing he can change, and that is himself.

Matt Doherty is the last survivor of the Jackett seasons. The one player who has transcended all his demons to remain at this moment an integral part of this whole Nuno madness. For that he is to be applauded and treated with the utmost reverence. The things this man has seen in his time begs some mad contemplations. The stories he could tell, and yet he remains on the team sheet every week despite suffering the ministrations and calamities of Championship football last season and taking part in a few rough head times this season too. He has changed himself, constantly. But more importantly he has become responsible for himself.

You see…when you are faced with a battle like this, to stay within a side even if it is filled with beautiful talented footballers from sunny places, you have to have courage. I think Matt is probably one of the most courageous footballers within our team at the moment and this bravery is a challenge and it makes you suffer. I suspect that this suffering gives Matt a meaning even if he is crawling exhausted off the training pitch or lying on some emerald green football pitch in some gigantic stadium as he tries to clear his vision of the stars erupting in his head after smashing his forehead against some hardnut after a fifty-fifty header.

I wrote this because Matt has been in my thoughts lately. We applaud and wax about beauty, about Neves, about Patricio swooping across our goalmouth, of Costa, of Vinagre and of Jimenez…but we forget sometimes the hidden battles players like Matt Doherty has, and the courage and fortitude he has shown. Fair play Matt Doherty…I thought I would wax and say this in ending…

Once more into the fray

Into the last good fight I'll ever know.

Live and die on this day

Live and die on this day

But I think my feelings were summed up by Matt Dohertys biggest fan the beautiful Anita Millard who, outside some shithole Championship ground grabbed hold of me and said 'I fucking love Matt Doherty, I mean I really fucking love Matt Doherty'. Me too Anita, me too.

But I also think sometimes about our love for our football club, especially now we are in this Premier League. Is our love large enough and powerful enough to fill in the gaps that this incessant pace from Fosun is making? We are going places, straight to the top maybe but have we as fans got the energy to keep up? Have we got the Philosophy in place to understand any of it? Maybe this search for Nuno is also a search for ourselves maybe. Not what we are now but what we may become. So finding Nuno may also end up with us finding ourselves maybe?

After the West Ham game I found myself at the top of the garden again. It was 1.29 am on my watch and every now and again the ambulances that constantly trawl up and down the Lichfield road throw these blue flames on the houses around me. Reflecting urgency and speed, a crisis maybe. Even the Bats are quiet tonight and there is nothing in the air that's alive as far as I can see. Insomnia is like a bad video cassttee. Moments of clarity interspersed with jagged and static filled screens that you can see, if you look closely enough, figures within and garbled speech, roaring mangled audio tracks, miscommunication. What is going to happen in the future?

Chapter 13

Lancashire Gollums, Stanley Kubrick and a few nights sleeping rough

I had a Stanley Kubrick incident I'll admit. Five hours after the Burnley match had finished I was walking, plodding on a mountain road to Bala Lake, it was twilight and I looked at my shitty IPhone 4s for the last time, all nestled there in my hand bleeping away. You remember the Apes at the beginning of 2001 A Space Odyssey? Throwing the bone in the air? I chucked my black Monolithic phone into the distance and it tumbled down somewhere into the darkness below. I was the enemy for everybody lately, the target of blame and the 'dark presence' I suppose. I felt like I had to go away for a few days to recenter myself. It was self flagellation too. I mean't to walk until I dropped dead like some death metal Forest Gump to be found by some Welsh Farmer on his way somewhere to do something. But I'm alive.

Thank fuck. Now it was just me. It was getting dark. At that moment I was a useless waste of space and I trudged further up the mountain, the tops of these weirdly named hills were just deep purple smudges in the half light. I could fall off the edge if I wasn't careful, and I wasn't. Fucking hell Nuno. I want you to phone me up and tell me to work harder and inspire me…but I've chucked my phone away. But the rhythm of the walking and the miles that passed also brought a hypnotic succession of idle thoughts…and I could see Nuno coming to rescue me and he's on a Golden Chariot with coal black horses with eyes aflame and the beat of their feet like the roar of a Molineux crowd and he would offer me his strong brown hand as he rode towards me and I would grab it and he would pull me onto his chariot and he would throw back his head and laugh loud, he would say some powerful magic words to his horses and they would rear up screaming with pleasure as they ran off the edge of the road and we were flying…to Nuno land probably. I have stepped on a squashed Rat in the road. At first I thought it was a Squirrel…but the bald tail and those sharp teeth, the cloudy Rat eye. It was getting dark but not darker than my mood. The tops of the mountains and hills looked like hooded dark wizards against the dimming sky. I could feel them watching me, only mildly interested in this confused and fractured human. What price human emotions against this backdrop of ageless geology? What effect do we have and how powerful can one human be against the pricks of daily existence?

At Molineux earlier I had watched the whole Nuno thing in relentless operation. Here is a man that can rally his strength to move a cumbersome football club into some sort of dynamic shape, to mold and cajole the clay of our club into this graceful work of art on display today. Can I draw a parallel with Hitlers incisive Blitzkrieg into Poland? I'm scratching around for angles and dangles of how to describe our football at the moment. We don't fucking stop do we. It's a constant stream of beautiful madness as the ball is pinged across the pitch, controlled, moved off, space, a threaded angelic ball, sacred geometry mate, boom, a chance. I don't know what I'm watching here to be honest. I have the same feeling when I'm looking at beautiful art or listening to good music. I've watched bands play a gig where everything all of a sudden hits a zenith. The band are locked into their music fully, the audience are reaching a paroxysm of joys, the whole place is rocking. This was the same, this was that moment. Every ball is a joy to behold and every tackle a moment of divine treasure and this one the treasury of our expectation I suppose. Nuno had put all our expectations and hopes into a black top hat, he shakes his wand over it and mutters some incantation and there we have it, he pulls a Rabbit out. Yay! We all cheer...

We are taking these Claret and Blue scalps with aplomb in the same way as that Panzer driven lunacy over a border way back in time. Moutinho is the driver of the whole show, it seems like he is connected to Neves by an invisible magic string. They devour midfields these pair, like hunting sharks, they gather their prey just where they want them before attacking, ferocious and contact between Neves or Moutinho and an opposition player ends up with the ball at our feet and another bloody rampaging load of beautiful madness as we move further into enemy territory for the 100th time.

How many shots did we have? 30? or 40? Fuck knows. I just stood there with my mate Pottsy who was waxing highly lyrical at this display. Every time we moved he was jabbing me with his elbow or turning me around so he could shake me into some sort of consciousness. Because I was confused. We play the ball and the whole match is like a snowball going downhill picking up more and more momentum as it moves along until everything is crushing and madness. Otto is in there again mooching and pimping the corner, chewing chunks out of and claret and blue balloon that floats into his sphere of influence. Jonny Otto ladies and gentlemen, I don't want to annoy him in any way put it that way. Lovely player. Everything is fast.

You see the football was moving a lot faster than my poor old brain could register. This was light speed bollocks. I've said 'relentless' before. It was bloody relentless, there I said it again. Not only for Sean Dyche and his rag tag band of weirdos from the North, but for us too. Burnley are on the arc of hopelessness, swirling into the pit…you can tell. Their football lacks context. But us? We are grinding them all down. These teams are becoming the errant loose sleeve in the cogs and gears of the great Nuno Machine. They get dragged in and smashed between our midfield and our three man defence.

Coady leaps out to smother a threat, a fucking rare threat to be honest, Burnley are a team afraid to stretch themselves in case they get their arse well and truly bitten by our ceasless movement. Coady dispossesses their man, Sam Vokes I think it was. Old Wolves lad now plying his trade in the diaspora of the North. I wonder if he recognises this place now? Vokes tries to get the ball back as Coady is directing movemnt with the ball at his feet. Coady is shouting and looking, Vokes moves closer. Coady puts a hand on him to keep him away, always talking, he pings a sublime ball straight to Neves who doesn't even look at the ball he just received. Of course the ball will land there, it always does. Conor Coady. Amazing.

You see this football is hypnotic. The steady tick tock of manufacturing goal scoring opportunities never actually stops. The ethic is of course hard work. Nuno tells us that every week. It's the time we spend on the training pitch at Compton that gives us this seemingly effortless chop chop chop of recycling the ball from the back, up to the front end where Jota or Costa or Jimmy can get a foot on it. Goal scoring chance. Jota puts it slightly wide. I mean who knows what blurb will be written about this game elsewhere but the one I watched was domination from start to finish. Clearing balls off the line, Sir William of Boly having the odd whack at goal. Jimmy flinging himself at everything. Little Jonny popping up like some mad little Corsican mafia assassin.

You could see the Burnley defence going 'Who the fuck is this nutter? How many people have they actually got playing?' That was the scope of the whole thing, the whole show. Domination from start to finish. I'm dizzy a little, probably due to the four pints of some funky IPA I drank in the Royal London beforehand. I am with people I love, to watch a team I love. I stop for a rest on my walk, I'm on maybe mile 24 and it is pitch black, I'm watching the white line on the side of the road and I'm concentrating, I could be over the edge if I'm not careful. My left leg feels like a piece of wood now, it has no life just a fire of ache and gnashing bone and my foot is slapping the tarmac and it's 'slide-shuffle-slap' also hypnotic, also mantra like. Now my mind is quieter but still dark I fancy I can hear someone walking with me, just behind me, I can't see them but I can feel they are there. I had the same feeling years ago standing by myself on the Southbank when not many went.

I was sure there was somebody standing beside me, just behind me, watching. Ghosts mate. Materialisations. Trouble is, standing there now, I also feel like a ghost, like my body is slowly becoming transparent and all thats left are a few hundred thousand words about football I wrote and that honesty of last season is now like a shroud around me as I walk and talk. You give more and more of your heart to this club and you are trapped within the whole circle of madness.

It's always Wolves, always the club or it's always you, never the victim but always the accused. I fancy I can hear people singing 'Silver Lining' in the blackness but it's just echoes from the ceasless internal monologue. I understand now...something that happened as I went for a piss ten minutes into the first half. I edged past a dude who just shouted 'Costa you fucking useless cunt' at full volume. I looked at him amazed and he looked at me with a blank expression. Yes, I understand fully. It's not Costa or Jota or Doherty or any player we want to pick out for villification. It's us. It's that internal monologue we have with ourselves. We harry and judge ourselves constantly, wondering how we fit into this madness we call life. In this one sided conversation the tone is always dark and violent. It's not Costa who is 'a cunt' it's us, it always will be.

Sean Dyche on his touchline was doing an apoplectic Pub Landlord impression. He looked like somebody has shit on the floor of his toilets or robbed his gambler. Jesus Christ man relax. just enjoy it. His head looks like a burned Orangutang, like a tramps hernia, his hair reminds me of hoovering under the settee or pulling the cooker out to clean the floor. He must have felt like a right banana seeing his team taken apart like this. I could see him getting redder as the game went on and I expected a 'Scanners' moment where his head would just pop brain and bone all over our pitch the red blood mist would be blown over to Nuno who would just step back and let the misty red Dyche plasma blow past and everybody would just sigh and pack up, go home. Tick Tock. Every movement of the ball was another hard won afternoon at Compton. It is relentless because Nuno wants it that way.

I went for a Coffee in the week. Aromas of Portugal in King Street, a lady named Monica owns it. She is lovely, from Portugal. Show her some love and go there next time you are in town. The Portuguese egg custards are bad man fodder, have two Espressos, they will blow your head off. So yeah, Nuno had just been in, I missed him by ten minutes. I could probably have still smelt his aftershave if I tried, hanging around the coffee smells like some abstract strange aromatic melody, it would be powerful but understated with a scent of Brimstone. As I stepped back outside there was a Spice head picking his arse and looking at his finger like there was something stuck on it. He howled to the sky as I hurried past. Spicehead stinkfinger is not a thing. I missed Nuno by ten minutes. Hart is smoothing his weird Metrosexual trim with his gloved hand. Wont some bastard put a small compact mirror on the goalpost so he can check his face for dirty marks. He looks towards us again and says something. His face is like a wax mask.

Somebody has said something to him as he strides towards the Southbank goal. He is pissed off and intimates some abuse back. Somebody is clapping his arrival in the goal. Probably the same doughnut who clapped Pickford the other week. I wonder what the stats are for us scoring at the Southbank end over the season? Somebody tell me please. Joe Hart is still mouthing. Weird eyebrowed dickhead. Fuck off. Somebody shouts 'Hart you wanker' and he winks. But he is hurt. We should use this tactic a lot in the next home games. Be relentless in cussing the opposition goalie. Halfway through the second half Hart sits down and chills out in his six yard box. Bloody hell. Dyche, this is your idea and philosophy then is it? Your goalie sitting down. Jesus Christ. I have a quick squint up field at Rui Patricio. Our goalie is shouting something at Coady. It's that loud I can hear him right back here with me mate Pottsy shouting in me earhole. Patricio and Hart are polar opposites, one dark and sultry the other pale and ethereal. Yin and Yang.

What ideas Burnley had were of the World war 1 variety. Throw bodies in front of it mate. I kept hearing this word 'clinical' as we busted goal scoring shapes all over the place. They were sticking their pale little bodies all over the shop these Burnley players. How many did they get off the line? Little Jonny Otto busts one goal wards and I don't know what happened but we didn't score. Jonny runs back up field like he has just cut an ear off one of their defenders and is now running back with it in his possession. He's a right mad little sod ay he? Only little, but again one of those blokes you pick on after a few pints and he ends up punching you in the face for ten minutes and your tshirt is pulled over your head and he boots you a good one right in the nuts and you wonder if you should have just gone home. Leave it out mate.

There were times when we should have fucking toe bunted the ball into the net maybe eight or nine times. The Costa chance was one of them. We are so nice and polite it's silly sometimes. Not every goal has to be as beautiful as you ya know. Sometimes we just want to see it in the back of the net so we can collapse over the seat in front grabbing hold of whoever. We are trying to walk it in.

The pace of the game leading up to any attack is so fast and popping that it seems like the money shot still has to be beautiful. It doesn't of course. There will be plenty of time for steezy 30 yard volleys and sexy curving balls that drift into the net. Trouble is...or maybe not is that now the actual play is becoming greater than the stage. Last week at West Ham all the theatre was in my mind at least, was a defunct 'souless bowl' to paraphrase the current meme. But it was a grand architectural marvel to be honest. It was massive, it should have been gawped at open mouthed by us simple Midlanders as we walked around it confused by the speed at which everything flies in weird shithole they call London.

But I suspect we now see the play on the pitch as far greater dramatic magnitude than steel beams and swooping stadium roofs or a day out in the madness of London.

Fancy missing Nuno. But what would I even say to him? Thanks Nuno…or just stand there like a knobhead singing 'Nuno had a dream..' showing him how few teeth I had. Muttering some heartfelt but dysfunctional thank you as the sweat dripped down my back and I wish I could talk as easy as I write. I dunno. Boly stretches to the ball as it oodles and noodles across the goal line. Fucks sake. But 4.5 seconds later the ball is back in the danger area again and Joe Hart is fannying around.

It looks good don't get me wrong, but it's fucking pointless movement from him…we are our own worse enemy and Jota takes 0.3928 seconds too long and there is a Burnley neck in the way, throwing his body in the way for Seans and Burnleys one idea…and if anybody knows what that idea is put it on a post card and send it me because I haven't got a fucking clue. These Claret and Blue teams make me feel ill. They should ban this colour strip. It looks like medical emergencies and illness to me.

I had a look at Patricio up the other end at one point in the game, still as the Bronze Stan Cullis outside the North bank. Somebody should have took him a chair and a paper…maybe my book. At one segment of our domination I'm sure he was reading the adverts on the video display thing. Doherty has just had a thing with Costa where the ball pinged beautifully confusing the Burnleyites into tumbled messes of neck and bad trims. But the ball goes somewhere else and it's probably chance number twenty something. It's entertaining shit there's no doubt about it.

I realise of course, I'm at the top of this mountain road now and it's pitch black, maybe midnight and I'm ten miles away from Bala. I stop for a roll up and sit awhile smoking then notice a star reflected in a puddle at my feet, then my eyes readjust and I see it's actually a farmhouse light maybe a thousand feet below and I'm sitting on the edge of a cliff I never knew was there. I turn around and go back to the Lake. It's good to walk and get that madness out of your system, it's therapy by mileage. I guess it's why people run or jog too. I haven't seen anybody for hours now, just a few sheep which were huddled by the side of the road in a group, their white newly cut wool bright against the blackness flashing when the moon has a quick look through the clouds before she pulls the mist back over her eyes and goes back to sleep.

Jimmy flicks the ball off his foot and the ball hits the post and goes in. Three fucking points mate, cheers. Sherpa Van trophy, Andy Mutch, Bully, scrapping Chelsea fans in Kings Cross station, fighting through Burnley fans at Wembley, Wolves were everywhere that day. Jesus Christ we were beautiful that day as well. I missed Nuno I suppose but in other ways I meet him most the time I watch a game at Molineux. I suppose Nuno is what we see on the pitch and his personality runs through the team like a golden lode through thick rock.

Yes I am sure I meet him like this. The wider aspects of the victory must be left to others to work out. We are still in the early stages of this revolution. The start of it has been positive and good, everything looks dangerous and ready to explode. The goals are going to come, I can smell it in the air when we play, it's anticipation, it's fucking relentless this Wolves Machine.

I suppose I was on mile 41 or something when I eventually decided to stop walking. My feet have two massive blisters that had burst. Socks and boots were soaked with rain and pus. My hips were iron fire and my knees felt like I was balancing on razor sharp knives. But my brain was empty at last I suppose.

So I just sat in the forest for a while as the rain splodded big drops of water down my neck and I kept my roll up alight in cupped hands. Sometimes football isn't important at all you know. It's someone elses ideas not yours. You are just the beneficiary of the hard work put down for your entertainment every Saturday Friday, Sunday, Tuesday or whatever day the Great Satan at Sky Sports picks. No, sometimes it's not important but it is needed. It gives you something to pin your hopes onto when everything else seems a bit dark and unlit. Out of darkness cometh light?

I keep coming back to that mantra like a habit or something. Like it explains in it's own way everything about life. But I did realise a few things on my walk around Wales after the match. There is always hope and there is always a glimmer of light in the darkness. We don't always recognise what that light is I suppose when it does come. Sometimes I think we mistake that light for something else like I did with the star reflected in the muddy puddle right on the edge of a thousand foot cliff.

At the end of my walk I stood beside the Van and looked at my reflection in the glass. I looked like a deranged lunatic. I had leaves in my hair which was plastered across my forehead by sweat and dirt. I had waxed long conversations and arguments with myself at the edges of cliffs, I had looked at the black lake on a low shoreline and pondered walking off into the inky cold water with a few stones in my rucksack. I had wept and I had laughed like an idiot. I had scraped Rat intestines off my boots, I had put my hand in a pile of fresh Sheep shit. My hands were shaking, my legs were trembling, I hadn't eaten in 48 hours and before that I had eaten half a bag of Walkers Ready Salted Crisps and drank four pints of IPA. I had £2.90 in my pocket, a British Army Pen knife, a packet of tobacco half full, pack of Rizla, a temperamental Poundstretcher lighter.

You have to let your Star shine bright inside that blackness you know, you can't let the darkness win. Sometimes that star will be dim and you can hardly see it, other times it will shine so bright you can't actually see what's in front of you. At the moment for me personally that light is a little dim and far away, but I know it's there and I know one day it's going shine so bright it envelopes me totally. Mad times bro. Manchester United next Saturday. I hate Man U.

Chapter 14

Yanited Gollums and The Great Red Tomb

How do you denigrate a great lumpen mess like Manchester United? For me I just open my mouth. Me and Horace are bumping along, standing up on a train to Manchester, In front of us sitting down are two Wolverhampton Reds. Man and woman. She doesn't like Wolves fans apparently…but nobody actually asked her if she did or not.

She has tits like a couple of leftover Samosas at a Wake for a dead man nobody liked. Does anybody want another cup of tea? Her eyebrows looked like somebody who didn't know what an eyebrow was had drawn them on. She has a Manchester United coat on. Fucking Lizards. We've been walking around Manchester and the ground for two hours and I've only heard one Manchester accent. Her husband looks embarassed to be travelling with her. He doesn't look committed. She looks like she wants an argument or has a lot more to say about Wolves. Negative things. But she is biting her lip which has that sheen of lip gloss which shines as she curls her lip, then bites it to stop it waxing. They have bought that bastion of Jurnalistic truth 'The Daily Mail'. What a comical newspaper. What a comical couple really. I am thinking of pouring her Costa coffee over her head.

'We are the foundations of European football' she says. But I'm not bantering today. Manchester United are walking on foundations Wolves built with their own feet, blood, snot and tears back when Manchesterites were still wearing clogs. We were the champions of the world bab. There is a piece of sausage sandwich stuck on her top lip and I'm concentrating on that, up and down it went, trying to keep up with that sneer on her lip as it moved up and down.

We built the foundations for these bastards and I'm thinking about this as I walk around old Trafford. But I'm thinking yes, solid foundations mate, but you've built a house of shit on top of it. Is there anything more dysfunctional about Old Trafford than the hawkers selling shite outside the ground and the silence of 67,000 of their 'fans'? Half and half scarves, mementos of Alex Ferguson. A childs bib, a foam hand, Red Devil horns, all the fucking tat mate, all of it. It spills over into the road and you have to walk around this mess, this unclean merchandise.

What a God forsaken place. Now I'm all about having a go at atmospheres at grounds but this? I can't find words…but 'Propaganda' and 'Disinformation' spring to mind. I suspect this Manchester club are now a political entity in many aspects and nothing devours creativity and dynamism more than a political philosophy.

Somebody shoves a half and half scarf in my face and I nearly deck the scarf gyppo selling them. The sole of his shoe is falling off. So the bottom feeders scuttle and feed from the crumbs that fall from this gigantic behemoth of nothing much at all. I'm feeling a little homesick for some Warnockian madness to be honest. I watch him on Match of the Day later on that night and I want to pat him on the back. Oh Colin. Got a kicking day ya?

'Mourinhos right ya fans are shite'

Nunos 'ideas' of course fill the ground. In the football and the madness off field. And how precious that Idea and Philosophy is. I mean you never know how something is so precious to you until it's gone. Of course at this ground it has gone. There's nothing here for us at all. In a way it was worse than West Ham. There isn't much sound...listen I'm not a writer so I might just tend to repeat myself a lot. There is little sound from the crowd, you can actually hear the players booting the ball and shouting. All you can hear is Wolves fans. Yamming songs, we have a great repetoire and we are showcasing it to these Yanited fans bereft of belief. Something is wrong in this place and for once it's not us.

This great Red Tomb is now a trap or a jail for any idea Jose has to reinvigorate whatever pulse these bastards had in the first place. On the field Moutinho doesn't give a shit about that history either. Pogba is picking his arse in midfield again as Moutinho dispossess him. I don't think Pogba even knew the ball had gone. He looked like he was stoned. Mourinho flaps around in the technical area like an old crow in his black overcoat. His internal dialogue must be like the Wolves fans here in the corner. Shouting and whispering, singing and slapping backs. Never trust a Coach that has a very small head.

On the way into the ground earlier it was quiet and morose apart from the odd group of Wolves fans who were yamming all over the place, singing, dancing, having a laugh. We have lobbed a few smoke bombs around, there has been a few ejections, injections and rejections already. The stand above which is full of Reds is hefty with the odd one leaning over the edge and giving us lot below some verbals. But every doughnut looks Spectrum Special up there. What are they really going to do? Block you on their PS4s or something? Fuck off. They are even doing it in one of the corporate boxes.

All I hear is Cockney or 'Suvvern' voices from their support. That's mad isn't it, that a Manchester club has all these drongos from other towns supporting them. These doughnuts make up all sorts of excuses why they don't follow their local team. Glory hunting fuckers. They make up stories about why they support them. Strange stories that don't make any sense. You can tell they are made up fantasies because when they tell you they support Yanited they look embarassed.

"Yeah my Great Great Grandfather was stationed near Manchester for the Boer War..I mean he never fought but was in charge of cleaning spuds, so you know....it's traditional. I can't let the side down" they say...or words to that effect. It's like the hawk faced woman on the train at Wolvo station. Glory hunting bastards mate. They make up any old story or embellish some tenous connection with Manchester to make it all sound plausible. But you should always support your home team. This international Red bollocks is annoying and sad. I keep saying 'Glory Hunters' a lot.

One of the prongs in the executive box has a haircut like a fucking

Walnut Whip. His mate stands there 'on guard' like Horace is about to pull Walnut Whip head through the window. Walnut whip head turns to his mate and says something to him. Walnut whip head has fucking make up foundation on no shit. You can see the line on his scrawny neck. Why does a man wear make up to a game? Why do they wear shirts that look that shit I would be embarassed to pull it on. It's very tight. It looks very much like a shroud. I would love to turn around and give the verbals back but the gap between the seats is shin to calf and it's like reversing an articulated lorry trying to turn around in this place. Stack em high bleed em dry eh? I don't want to get thrown out thanks.

I think about Walnut Whip head wearing make up. Jesus Christ if my Grandad was alive to see this he would be apoplectic with confused memetic grooves. Ok he would be laughing his tits off. I'm all for people wanting to express themselves to the world but dude. What thoughts were going through your head as you put your foundation on . He is laughing at us from the safety of his smoked glass enclosure. His mates are laughing too.

We are laughing. Horace is telling him that his make up application skill level is quite shit, You can see the line under his tight shirt Grandad collar (ASOS £19.99) The doughnut is rocking mascara too. He's ticking all the boxes. The Feds now turn up and are watching closely from the sidelines in case one of us bangs the smoked glass and does something...well...mildly violent to be honest. But that's never going to happen. I'm a little sad too. This is the famous Prawn sandwich crew at

Old Trafford then? I want to run in and ruffle their quiffs. Half and half scarves, dudes in make up, dudes in very tight shirts, dudes with Walnut whip heads, Jesus Christ man. Horace is scaring me as his face is beaming with smiles as he banters with the glass between them.

When Horace smiles like that it means something badly weird is going to happen. Even Mascara boy is a bit reticent, he can obviously pick up some unconcious vibe from Horace and old Walnut Whip head is smiling a little too forcibly, bantering a little too loud and I think he wants to run away into the toilets to get away from Horace. I don't blame him. When Horace is smiling then something bad is about to happen. Walnut whip head has legs like pieces of string or cord. They are fucking stringy little things clad in black denim and with this ensemble he is wearing a light brown pair of fucking winkle pickers. The toes of these shoes curl slightly like some medieval pair of fresh creps.

Then I realise, the make up, the shoes, the comical hair...he is the Jester for the day, the great joke and I realise this whole Manchester United thing really is one great Pantomime. Horace is shouting through the glass at Walnut whip head and Police are at either end of our row. If the Police start beating Horace I'm going to help them. I must remember to tell him as it would make him laugh but of course I forget until now writing this.

Just before kick off they trundled old Purple Nose Alex Ferguson out for the crowd. A puff of pyrotechnic powder and sulphur and there he is looking like Satan trundling his Sports Direct suitcase to his Saga holiday. He loved the Wolves did Sir Alex. I couldn't give a fuck. Some Wolves fans are clapping him and I laugh. Probably that silly bastard who clapped Hart and Pickford at Molineux. Will somebody please tell this Wolves fan to stop clapping the enemy?

The Red Tomb loves it's frail and crumbly heroes for sure. I bet they drag the odd one out of their retirement homes in Lytham Saint Annes every week for the delight of all the tourists who haven't got a clue who the fuck they are but they will blow their Red Devils whistles (£4.99) until their fucking eyeballs fall out.

Here he is Stanley Bucklewright aged 139 years old who once played ten minutes in the 1929 Stepman and Gumph Cup winning match which United won 5-0. Stan looks confused about where he is, his Grandaughter struggles to walk on the pitch in her fuck me heels and tight mini skirt and she hopes Great Grandad Stan doesn't shit himself again because she's left the wet wipes in the car and she can't wait for him to kick the bucket so she can put all his mementos on Ebay...maybe get a holiday to Ibiza out of it with a bit left over for some snort while some Spanish dickhead with a hard body, stubble and a pony tail hangs out the back of her.

I mean you've paid all that money to cross Old Trafford off your gap year list why not enjoy it? I expected Sir Alex to be on strings like some weird puppet jangling up the steps to his seat, his conk shining like a darkroom light. In the next few decades you will see an Alex Ferguson animatronic dummy with a tinny Scottish electronic voice going 'It was 40 years ago when I blah blah' and his nose will start to flash until you put another pound coin in the slot on his head. I've always disliked the bloke, I mean theres no way you can cuss the mans footballing pedigree and knowledge of the game. No way at all. But I can take the piss out of what he is. A Racehorse owning, Red (what else?) wine guzzling, champagne Socialaista. One of the living ghosts of that place for sure...and he's a sweaty.

Our team is unchanged. I love that whole madness. We go again. Second verse, same as the first verse. Have United played 182 games already? European something or others? Who cares. We define the tactics now. Nuno puts out a team to stamp and impress his ideas here today. He doesn't care about the enemy only the beauty of how we play, how we press and how we jive that relentless pressure again. From the back. Boom. Again and again we shatter whatever United are today, which is a bunch of highly skilled players with only a distant memory of why they started to play football in the first place.

They have forgotten for sure. Forgotten not how to play attractive penetrating football, but forgotten why they are doing it at all. They look like puppets for sure. It's all an act this Manchester United thing. A house of straw and the big bad fucking Wolf has turned up.

They score of course and then all of a sudden I am aware there are actually Manchester United fans in the ground. Well bloody hell eh? Whooda thunk it? Patricio was unsighted I'm sure. He wasn't far away from it at all. Apparently a bloke called 'Fred' scored it. Fred who? This was on the back of a number of potential goal scoring shapes we were carving in front of Uniteds goal. But we knew it wasn't going to be one of those days at all. We carried on singing and shouting. Of course we were going to get one back. It's the Nuno way. Don't let your heads drop. The idea is everything here and you have to believe it will come good. It always does if you believe. There is no post mortem as we wait to kick off again. Nobody is talking in the Wolves team. They just wait. We know something deeper is happening within our idea and tactic, our ideas are strong, much stronger than Yaniteds.

Now don't think for a minute that this was some sort of Apprentice versus the Master moment as Nuno meets Mourinho. It's a silly analogy. Who knows what mad knowledge Nuno chose to pick from the people he met through his life. What information that he assembled to make his own philosophy, his own beliefs. Who knows what Nuno decided would be useful in building his own idea of what football he wants his team to play. . What would Mourinho have told Nuno? To spend big? To bluster results? To denigrate any idea of football as an entertainment? To slather your emotions and salt over every press conference?

It was never Master and Pupil. Nuno Espirito Santo knows intimately the zeitgeist to invigorate a system with creative centres ie Moutinho and Neves, add a dash of the stoical with Doherty and Bennet, Jonny and Boly, then pour in some Jimenez-Jota and Costa to froth the whole Wolves madness into a frenzy. Somebody had forgotten to sugar this United team. The Referee had tried to help them of course. Every touch on a United player ended up with said player rolling around like he was trying to put out a fire on his back. They were looking for easy routes here. That showed me United had if not lost the game had stopped believing in it.

Jimenez again was rocking the funk all over the place. He was everywhere this lad. Pulling and splitting the United defence like he owned it. He's a gorgeous thing to watch and the lad ran his heart out making the dreads of Smalling wave around like the tentacles of some faintly dangerous deep sea fish. His hair is hilarious to be honest. I am laughing at it. Shouldn't this place be somewhere to fear. It's all comical. Yaniteds defence are confused. We move around them like Assasins.

Corners were the finished product of much of this movement. Moutinho started to stick some right spiky balls into the box. Ryan Bennett wanted some, his header choked over the bar. Sir William Boly dives in. He wants a go too…hang about, we are playing these Euro giants and our fucking defenders are all over their box? Fair play lads, get in there and have a sniff. Doherty dives in as well.

It's crazy…I'm expecting Coady to think 'fuck it' and pegging it up the pitch so he can have a dabble as well…but Coady knows. He might get picked for the next few England games. Well, I did say a few years ago he would be an excellent addition to the national squad. You see he's picking balls away from Uniteds players like he does it every day. He ay scared mate. He ay bothered.

I have a look around the place while there is some United possession. It's certainly a big place this Old Trafford thing. I remember coming here in the 70s and it was a roaring cauldron of madness inside and out. Now of course it's the Red Tomb and I throw that term around my head a little as I look at the crowd, sitting, farting, bored of it I think. There is a 'singing corner' of Reds to my right but I can't hear what they are singing. We ourselves are in fine voice again of course. I see the corner Reds clapping something but I don't know what it is. Probably Fergie going for a piss.

'You Brummie bastards' somebody shouts from the stand above…yeah well fuck Manchester and Yorkshire too, fucking Scousers. I kind of hoping one of them falls over the edge as he leans over. That would be funny. On the pitch we are in control. Boly is leaning into the territory of legend at the moment. He is just picking balls from Uniteds feet for fun I think. Boly and his movement is refined and sublime. We are all running around of course but now that effort is controlled and managed...just like us really. We look as if we are carrying on the Burnley game and all we did was just stop to change our shirts.

You would think that with all the skill levels on offer to Jose that this team would be instilling whatever ethic Mourinho has given them into concentrating on controlled possession and attack. I mean there are moments when United get a groove on and start to throw delicious shapes but everything has a patina of artificiality to it. Like it really is an errant dust smeared computer disc that keeps crashing.

Horizontal lines, static and Pogba is frozen again, he's gone into 'stand by mode'. United players keep freezing it's as if they are updating their system files and stuck on 99%.

Moutinho splashes a few sexual efforts around trying to start some attack. Costa again moving like a snake through the vine ridden dankness of the Untited defence. He skins them this lad. Something is going on in Helders head that I like. Maybe he too has failed to see the massive mausoleum of football in historical terms and now sees it as just another set of points, just another unsympathetic architectural edifice to be overcome with dashes of quality like he's showing. Luke Small who is the doughnut tasked with keeping Costa at bay is having a torrid time. He looks like he's on a reality show and everybody has just voted him 'Most likely to be caught in a stranglewank incident'.

Fellaini or whatever his name is falls to the ground again. Amazing lack of balance mate, so the breeze of Mountinho running past you actually blows you over. Not surprising with a trim like a Dandelion. I'm not always impressed with weird haircuts and I dislike Fellaini purely because of his hair. In fact there are some bloody shocking trims in the United side. No more the classic Thunderbird haircut of Keane, the delightful 'Postman Pat' Gary Neville trim or the Settee horsehair stuffing of Scholes. No, the united trim content is now into Manga territory not British kids TV. But Traore is warming up and I shut up. That's a funny trim Adama, you remind me of 'Blade' for some reason.

Patricio now has his own shapes to throw and he does, a lot. I mean Uniteds team have gazillions of quid to their names. Of course they are going to bung a few incisive glorious balls in and out of our end. Of course they are. They ay daft. Mourinho ay daft either. But the thing is, they are doing it without a smile on their faces at all. It's like they would rather be doing something else. Do they make their players clock in and out? It seems like it. Lingard throws a few shots in, it's obvious United have a hard on now but they are walking around with it in their hand like they don't know what to do with it. But that Lingard bloke is a fraud. He's all bluster and no bollocks. You can tell he doesn't care any more.

Now United are playing with their backs to us I expected a goal. You see it's always the Southbank where I sit or stand., It's always home wherever I'm surrounded by half pissed lunatics from my town. Somebody chucks a smoke bomb and I'm laughing. I love smoke bombs. The ball wangs around a bit and there is Moutinho. He collects, has a saunter around then curls a delicious swerving ball right into the money box. Goal. 1-1.

Smack. Cheers Mucka. I fly over the seat in front of me. I get punched in the ear, my quiff goes mental under an armpit, Powelly is laughing his head off, Horace is trapped between seats, I fall over again, I get a knee in the leg, somebody steps on my foot, I get punched in the other ear, my glasses are falling off, I try to sing something but forget the words and I'm singing something unrelated to everything else. By the time I can see again we are kicking off again. Fucking hell 1-1. We can nick this but nah. United throw everything but Fergies nose into the mix and we are diving all over the place to block shots and make sure that ball doesn't break our hearts.

Was it a Cup final game? Nah. Jose you are mistaken. Every game we play now is a World cup game, every one. Whether it's against some doughnut league 1 side in a cup game or playing here at the 'Home of blah blah blah Old Trafford'. You see our sight is set on bigger things than playing these Dinosaurs. Manchester United don't have Heroes any more. We didn't come to old Trafford to watch these mighty Reds play. We didn't come here to see Mourinhos side. We didn't come here to have a day out in the madness of Manchester. We came to see our team play, not theirs. This is how far we have progressed, these are our ideas.

We have come to see Nuno and to sing songs to him to show him how much we love him. We have come to see Moutinho-Neves-Costa-Jimenez-Traore-Jota and fuck me we even came to see Bennett. We came because we believe and we came because we love, it's as simple as that. Their 67k fans had come because once upon a time this great Red Tomb used to be like Molineux.

Back in those days they too believed in a philosophy, believed in their team. Now of course the place is filled with the ghosts of those times and whatever those ghosts had done in the past, those great games, the typical United fan now sucks on what energy those ghosts have like a baby on a tit. I wonder if we have broken them again. We probably accelerated the slide they are about to face. I have seen this before you know, with Wolves relegation seasons. The acrid smell of stagnation, the civil wars online between fans, noises from suits from men that look like sharks. We dream, Nuno dreams and everything is beautiful.

I had a daydream Nuno ran a second hand car business while we travelled back into the center of Manchester. Or maybe it was the

Manchester Metro rocking from side to side as we made our way from the dystopic stadium of the abyss into the bustling and dangerous Picadilly Gardens where men walked and they had crazy eyes and feet that wouldn't keep still. Hypnotising me really, that gentle throb and click of the tracks.

I'm trying to be clever in the Italian restaurant and remark that the seafood Rissotto is undercooked. I got confused with Paella. The mussels are delicious and I am surrounded by beautiful people and Manchester hipster serving staff with that face that just can't smile any more. There are beards, many beards. There are tight jeans and tight tshirts even when they are fat. There is Horace doing his Horace thing...I offer to pay for the meal and throw my season ticket on the plate. He laughs.

The train from Picadilly back to Wolverhampton was filled with pissed as a fart Wolves fans and angry London Reds who have taken issue with the bad language, the songs, the burning spliffs and the copious alcohol abuse. Me and Horace just sit in the middle of this beautiful madness. We of course remember pitched battles with the Police on trains back in the 1980s. We remember throwing seats through the broken windows, we remember everything of course. So this insanity is perfect.

The behaviour of our fans is anti-social and it is loud but we don't care because these nutters are our nutters. They are us twenty-thirty years ago. This is everything we were and maybe still are. Voyaging up and down the country with our team has always been high drama and exquisite play writing. You might get a hard on over the vandalism and political posturing of that Bristolian Banksy but we too have an art and a way. I watch a young kid break open a can of Cider and tip it down his neck. I watch a man spark up a big spliff which fills the carriage with pungent herby muskiness, I watch a disgusted couple move carriages to avoid the falling drunken bodies. Her face sneers, he looks frightened to death. Its all art and all beautiful just as much as Banksy, just as much as some Grime rapper doing his thing, just as epic as some abstract corporate sculpture. They are the couple from the train up here, the one with the sausage bap and the husband who was scared of us. They don't look happy. They look like the kind of people that will pontificate about how their teams crap as soon as they start doing a bit crap. Manchester tonight reeks of unimaginative football. Yanited are dying a death and we have smelled that rot, that sickness, and so have they. Things are going to shit up there. I laugh as a veteran lad from Wolves sways backwards and forwards in the aisle with his eyes closed.

Maybe Nuno is an artist rather than a football coach. Maybe his intent has bled into our lives too and every act we act is pumped up with an artistic Nunovirus. A few of my brothers walked around Manchester City center and bumped into Nuno. They had their photos took and I was ten minutes late again. We passed like ships in the night again Nuno and I'm still no closer to finding out what exactly you are. But I will keep looking of course, keep searching.

Chapter 15

Shampton Gollums Cup games and Hipster Beers

'Can you imagine Wolves going to Barcelona or Madrid to play European football? it will be brilliant'

Yes it would, I'm listening to fans waxing outside the pub while I am having a break from the press of flesh inside…but there was me smoking a roll up outside the pub listening to it all and feeling a bit weird. Why weird? Well, I can appreciate us playing European football but I don't really care where we play it. Somewhere warm and cheap for sure, but I've always looked on teams that weren't Wolves as being a bit lacking in… well Wolves to be honest. Barcelona or Madrid? Well yes. You see I'm still a bit stuck in League 1 to be honest, mentally at least. I haven't quite caught up with the Nunolution I still think that Barcelona or Madrid will be privileged to watch my team and have our fans at their stadiums. But I'm also still thinking about Tommy Rowe and bantering Leyton Orient fans, so Southampton. What do I make of that match? We were below par. But we won. The Gods are still smiling on us again. We are five games unbeaten and I still think there is more to come, more in the tank. I suspect we haven't seen anything yet. But I'm still counting my 12p change in the Royal London Pre Match.

This IPA is a weird cloudy colour and it tastes like fucking Lemons. The bar staff in the Royal London all look pissed off. None of them smile. I don't think Wolves fans are Jazz enough for them. Perhaps we dont really look at them that closely. They have a high turnover of staff. But beards are in plentiful supply at Wolverhampton University. These people are our future...God help us. I'm day dreaming again but somebody treads on my foot and to be honest I'm quite glad of it because I'm awake again and not staring at the dude with the beard handing me my change. I must look like a mental. I piss off quick because it's obvious he has made some sort of joke I didn't hear and if I ask him to repeat himself the joke would be dead then and we would both be embarassed and ashamed that we are too shit to communicate simple memes. Southampton in the Cup...I forget which Cup it is now. The games are everywhere and my poor brain can't keep up. Is ity the FA Cup? The Caraboa?

Were we confident? I suppose we were, wasn't the last time we played them an F.A Cup thing? I'm reticent to cuss their town as Southampton is very, well, weird. It has a defunct and just 'thereness' about it, like it's forgotten what it's about, why it's there. Kind of mirrored by Mark Hughes the Southampton Coach. You know he only dines at the best restaurants and enjoys the fruits of his career but does he know why?

I'm watching pre game fireworks and phone videos of Liverpools goalie porking a succession of be-eyebrowed Cheshire Pussies in a hotel room.Dan is showing me them. Dan sits in my row, has done for years. I suppose I've watched Dan and his mate Ryan grow up in those seats. We have watched some awful shit in them I know that. Liverpool Goalie porn, Dan is laughing. The Goalies dong is flapping around like an elephants trunk, like a babies arm holding an opple.

Cavaleiro is on the bench. Someone is screaming over the PA. It's the shouty woman Wolves put on the Microphone every game. I haven't got a clue what she is on about but there are plenty of woops and waheys etc. Explosions in the sky. Football. Singing. Oh God I love this shit. What do I like about it? Every member of the Wolves team steps out onto that pitch with a furrowed brow. They are assimilating their Coach's pre game match. They are working through the moves and the tactics, the planning, the homework done at Compton. I bet some egos are left shivering and running out of breath on those pitches as the first frosts fall. I bet those egos die on that pitch. Play or Die I suppose. I think we have an idea that Nuno is this fucking wizard like Sage who wafts his wand over the players and they all explode into this stardust Unicorn studded football we are playing and everybody joins arms and dances around like lunatics and we sing the Nuno had a dream thing again. I was totally on that level. Being cuddled by Nuno, tickling his beard by an open fire, Led Zeppelin on the turntable.

"Nuno? Talk to me about football", as you lie back and cram another eight stack of Pringles in your fat gob. My mind is changing of course. It started at Old Trafford and for a few idle minutes I just watched Nuno in the technical area. The way he moved and gestured, shouted, moved a position, debated substitutions or something with his staff. There was something there but for a few moments it wasn't magic and it wasn't wizardry. It was violence.

Not the way he moved of course, everything was measured and beautiful, that beard, that skull. I think there is a Wizard Nuno and I think he is channelling a footballing Muse somewhere, a Muse that maybe delicately arranges raw ideas into tangible forms on the pitch. But there is another side to him. At Old Trafford I was shocked to mentally discover that in our players faces there was something else too. apart from the tactics etc. I think that was fear. Not of the opponents or the match. I think they suspect Nuno will pull a plastic bag over their heads, gaffa tape it until they stop kicking then drive cursing up to Cannock Chase to find somewhere quiet, where he can enjoy a few hours digging in the Cannock dawn. I think the Nuno we see on the telly and on videos is the friendly version. Would you cross him? I've lost and won some fights against violent people but I don't know whether I would like to tangle with Nuno. I think there is some of the Romany in him, quick to smile and love but also quick to slit your throat for transgressions. I think Nuno says 'Fuck' a lot.

So with Goalies willies and fireworks still wanging around my head it was kick off and we were away. Well nothing really happened in the first half, it was like the Burnley match part two. We were playing a bunch of very wise players in Southampton FC. They were a bit elbowy to start with. Wise and again stoical, plundering, incessant, sparkles of pure art among the hues of bland greyness and looking at the seagulls, the flags, the Billy Wright, oh…the Southampton fans. Hello. You're quiet. They were moaning pre game about Wolverhampton being unwelcoming. This.

From a load of Southerners. Jesus Christ. I hope we are unwelcoming to the enemy. That's good. Watch the game then piss off. This isn't Alton Towers or fucking Drayton Manor theme park. This is tribal football. Thirty years ago you would be getting half enders bounced off your heads...oh God I'm channelling thirty years ago again. I have to stop doing that. Times have changed thank God....but it's only a little murmured thank you.

We haven't been beaten for four games and I am quite happy. I enjoy parts of the game where Jonny is being a massive lunatic diving around nibbling away at people with the ball. He's like a little Staffie, once he gets those jaws around the ball it's his and you can piss off. Passing it gives him real grief I think.

I suspect in his head he's visualising charging down the pitch, scoring a goal. Kicking off and he does it again. I think playing with a load of other blokes pisses him off to be honest. I watch him make a run again from deep into our half and into theirs. He's palming off Southampton players by shoving his hand in their faces. Like he wants to pull their eyes out. But it's restrained by Nuno again. Or his skillset I don't know. But underneath Jonny is something Nuno identifies with. Controlled violence.

Jota is also of the same mold. His play has been as always beautiful and sublime. He's not having a tough time on the pitch, not for me at least. But I think he is tense with the whole idea of playing in the Premier League. He needs to relax a little, chill out, kick back.

Atwell the towel boy is Ref. He doesn't really know what's going on in the first half as he loses control of the game for long periods. Of course his dimply fat hand and protein bubble muscle arms flick out a few cards to incredulous Wolves players. What for? Fuck knows.

Atwell comes out of the Puregym. Those 5kg pink dumbells are a killer. fifteen whole reps and his arm was falling off. He takes a swig of his MUSCLE KNOBHEAD protein drink. It's full of Testosterite and Muscleoids, and maybe the adrenal glands of the lesser spotted groat. Fuck knows, he bought it off Amazon. £29.99 with a free Knobbo protein bar. He watches his bicep flick into some life in the smoked glass window of the gym as he lifts his free RAWKNOB plastic bottle. Jesus Christ Atwell you fucking fruit loop. I bet he has a stack of Soft Cell and Depeche Mode CDs in his Audi.

Traore is looking leaner. Who knows what the Boffins at Compton have found in him. Some need to lean up, get that upper body muscle off while keeping his core intact. I bet there are spreadsheets and graphs all about Adama Traore. We are building him into something 'fantabulous' for sure. He bursts everywhere.

How can we top this? How can we add to this crazy show in the second half as we constantly attack the Southampton defence? Fuck knows! Oh shit Cavaleiro is coming on. Oh my days look at them! Cavaleiro on the left, Traore on the right with Jimmy running things in the middle. Jonny is in the box, everybody is in the Southampton box even Benno! Of course Cavaleiro scores. Pulling the game up by the scruff of the neck he boots it smack in the balls and wakes everybody up. Ivan you beauty. I am emotional. You have been missed. We talked about when you would be back fit and running around with Adama. I'm getting a Dicko-Afobe-Sacko feeling. I told you I was stuck in League 1. Who would be the missing link between them? Would it be Jimenez? Costa playing more central? Some unknown buy in January or somebody about to break into the team? Who knows. For the last twenty minutes everything is crazy. Southampton have to stretch now and stop playing scaredy cats in their own half. They boost out in number, now there are gaps and Jonny loves to fill in the gaps. Boom. 2-0. Even Atwell in his dopey protein addled head doesn't feel the need to add to the drama. That's five on the bounce now and we end Saturday in 8th. European places are there look. But it's too early to think about that. In all fairness we played a C class game for sure. A few players maybe shouldn't have played Leicester in the week. But who am I to comment? I don't want Nuno coming around here booting my door down.

In parts it was almost Warnockian this version of Mark Hughes ideas. So Jota gets kicked around the floor a few times again and Atwell runs off waving play on waggling his arse to his 'adoring' fans in the Southbank. There are elbows and errant feet. Costa goes down under a tackle, Moutinho is nibbled. Great. That's what I like to see. If they have resorted to doing this so early in the game then they have run out of ideas. They are fucked. I go for my halftime roll up content that we will beat this side. They will be going home sad. Trudging up the steps of the Steve Bull stand with heads heavy, muttering post mortem match bullshit. Moaning, long trip home in sadness, It's hilarious. I'm laughing my tits off already. Confidence you see. Nothing is going to happen during this match that puts a handful of sand in this particular gearbox. Those gears will go up a cog. It's like watching a video of a bloke getting his balls punched by some woman. You wince at first then you start to wonder…when will he tell her to stop. That's how Southampton look. Like they are getting their eggs minced.

For sure we have encountered a right smorgasbord of tactical grooves from teams we have played so far. The brilliance of Manchester City was tempered, and we have broken Manchester United again, we shocked West Ham United with our belief and we have sent Burnley back home with things to think about. What is the zeitgeist? We too have answers to all the questions an opposition coach may offer. We are adaptable and creative, we can change our shape at will and with minimal fuss. We defend with bravery and belief. Boly-Coady-Bennett are a wall of belief and trust. Patricio rarely troubled but when called upon is brave, astute and fast to snuff out penetrations and dangerous balls. Loved all of it. Don't fuck with Nuno.

Chapter 16

Shitsall Palarse, The Great Owl and another trip to London

Moor Street station in Birmingham (where we are catching our train) is a beautiful place. I love the wrought iron work, I love the Gingerbread roof, I love….oh fucking hell. A load of Aston Villa scruffs walk past me as I am gazing at the architecture. They are a highly dysfunctional bunch. Mind the gap? Nah, pull your trousers up Aston Villa, wipe the drool from your lips. One of them has a carrier bag full of Carling. Jesus Christ, if you are going to pre drink at least buy something that has some taste…HEY! that's pretty much a mantra for their team.

I laugh to myself a little bit as Horace slurps his coffee next to me and I can feel there is a bit of violence in him. Last March, me on the cold streets of Witton, Downer and me sharing the pain killing gas and laughing. Aston fucking Villa. There will be loads of them on the train but I'm past caring about them for a few weeks at least. They have sacked Steve Bruce and thrown cabbages on the pitch. I laughed that much I nearly had multiple fractures of the funny bone. Fuck Villa.

The train to that hole London. 'Us' the Wolves. It's a collective term really that encompasses the whole zeitgeist Nuno and Fosun have made. Now the 'Wolves' is all of us, everybody. It's a strong seedling that's germinated in the tear soaked soils of Molineux. Fucking hell we have had some pain here. Now of course we can look forwards to a visit to London.

Is laughter a prerequisute for every trip now? Horace is on the floor laughing at one of the stories being told. His laughter shakes the windows and makes the other passengers tremble. I hope he gets thrown off. If I had a phone I would report him to the Transport Police.

There are shoppers on the way to London. They are not happy. I mean I wouldn't be happy either going to London but I think it's Horaces laughter that is grieving them and all of a sudden I realise...bloody working class oiks on their way to London. I think it was my story about my blonde Cop I had an affair with. She was insane to be honest.

We are loud and for the most part have been stuck in anonymous industrial estates or shitty offices all week. It's a wonder we have the energy to laugh really. Touch Horace and I will kill you. The countryside rumbles along outside. There are Villa fans down the carriage, they are quiet. They must have heard Horace and his maniacal laughter. It's pissing down with rain in London. It makes it all a bit harder.

My Adidas (which mar mate Andy gave me) are dry. No wet foot. Here in London are deep puddles which every body else jumps over. I of course have to gingerly step through and over them so each step is a concentrated manoeuvre so I don't fuck my leg up. Twenty minutes into the walking and I am exhausted already but the need to see this team overrides any pain. I would crawl through broken glass to see them, to sing at them, to venerate them. It's a journey for all of us really. It does give you a spring to your step as you navigate through this London, this most horrible of places that has an even darker underbelly. South London, it's a hole. Not something like a cosy Rat hole but a place where ideas are thrown never to be seen again, We go for a pre game pint in a plastic pseudo pub where the staff is one fat disinterested Cuban and one Czech sex fantasy with a bogie stuck in her nostril. Her boobs are nearly falling out and I am mesmerised by her tits on the one hand and the snot on the other. She is asking me what I would like and is annoyed because I'm not listening. The bogie and the tits. Fucking hell. I order a hipster beer. An IPA called Hopadelic and I want to throw it over them and smash the place up a little. Fetch out your Riot Gear. Wolves are here. But I hand my fiver over and get 2p change. Fuck off. Her bogie is blowing in and out of her nostril and I am hypnotised by it for a moment. The Cuban dude pantomimes to her that she needs to get rid of it and she goes off into the kitchen to grab a piece of kitchen towel. or something.

Surrounding us is the detritus of the place. Tourists laden down with overpriced shit they have bought. Getting the 'British pub experience' in this plastic insane place. They have bags and trolleys, suitcases. Everybody looks like they want out of this place. The only laughter here is Wolverhampton laughter. It is genuine laughing because it's deep and rumbling honest and pure. I choke down the first pint and outside the rain is in sheets, incessant. It will do this all day.

'Nunos the special one, Nunos the special one'

Crystal Palace is wrongly named. Shitstal Palarse more like. The trip over the green murk of the Thames and we enter South London. Rows of roofs slate grey, gardens full of shit, rubbish being blown on the wind, half a greenhouse, youths hanging about, windows curtained so the inhabitants can shut out the environment. What are we doing here? Nuno tells us to come. Nuno demands that we come here, to these places. Who are we not to answer that call?

He doesn't pimp ticket sales of course. His message is deeper and he pulls us towards every match with his idea and his intent. Is Nuno the special one? That would mean entering the shoes of another 'special one' and I don't think Nuno would accept the place of another. Nuno isn't the special one…Nuno is the one. The rain sticks to your skin here, like oil, there is a grime within it. The passive slack faces of the inhabitants are in stark opposition to our faces which shine through the gloom. A raindrop from an awning over the entrance to a 'Money exchange' shop staffed by a slack jawed bucolic Syrian fat man drips down my neck. I am transported instantly to Swansea away last season, cup game, rain, storms, wetness, having a piss on the grass at a petrol station watching my piss get blown fifty feet into the air it was that windy.

My leg is being a bastard. I can feel the screws in my ankle grinding together. I can feel the foot swelling. It doesn't like this for some reason. I am wet and we trudge. It's like the retreat from Moscow as Napoleon watched his troops fall one by one into the deep snow as the icy winds swiftly covered them up with a light dusting of snow. But this is existential snow…rain, traffic, humans, London. They scurry from every doorway and peer out of every window like slack jawed lunatics.

Crystal Palace. A journey to Hell indeed. We talked of Galatasary and their 'Welcome to Hell' banner but a Turkish painted bedsheet is a vapid devoid idea really. This is hell, this cold rain, these Londoners rushing to nowhere. Nobody talks, everybody rushes, everybody has earphones on, everybody looks sad.

Hell is cold and damp not hot but our faces shine anyway. This is a pilgrimage not a visit to watch a football match. This is something else. That glow in our faces? Direct from Portugal mate, a fire inside us. Another tube station platform and the sounds of 'Nuno had a dream' comes floating down the platform, bouncing off the walls. You cant see who's singing of course, there is a crush of damp bodies that press and move. The song is of course a mantra. We have to keep singing it because it is the only way to understand what is happening when we watch our team. It's the only thing that helps us make sense of all of it. The walls of the subway reverberate to it and adds it's own magic to whatever pain these tiled walls hold. Then the song is quieter as whoever is singing it turns a corner and you walk a little faster so you can still hear it.

Roy Hodgson is a fucking idiot. We all know it. He managed 'Them' once. You know who. He has a face like a sick mans pillow, like a pair of old stained knickers caught on a canalside Hawthorn tree. We remember you Roy. But you got out of North Birmingham fast. We don't blame you mate.

They start the game on the front foot for sure. Their team move the ball ably and with danger. They press high and seem to be pushing back Doherty and Jonny into weird deep positions. We aren't getting them up front to support Costa-Jota and Jimenez. They of course have occasional forays into dangerous positions. But these Palace players. They play almost the same football as us for large slices of the game. Coady is omnipresent. Here is a lad not far from the intrigues of League One football who has thrust himself on to the worlds biggest footballing stage. Watch him snuff out another attack. Watch him destroy another Crystal palace move. Watch everything he does. Southgate doesn't want him in the England team yet. I want whats best for Conor. Will he write his name large within an England team that are clique filled and arsey? Can Conor do that same thing here? At Wolves? and disregard the fluff and flannelling from the madhouse that is the England set up?

Coady is attacking every attack, he doesn't defend this man, he doesn't retreat and block, get his body in the way although there are aspects to his game that require it. He dampens the opposition attacks and disintegrates the movement splitting up Palaces tactical offense. He is the 'Terminator' of CPFCs premier league quality, it seems effortless but I know it isn't really. Hard work Nuno keeps repeating. I know Nuno is right.

Bennett and Boly either side of him and they are a power trio, a veritable Motorhead of defences. We fans stuck under a leaking roof and a view I would describe as 'abstract' and 'shit' keep singing. We understand perfectly well thank you. We withstand this barrage of Palace silkiness with more singing, more shouting, we are not disheartened of course because 'we know'. We are a few weeks into this season of Premier League madness and already we have withstood the intricacies of the Manchester teams and deployed our philosophies perfectly well against the other quality laden sides we have faced. We know that Nuno doesn't have a dream, he has a plan, and we stick to it like the London grime to damp skin. Horace is chewing his knuckles again, but he knows.

Rui Patricio our goalie stretches and flies again across the goal. This man is world quality. He shifts his weight from foot to foot and he is springing around like an insane mountain goat. Here he is throwing himself into a tangle of bodies, a loose ball, feet everywhere, the ball pinging around. Coady protects with an almost violent passionate attempt to dissipate the attack and get the fucking ball away. This incisive violence and passion of Conor Coady the perfect foil to the almost Zen like quality of Patricio.

They have many chances of course. They are a Premier league team. But as the first half progresses we start to see a sort of lethargy creep into the Palace side. Not a physical lethargy of course but maybe a metaphysical one for sure. They tactically fumble their way to the break. They are trying to pick a magical lock with a ten quid set of lock picking tools off ebay and are tired of poking their intent at a footballing idea that defies logic. It is an ideological malaise for sure.

What ideas will Roy Hodgson explain to Zaha, what foundations does Roy build his ideas upon? Here in the murk of South London? Jimmy has a chance, ten yards out. Its a fucking miracle he can twist his body around and put a thundering shot just wide. He is leading the line like a Warrior, he is everywhere pulling Palaces defence here and there allowing Costa or Jota to move and to probe spaces. Costa is beautiful bounding around Palaces defence like it isn't there. Jota gets hacked down again. He's back up instantly. Jota is a fucking machine but he needs a goal just for him really. I wonder if Jota is carrying an injury. Diogo is a pleasure for me regardless of whether he scores or not. Interplay now, Costa to Jota to Jimenez, it's fluid and magical they can do this here in this strange place.

I suspect that Palace had locked down Ruben and Moutinho with some tasty man marking at some points. We were not clicking there for sure. It was more a case of hang on tight possibly for both of our midfield dynamos. There wasn't much time to spend on the ball and todays murk required maybe another fraction of a second for Moutinho and Neves to define where the ball was going to go, we didn't have it, not for large parts of the game anyway.

'Where's ya famous atmosphere'

Jimmy gets the ball and slinks it to Doherty who rages towards goal and splashes some colour into the greyness. Boom. Straight through Hennessy…remember him? I was vitriolic towards him when he first ran onto the pitch, I booed every time he touched the ball and I did this for half an hour maybe. Before Hennessy meant nothing at all. A redundant meme under the glare of our team. 1-0 to us. Crowd goes wild. Everybody is hugging everybody else and for a moment I don't have anybody to hug and share the moment with so I grab a dude in the row in front and rag him around a bit, then my glasses fall off again, I go to pick them up and somebodies knee hits me in the face, my Adidas have a big foot mark on them, my knee is hurting, my glasses have steamed up, somebody punches me in the back of the head. 1-0 Jesus Christ. Doherty. I was moaning about him ten minutes earlier. What do I know about football? Fuck all mate. 1-0 Jesus Christ. Palace fans start to walk out the stadium, I laugh. Then I weep a little bit too drying my eyes on the Pret Napkins I nicked earlier on in the day.

We are all Pilgrims you know. Now the whole Wolves thing is turning into an almost quasi religious thing. I know supporting Wolves needs faith at times but it's becoming an almost revelation to see beautiful, passionate and hard pressing football that we are. I look at our team and I have to pinch myself that they are my time.

Here's another word. Healing. Those days at Gillingham and Burton, Brentford and Rotherham watching our team disintegrate under teams that should never be allowed to put their stinky feet on our hallowed turf. Wounds we had for a long time. Open wounds. Hoddle, Lambert, Saunders now being healed by this football. Our football. Nuno calls and we answer him, we travel and we attend these sacred events with happiness that we have been delivered from the evil football we have had to endure. I think we have ceased to be fans and are now Pilgrims. Nuno comes over at the end of the game to clap and applaud us. I am weeping a bit again. It's emotional.

There are Villa fans on the train coming back and they are happy for some reason. I suspect they are just stupid. Their songs are too shrill, too loud. Their laughter is forced and too long. They too are drinking Carling. One of them tells me it was a bad idea beating us last March. He thinks we broke them. I hate his accent, I hate his team for what they said about us. Horace is staring at him. Everybody is staring at him, everybody Wolves any way. But this Villa thing is in the past. We have left them behind in our wake and they know it. They will never have what we have, they will never suffer what we have had to endure over the years. I ask him 'are you ever going to eat cabbage again?' and he looks at me like he is confused. Standard.

Chapter 17

The Elton Gollums- Stockhausen-IPA

I sometimes think…I mean I'm being metaphysical here, that some things are not meant to be. A victory against Watford. They are not a 'name', they have players though. Are we on that crazy train again? Are we going to bust through them as we tend to believe most pre match waxing? Nah. It's weird isn't it? Losing a match like this and filing out of the South Bank like sad things…like some of the teams we have smashed up so far.

I'm watching the moisture from a pub full of Wolves fans drip down the pub windows pre game. I've ordered this sour blackcurrant IPA that cost me nearly five quid. It's fucking horrible. Major mistake on my part. I look at it on the table while I'm talking and already there are a few pangs of self doubt starting to needle their way into my belly. I've had that feeling all week.

I've shaved my beard off and now I'm looking at my own stupid bare face in the pub window as I have a fag outside and everybody cheers a Manchester United goal inside the pub, I shake my head, an African dude trips up over the kerb and is sprawled across the road. My fag goes out and the lighter is a shit Poundstretcher one that only works when it wants to. Click click click click click and a bolt of flame shoots out that sets my nose hairs on fire so my fag tastes like burned animal, black currant and desperation.

The great Tit of Nuno has been moved away from the mouths of some for sure. That golden beautiful liquid milk of Fosun-Ball and Nuno magic stopped flowing and the hungry mouths of 'some' are open and looking for the Nuno Nipple again. We are shocked and angry, we are lyrical again. Moaning really. And of course I suppose anybody will have a moan at anything. Maybe they should go back into the pub and watch another team play…maybe cheer goals from these teams too. I couldn't give a shit about Manchester United or Chelsea unless we are playing them. I go back in. Somebody treads on my foot, somebody nearly trips me up, I'm sweating and it's clammy, I want to be in the ground right now.

Our little Wolf is bothering me a little. Diogo Jota is getting some neck off people around me, in the South bank, who would be hard pressed to have the athletic groove to run for a fucking bus yet alone razz around on the pitch for ninety minutes. I despair sometimes. No, I despair most of the time. I write little messages of support on there, little stories not many people read. But that's ok. It's just for me really. But outside the pub I watch people moving to and fro into Town. I watch and I observe. It's something I do a lot of and I think sometimes it's the only thing I am good at.

The thing is dear reader…when we have shit times, like Jota is at the moment. It's hard to really grasp what the fuck is going on when your game (or your life) is falling apart. Sometimes ya know, we tend to think we are searching for some kind of truth in what we do. We lie constantly about things we do, that's just because it makes life easier sometimes when we have some sort of mad fantasy we can build up for ourselves to protect us from real life. But truth today is hard to come by, instead I like to try and find some meaning in what I do from day to day. That's one of the reasons I write. Outside the pub see...I'm a wreck of a man in many respects. The truth has gone right out of the window and I've got five quid in my wallet and I don't want to go back in just in case somebody wants a drink and I have to stand a round. I'm hiding here, watching the Taxi drivers attempts to kill pedestrians...wondering about Jota.

You see, we sometimes think that players we have are just abstract goal scoring bodies or names we may denigrate at our fancy. I still watch Jota at the moment and wonder at him, his skillset and his ability now being crunched and munched in the cold LED lights of the new Molineux floodlights. I still see him as a gift, an absolute prize of a player and one who brings my shins to the hard plastic edge of the seat in front of me, I wait for him to explode. I try to will him to excell and to fly. I made him my gift if you like and I can only see him in this light. So when he is in the shadow and he does seem to be struggling then all I can offer him is a bit of love.

Yes, Diogo, our little Wolf is getting some stick and it makes me want to weep as I watch our team. It actually makes me want to hold my head in my hands and cry. I'm a man, a big bloke, I'm not afraid to weep. Of course a few years ago I wouldn't have. I couldn't shed a tear over George Saville playing on the wing for sure. I couldn't have shed a tear over Grant Holt throwing himself around the pitch like a headless chicken. Or Sagbo for Gods sake. Now of course, emotionally any way I have nailed my heart to the mast of the good ship Nuno. Everything that happens on the pitch is of course translated to 'how I feel' instead of the game being some strange thing men and women do on a Staurday afternoon (sometimes...cough...before Sky Sports).

It sounds very emotional I know. I can't help it. Last season was a turning point for me personally. At last I could start to get over the years of pain before and start to actually hope that things are getting brighter and more brilliant...and they are. I started to see every bad thing, every dark episode last season and the seasons before as some sort of construction as to who I actually am. I suppose this manufactured entity of 'me' is a product of those bad times and the good ones maybe.

But when you look at our Jota of last season and many times this season too despite the criticism I see someone who gave our community, the community that surrounds our club, the courage and hope that we had been lacking for many years. In running his heart out on that pitch and all the other desolate stadiums that season he gave us everything. With his team mates too he produced at last a meaning for us. That brings me back to the truth aspect I was waffling on about earlier.

When truth is an abstract weird concept in this mad life sometimes the only thing worth holding onto is that meaning. You see without any meaning in our club then we dont have identity. Man, how that identity flourished towards the end of last season as well. All of a sudden we knew who we were again instead of being some meaningless former great club now doing it's business in the arse end division of a football league that itself lacks any kind of viable zeitgeist.

Maybe Diogo has to start to look at himself a little and decide whats more important here. Losing onself in the greater identity of Wolverhampton Wanderers, losing his self in the machinations and madness of the club or actually forging ahead with finding some meaning about why he's there in the first place. What his football means, and how that football should be played. I often get maudlin like this. Keeping the roll up alight in the wind that always blows around Wolverhampton City center. I did the same for Helder Costa and Matt Doherty. Writing a few thousand words about some twisted and bent idea of Pyschology I have rolling around my poor mind. I try to inspire our players maybe, in the great electronic weirdness of the internet I try to affect the world through my own search for meaning. I'm singing for the team that never listens, who's own perusals of comment and opinion are probably highly edited in their browsing.

All these games where Diogo looks off colour and insipid are vitally important things. They are the building blocks of his re-emergence I suppose. The bad games are what he is built of as well as the good games. It all builds the meaning into servicable memes that allow Jota to build a new identity within Wolves. He is not the same player he was when he came here. I don't mean in terms of ability or athletic prowess but in what Jota is as a person. Somebody else has fallen over the kerb. Shopping everywhere.

I'm shutting up about this stuff now. This stream of madness I write down can be entertaining I suppose but I can't half waffle. I should stick to writing on toilet walls. C games eh? I'm having a C day at the moment...not an A or a B but a fucking C day.

I said a few months ago we would have 'C' games against teams who are quite prepared to have 'A' games when they turn up. Add into this stew pot of cognitive dissonance a dollop of shit refereeing in the strange piss drinking anathema of Lee Mason and you get my drift.

I forgot that you aren't supposed to touch players now without them twisting to the ground like someone has shot them in the knee. I forgot, I'm sorry. The bald head of Mason shone, unlike the game. Why do all these Premier League Referees look like they go to Pure Gym and Sex clubs? Why do they all look like they wear tight shirts to show off their Soy muscles and protein pecs? I dislike this doughnut immediately and my thoughts about him are confirmed as the match progresses. Mason you are a weird one for sure…I don't like you. He books Neves for an innocuous challenge and Jota looks like he wants to fly kick Mason in the head. Please do. Jota and Helder are bothering me, they need love these pair. It's not flowing for sure.

A Willy Boly back heel is cleared by Ben Foster the Albion reject now plying his trade with the Eltons. Same kind of club really. Watford is to London what West Bromwich is to Birmingham. An armpit of a place. At the end of the game Foster is celebrating a little too hard, a little too forced and you could tell we had got to him for sure. All I'm doing in the second half is dumping abuse on his fucking Basketball head. Wanker. I bet when he's sad at home his Missus brings him his favourite DVD which is probably a decrepidly produced Sandwell bullshit DVD with games against Wolves where Albion score weird Albion like goals. He sits there in the blue light of his spunky plasma TV and rubs his head manically while he watches them. Knobhead. Sorry Ben, football tribalism eh?

It's hard I suppose to extrapolate the cackness of this match with the glitzy videos and the Titanic music that normally follows a Wolves victory. In these glitzy websites we wallow in our golden victories and wax grand lyrics in podcasts afterwards and everybody is happy and back slappy. But these days? It's never easy to take defeats. It spoils the day somewhat. I mean there weren't any fireworks. I like them. Perhaps this day was just 'another bad day in the office' for some, but I've never worked in an office. My bad days at work was getting made redundant, sacked, or smacking some doughnut over the head with a pin hammer…then getting sacked. This wasn't like that. This was just an outlier of a data point on the journey. It definitely wasn't one of THOSE days…remember them? A few years ago? That February in Blackpool, was it a Tuesday night? 1986? Some people wax grand lyrics about Chorley but that awful fucking night, the freezing rain?

The match? That extra Watford doughnut in midfield made things extremely weird for our magical duo for sure. Watford were clicking. I watched them play on Match of the Day a few times and thought they looked OK. But I thought the physicality of their players wouldn't really factor in our philosophical approach to football. How wrong can you be? Suddenly…well from the off, Watford were pinging the ball around like….well us really. Every loose ball suddenly had a Watford doughnut on it. A pass here, a touch there and Ruben was running around like his bum was on fire. There was work here definitely. So we couldn't get the ball out wide, this was like their Coach Garcia had watched us and done his research. So had the players he had brought to our ground. So we were being squeezed into this narrow strip of play where Watford had an almost effortless superiority.

They had big physical dudes in there who could play football, knew how to move, the extra man darting between Ruben and Moutinho to desecrate the day. To piss on our Parsnips. It was a double goal they scored I suppose. You couldn't get a strip of paper between either of them. Low and hard, smashed through a tangle of bodies, Rui unsighted and immobile. Two good goals from them and they were champing at the bit to score a few more. Doherty and Jonny just hung around during this time, having a chill on the touchline watching the madness unfold in the middle, waiting for some love that never came.

Jimmy was negated from the off dipping back into midfield to help out leaving Helder and Diogo feeding off scraps and momentary chances. You could see the frustration in Jotas physical movements off the ball, Helder pushes forwards again and he has three players on him, Jimmy is arriving late from his midfield duties or trying to hold things up and hey there's nobody there and a sad funk is setting in. Myself, I would have put Saiss in early doors to support our dynamic duo, pulled Jimmy off…but what do I know? How dare I question Nuno and his magic, because maybe it just wasn't an easy choice to make for Nuno. You see if the 'idea' has paid dividends before (which it has) then one must tie oneself to that idea regardless. Plough on, attack the day, keep your shape blah blah.

I see the whole game in a positive light for one reason. This whole fucking Premier League thing is a whole new landscape we are trying to navigate. You will get lost during it. There will of course be games when it all goes a bit mad. Are our team not human too? There is probably some formula to describe the match. I would enter a few things into it. We had eight players on international duty this week. Flying around the world with their countrymen, getting their cases packed, travelling, training with new ideas from Coaches who they only see a few times a year and in some cases who they have never met. Strange hotels, strange grounds, players around them they hardly knew and discordant rhythms after the smooth effortless chords Nuno enjoys having them play. Of course coming back into the pack after such sojourns are maybe jarring a little.

Maybe our players with their heads full of the sights and sounds, experiences and problems of international football were a bit way worn. Not tired physically as they are top athletes. But possibly mentally they were a little dysfunctional, a little weary.

Wolves currently is not a place where blame is attached or where the toys are being thrown out of the pram. Everything will be analytical now. Where did we go wrong? How did we react? Where did we react? Where did we fail to react? Quantitative decisions will be made as to how we performed for sure. The duties some players were given over the past weeks will also be looked at. How can we make our players able to deal with these international games better, how can we inspire them to play when they are tired mentally, maybe a little tired physically. It's a learning process, all of it. So this game will have value and it isn't a wasted day for sure.

Nuno has a short terse press conference but it will not be a Mourinho type meltdown, a tantrum of the shaman. It will be because Nuno will want to analyse and forensically perform a post mortem on the whole day. Chuck an 'incident' tent over the whole 95 minutes or whatever and get in there in the white noddy suit and the mask, start taking some samples. There is no time like the present to deal with a murder like when the body is still warm ay it.

Molineux is one of the few places where there is some sort of magic in the ground. Did the crowd unconsciously pick up on the zeitgeist pre game? I think we tend to. We knew unconsciously that the day would be some sort of dysfunctional non matches where we would get dicked. Maybe we knew the result before a ball was even kicked. So the atmosphere was muted for sure (apart from sections of the Steve Bull stand God bless them). There was a feeling I suppose that it wouldn't all go our way. Like we knew beforehand I suppose.

So Jonny gets hauled off for not being quite connected to the whole idea. Maybe his head too was full of international madness. He definitely wasn't himself but I see Ruben Vinagre trot onto the pitch and I elbow the dude next to me and I'm nodding my head with excitement. Maybe Ruben V will put some chords together, try and make the whole thing start to click. At halftime I'm telling everybody we will win 4-2. I'm channelling some idea that the whole game can be saved. I have sung and shouted that long I haven't got the voice to wax lyrical too much and add to the mix a few crafty roll ups and I'm croaking abuse at Ben Foster as I watch Ruben V slowly get pushed back up the pitch after a few initial forays up top. It's turning into a Stockhausen performance (YouTube him) all clangy and jangly.

When you tie all of these factors together you kind of get a good idea of what the day was all about. But I'm not disheartened by any stretch. We are all learning something here and like Nuno said it's a group experience, its a shared experience the whole fucking thing. What do we need now? Perhaps a subtle change here and there maybe? Introduce a few ideas that maybe Nuno and the Coaching staff have up their sleeves. A few tactical moves that would see fresh faces, fresh legs. I mean it's all about squad depth. In the pub beforehand I wax a little about naming the same squad game after game but deep inside my own feeble mind I'm aware that depth of squad is a much needed addition to the armoury for sure. It's a harsh Mistress this whole Premier League thing and maybe those eager faces on the touchlines, the Donks, the Giles's, The Gibb Whites possibly should be ushered in for a couple of games. Give key players five minutes to gather their thoughts and start to interpret their own feelings about how they should play the game. It must be exhausting not only pushing your body to levels of physicality some of us can only dream about plus the mental effort to understand the requirements of Nuno would have you banging your head up one of the Oak trees by the side of the Compton Park pitch. I know I would be.

Overall I am positive and happy. What an insane place this Premier League is. Brighton next week and I am looking forward to it. Their staff will be looking at this match and making their own plans to piss us off but maybe Nuno has a reaction to it. We've seen it before, the shape, the idea, the tactics a subtle change here and there. Maybe Brighton will be a bit shocked at the way we look and play next week expecting the same team to play them. Who knows, we go again, we plough on to death or glory and I fucking love every minute of it.

Chapter 18

Coastal Gollums and some minor train vandalism

"Give us some of ya hair stuff kid"

You slather the strange smelling shit in your thinning hair or whack trim to coax it into a bit of life. Oh man, it looks quite good to be honest. There is a semblance of a sexy on trend quiff going on there somewhere. You hope it stops there. Better than the state it's normally in during the week when it looks like a tramp has been sleeping on your head.

You spray some anti perspirant in your pits. Have a smell. That's ok. What about the beautiful Lyle and Scott shirt you bought off the internet… it was on sale. £25. It fits beautifully. Hiding your man tits and showing off the abstract biceps we have. It hides your belly a bit too. Lets strangle our balls with those new Levis we have to lie down to put on. They are a bit tight but look ok. Your bin bag full of bottles arse looks ok. Nick a few squirts of your lads aftershave. It cost £80 apparently. Better smelling than your knock off 'Paca Rabbin' you bought from Bilston Market that rots your clothes when you have a squirt and it tends to give you a strange trash on your skin.

Stand back…look in the mirror. Fucking hell, you look lovely. Handsome, fresh, relatively clean, smell nice. Ready for the night out. Put £60 quid in your wallet. Bank card for emergencies only, not the thirty shots of Jaeger you laughingly bring to the table at ten o'clock.

Four hours later and you are on your back in a kebab shop covered in cabbage and salad with a big loop of kebab over your face that looks like a question mark. Chilli sauce in your eye. Your nose might be broken and you are snuffling snot and blood. The arm of your shirt has been torn off. Your immaculate quiff now looks like its been trowelled to your forehead with a Nans shaky hand. You can only see out of one eye. Your skinny jeans barely cover your arse. You smell like beer and fags and fucking hell, you threw thirty good punches at him and he only threw one…see where I'm going with this? Coastal Gollums. Fucking hell.

Stop getting aggravated. We are still beautiful and everything is still going to plan. Us lot always look to the next match and the position in the league table and it's this thing, this outlook that gives us beady eyes and a furrowed brow, makes us moan on the Train or car coming back home. We scour the internet for prolific strikers and wonder if Thelwell and Company know who they are, we think about sending them an email. It's all mad all crazy. The ball just won't go in. It ay happening at all, we want to kick something, we want to moan at somebody about it but everybody is moaning but I suspect if we had been a bit louder as an away end it would have happened, our belief would have sucked that ball into the net. My kidneys hurt from an infection, I've got a sniffy cold that won't go away, I have hat hair, my legs swelling up slowly, Horace has just tried to break my arm and I have bellyache from the antibiotics. I might just walk into the sea like Reggie Perrin. I'd probably wash back up and lie still on the beach like an errant Jellyfish, dogs would come up and have the odd sniff, kids would poke me with sticks or throw rocks at me. I would just lie there staring at the sun with my pale Jellyfish eye....they don't have eyes.

BAFHA..Brighton and Fucking Hove Albion away. Jesus Christ. It's full time and I'm on the train terrorising people and trying to nick a Monkey poster off the wall. People laugh and I do to but I don't know why. Brighton fans are weird, they look like they have bought their clothes from Hiking shops and they don't quite understand why they are travelling to their ground…it's something to do with football they don't quite understand either. You see this is 'modern football' and it's more to do with Hummus or that Hoomaloomu cheese that tastes very much like training shoe rubber rather than sausage sandwiches, IPA rather than lager, speak Socialist but check your share prices. They will never know the joys of having a dart removed from your head by a laughing St Johns Ambulance dude and having your head bandaged. There are loads of 'antique' shops selling tat, expensive tat. We go in a 'bar' that reminds me of a shit corner sandwich shop…the bogs are outside and I'm a bit pissed and I nearly walk into someones flat by mistake. It's all a little bit confusing. Why the fuck have I followed people in here, I should be in a Wetherspoons or something.

On the football side of the whole subject well, we had transformed ourselves a little for sure. All of a sudden Neves and Moutinho had kind of grabbed hold of a few former ideas about how they should function as a midfield duo. Gone was the Watford strangeness and they were back to the 'old' partnership. Neves holding for sure and still quite deep I think.

Somebody should wax to me about that Chestnut, get my mind clear about it. Is Neves too deep? Doherty side foots into the side netting, Ryan Bennet goes close…bloody hell everybody went close didn't they?…but we walked out singing, well I did. You see I'm not alarmed at all. I thought we were sublime at times, I will go as far to say beautiful even. Brighton had one shot really and they bunged it in. 1-0 and I hate it when the other team score. I mean I really hate it.

All of a sudden the stadium erupted and I was aware that bloody hell, there were Brighton fans filling the place. Before that I hadn't even noticed. I was busy watching the football or the wonky North end of the stadium which looked like it had been modelled on me leg. Bent and twisted a bit.

I was sure that by the ten minute mark it was going to be one of those days again and I was right I suppose. Pinging balls into the danger area, a chance, another one and nothing was going right and I think the players knew it too. As we walked off the pitch on full time you could see the anger on their faces. They were pissed off. They knew it was their game but fucking hell the universe turns and someone has put a big dollop of sugar in the petrol tank for sure. Horace is biting his fingernails and not saying anything at all. I think this place has even got to him. I just feel like smashing things up.

I don't like it when decisions…from another bald headed bastard of a referee-affects the whole flow, the whole groove of our team. I don't wax lyrical about rythym-jazz-music and movement when I talk about the way we play. It's a concrete and real thing. But when you put some doughnut of a slap head in charge of the game, who likes to blow his whistle a lot because he's missing the cock he normally gobbles…ah man. I'm sure you don't want to read about the Ref.

The only part I didn't like about the game was the pinging of the ball into the box for the odd head to get on it when all we saw was their two neck centre backs who would nod it away every time the ball flew in. I mean our front lads ay the biggest am they? Jimmy might have got his head on it but he was back in the changing room by then. It wasn't a loss of ideas for sure. We have seen Manchester City get frustrated by us playing exactly the same tactics in the Cup game a few years ago. 11 man defending and us trying to thread a needle where the eye of it got smaller and smaller as the game progressed. Add a dollop of dysfunctional Premier League refereeing, a pinch of six foot plus big necks and some balls to the wall defending and you have the game there in a nutshell. But we looked great, we looked really good. But the kebab was definitely stuck in our hair at the end. But Brighton have to live with themselves thank fuck.

Doherty was lovely to watch again. All or most of the first half threats were coming from him via Coady or Boly. Forensic accurate passes were picking him out almost from the off and we were moving at times for sure. That's what this whole show is about. Playing it out from the back, constantly attacking teams and being beautiful and exciting. As much as I love Benno I can see why The Donk is a thought I keep returning to. If Coady and Boly (who I loved in this game) are the lads who slide that ball out to the flanks then I can see Donk being the fluid interface between defence and Midfield…perhaps even moving forwards a little maybe into that Holy land where Neves and Moutinho like to tread. I also see Vinagre doing something sexy and oversteppy up the other side. I mean fucking hell even with Helder and Diogo having some grapply strange moments trying to get to grips with Premier League footy we looked fluid and oily moving forwards. This league is a massive leap forwards for all concerned, even us knobheads in the stand who were bloody quiet if you ask me. Atmosphere was muted for sure. Perhaps we expected this was going to be a weird day?

Brighton knew what they were doing of course. Their number 17 had a big problem staying on his feet for large parts of the game. When he walked off he was covered in the dirt he had rolled around in for 90 minutes. He looked like he had been doing some gardening in the rain. I hope he's ok and his wobbly legs recover.

I thought it was a disgrace for the Brighton Coach to send him out there to be honest. Especially when the cold wind that blew in from somewhere kept sending him crashing to the ground like he had stubbed his toe on the Referees dildo. I watch later in the game as Cavaleiro is trying on his new coat in the Brighton box. His coat was weird, it had two arms and two legs and was the same colour as the Brighton kit…oh sorry it wasn't a new coat it was a player…he loved our new strip that much he was trying to get into Cavs while Cav was still in it! Referee waves play on, I wave to the Ref with two fingers and announce that he enjoys regular masturbation and has not known the love of a woman.

What's the zeitgeist? Well…"we need a twenty goals a season striker we shudda bought one ay it and we wouldn't be in this mess". Bloody hell. I'm listening to all the post mortem stuff with a slightly tingly ear hole. Revisiting the whole Striker thing makes me laugh although inside I'm crying a bit.

We don't play with a Striker…or two, we play with an interchangeable front three (at this stage) who move around like lunatics, they get the odd goal too. What we have here isn't a time for Fosun to get the chequebook out and splurge big dollars on Edmundo Rocket foot. No need at all. Who we have up front are totally fit for purpose. Everybody stretching back from Jimmy all the way back to Rui are totally the right people for the job. We can even tweek the whole set up and put Donk in for Bennet, Ruben V for Jonny just to liven up the whole shebang. Maybe go for a front two and put Donk in midfield, let him stretch his legs out a little, see what he is made of. Bung on Traore for the last twenty minutes just to liven up the whole show. It's all bloody academic and it get's us all tapping away on our devices when we should really be putting the phones in a draw or turning them off. Look up for a minute and look at the people around you that you love. Talk to them and hug them tight…

We got back to the news that The Foxes owner was in a Helicopter that crashed on take off at the end of their game against West Ham. We got back to the news that a Brighton fan had died at the game yesterday. I hate this stuff, loss and bereavement within the whole football family really is felt by all of us. It really is a shared loss regardless of how much we hate these people when we play them. We feel it because even though we all wear different colours we all share the same love of the game, we know each other intimately in more ways than one. You see one fan goes home in his Helicopter and another on a crowded smelly train or coach or bus but they are just fans ya know. For what it's worth in the madness of this writing I offer my sincere condolences and will light a candle tonight for people we have lost on our mad insane journeys watching our clubs. Now I'm a bit sad even if I never knew these people before this news.

So the journey in the Premier League is a thing isn't it? Rattling from one game to the next so far seems like a consensus is emerging...on my part anyway. What's wrong with these fans of other teams? Most of them look like the mad spangly unicorn of their lives has kind of rolled over and expired it's last lukewarm fart. Most of these new grounds and stadiums look beautiful and well...big. But something is lacking in them for sure. There is a lack of love in there.

Chapter 19

Tales Of Topographic Bastards, Z-Boys and Tottenham Hotspurts

I had held this beautiful double album gatefold sleeve in my hands for weeks. Gazing at the cover, trying to glean some idea of how the music inside would sound . But it wasn't mine you see...not yet. It belonged to Sundown Records and it was on a shelf marked 'Rock Y'. Sundown Records was at the back of the Royal London pub. It's not there now. But back in 1981 I would walk in there and go straight to it, open it, look at it, while I saved my money.

The sleeve had cosmic tropical fish swimming in the air, or the water, or the vacuum of space, but they just hung there in a proto alien desert landscape dotted with those rocks that Roger Dean (the artist) beautifully ladled onto his masonite substrates. In the distance, practically on the horizon was an ancient Mayan Pyramid. When I did save enough it was a Saturday and we were playing Tottenham, it was a big game, they always were. So it meant buying the album and taking it to the match. I wouldn't stand in the madness of the Southbank for sure. I would stay at the fringes. Keeping the purchase safe. We would win the game, then I would walk down Molineux alley back home and put the thing on my shit record player and listen to it.

I paid my cash to the sexy curly brown haired assistant in

Sundown...Sally? I forget. She worked there on a Saturday. I was a bit in love I think-she had these crazy brown chocolate button eyes and she was always nice to me even if I was a scruffy bastard, a bit of an urchin. So she slid the album sleeve out of its sun browned and foggy vinyl sleeve protector and I swear it went 'whoooooosh'. The colours. Oh my days the colours. Now they were beautiful and fresh and I think I gasped a little.

The Roger Dean artwork come to life, the grand song titles, she found the vinyl discs behind her and the sleeves look fresh the vinyl black and bottomless. She was talking to me but I don't know what she was saying. I was dumbstruck. Maybe too stupid to understand. I was sixteen years old.

I walked past the exact spot where the store was only last week. I was a little sad it had gone and felt a bit weepy too. Now nothing is the same, everything is change.

Coming out of the ground back in 1981, well it was chaos. It was always chaos. I am with two lads I grew up with and we are in Broad street. They want to have a go at Tottenham streaming out of the ground. I want to go home and play my new record. I've kept it so safe in the madness of the Southbank in those years.

Now we are running and I don't really know why I am there. I'm not in the mood for aggro today. But we run, they run, everybody runs. We have beaten Tottenham 1-0. We are happy. They are not. We get to the corner of the Lafayette nighclub, it's a Casino now. Tottenham are there too. It is madness. I avoid some Spurs fan in a flowing paisley shirt and ponytail.

He looks like he is in a folk band. If he was then he has a strange instrument. A piece of concrete with the rebar still attached. He swings at me. I hold my album to my chest. Duck and weave. I should have gone home. There's somebody on the floor and I try to boot them but miss. My Prog Rock album is curtailing my fighting shapes.

It's going off everywhere. A Wolves fan goes down and Wolves fans give him a kicking. We don't know who's who. I'm dodging everything. The Old Bill arrive and everybody splits. I dart to the side between a VW Beetle and a van. A Cop is there, old school tit helmet and overcoat. I smash into him, my momentum is mad. We both fall over into the doorway of the club. I put the album underneath me as the Cop starts to kick the living shit out of me. Another Cop comes. He pulls me up by the hair and to my feet. I have the album safe but I get punched in the mouth and blood starts to flow from it. He punches me in the balls and I'm limp but gripping that fucking record. An eggshell blue and cream Allegro Cop car pulls up. They boot me in the ankles to get in. My face hits the roof. More blood from my lip. I'm sat between two cops, big fuckers. One punches me in the face again. The other stamps on my ankle. I've been nicked. The short Journey to Red Lion street is punctuated by the fat Cop next to giving out abstract bored punches to my face which already looks like it's been through a mangle

It's November 2018, we are playing Tottenham. We park the car at Faulkland street Coach station right in the middle of loads of drunken Tottenham fans. Everybody is drunk except me. Everybody is loud and clear. It's windy and this wind snatches words and songs away before I can hear what it is they are waxing about. The night sounds like the start of Silver Machine by Hawkwind. We get to the art block and there it is. Beautiful Molineux shining in the darkness. What a fucking Jewel it is at night, a jewel in the darkness for sure.

What will happen today? Are we going to get another punch in the face off the Premier League big bollocks? We have lost two on the trot. We hear our little wolf Diogo Jota is injured. So Cavaleiro will start? Traore? Who?

I am trying to work out the current zeitgeist and the past keeps pouring through the cracks. My mate Andy has a Mod parka on. It's very smart. But I hated Mods when I was a snotnose. I bump into an old school punk rocker. Black leather jacket with 'Exploited' on the back painted in white gloss probably. For a moment I'm back in 1981 and the night is leaking for sure. Overlaid over everything are the ghosts. The rude boys, the rastas, the skinheads, the rockers, the mods...now it's just generic beards, tight trousers, shit flickers, bad attitudes, Northface coats, kids, Moms, Grandparents and I'm disorientated. Some lads are singing coming out of the subway.

'Nuno had a dream...'

...and that worries me too. What does that mean? Has the dream dissipated under the harshness of shit refereeing. bad decisions, stupid goals? The Premier League is bereft of passion for me at least. Has it sucked enough life out of us yet? At Brighton last week I started to smash the train up but nobody joined in. I was surrounded by Brighton fans who looked disinterested at my antics. What was I even doing here?

Tottenham have Harry Kane-England Striker. He is the epitome of the faceless uncreative kid that was hot housed in public parks, ferried to better teams, better chances to be seen. He is a grey man in football. Today he is the enemy. Around the ground it is packed with humanity. The Cops look edgy, the stewards look scared. Drunk people stutter and tumble around. Drunken men laugh and wonder why nobody else is. Jota injured. Two losses on the trot. We should have won at Brighton. I see us shithousing a 1-0 win. I tell everybody my prediction.

I roll half a cigarette before I go in. I check for my ticket half hoping that I have lost it so I don't have to experience watching my team fight, play, struggle to get that ball in the net. Fight and battle for three abstract points, just numbers that will never explain the turmoil and the agony of watching those you love fight. I don't think I can stand it any more. This is supposed to be entertainment, supposed to be fun. Now I feel like I'm fighting with the team but I have nobody to put an arm around my shoulders. To gently whisper words of encouragement and hope. I feel lost and alone in thirty thousand people.

Back in 1981 at Red Lion Street Police Station the Cops pushed/tripped me down the steps to the cells. There were about five steps and I hit the bottom and slid to the opposite wall where I cracked my head. Now I had a fat lips, a swollen eye, aching balls and a large egg shaped lump on my forehead. I was dizzy when they slammed the cell door shut. Somebody had pissed on the mattress so I crouched on the floor and tried to sleep-by counting sheep. I look at my shoes which look like dead squashed birds. They have taken my shoelaces out in case I hang myself. They took my album off me. Outside the Southbank the queues are building up and I absent mindedly touch my forehead and wonder where the lump is...

'Have you got a headache again?'

Of course not I laugh. But I can still feel that pain in my head, it didn't go for months and I am sure they did some bad damage to me poor yed.

I start putting the filters up. I've got my lucky pants that have more holes than a Politicians tax return. Lucky socks, lucky boots, lucky wallet. Always put your season ticket under the green laser scanner with your right hand...always. Never have a roll up pre game standing around. Go to your seat. Don't make eye contact with anybody. Just stare at the pitch mate. Concentrate. 1-0 1-0 1-0 a mantra. Who will be the match winner? Who will score our goal? My left leg is shaking and I don't know why.

There is a memorial service kind of thing for the Leicester dude that died in a Helicopter crash last week. The mood is sombre. It's supposed to be a two minute silence of respect but nobody told us. We are talking still. Spurs fans start to shout, Wolves fans react. The silence is peppered with abuse from both sides. I blame nobody as nobody knew. There is a strange unrehearsed silence too that was eerie. We remember those lost in Wars. The Steve Bull stand have a poppy display, a lone red firework blasts into the sky as the last post is beautifully played, note perfect. It is strange as fuck but lovely as well. I remember when they used to play 'The Liquidator' before the redevelopment of the ground. The snap crackle and pop of the 7" single and...

"Lez welcome our team WULVERAMMATUNONENERERS" Chunka chunka chunka... 'You're everywhere and nowhere baby..' That's where it's fucking at mate. God help my nerves. Please don't fuck this up. Please let every pass we make be a testament to our faith. I'm excited, I'm shitting myself. Win-win-win-win...another mantra going on in my poor head.

I look over at the Tottenham fans. They seem angry. They haven't got a stadium have they? It's still being built, the timetable has gone to shit. I wish it was the 1970s and we could run onto the pitch over to the away fans and start swapping angry misdirected crap punches. It's our towns honour at stake, it was for me anyway. Now of course I have to walk carefully everywhere, especially down concrete steps, not run. Wolverhampton is like me, half crippled, half insane, short sighted, scared of a future we lack the power to define or change to our benefit. The fucking crazy train my friends, you just have to hang on until the end hoping you don't fall under the wheels halfway there. I've tried to understand this whole Premier League Global football thing but how do you expand a mind that's been battered by the past?

I keep talking to people about Sammy Chung and most of our fans don't really know who I'm talking about. Where the fuck is Horace? He would understand.

Conor Coady is on the pitch doing the Coady thing. Directing the troops against this shiny Tottenham top four thing. Spurs are very good, they are floating these players into positions with beautiful football. It's nice to watch after the arse fisting horrors of Cardiff and Barnsley last season. But on the other hand it's nerve wracking.

But what a sight Coady is. I loved him as soon as he came here to Wolves. He was gangly and looked too happy to be playing football. There was none of that thousand yard stare most modern professional footballers have, no. He smiled and the whole stadium smiled with him. There was none of that grey faced kids who have been hauled from one playing field or park to another in the back of their Moms or Dads car. Another team where they could be seen. Another chance at glory in the mud of a municipal pitch covered in dog shit and angst.

How many dreams are shattered on these parks and pitches with Dad screaming abuse, fist fights on the touchline. It's meant to be fun you know. But Coady was different. He is directing the troops. Barking orders at Bennett and Boly. To move here and there, to watch Kane moving, to keep an eye on Spurs stars desperate to do something. Coady has passion, but these Spurs stars have eyes that have suffered under the spotlight of TV views. They are automatons for sure going through the motions.

These footballers wear fashion they have no idea about, no understanding. They listen to music about lives they will never understand. Through headphones that cost a good weeks wage, wearing shoes that will be discarded after a few weeks. Coady has pride though. His passion drives him and his pride defends him. All he understands while he plays is his role assigned by Nuno. To defend-and when defended...to provoke attack. Under pressure he floats the ball to Neves.

Problem (Kane)-Reaction (Coady)-Solution (Neves)

There is still an ethereal pyro smoke still in the air. Everything has that unreal almost artificial atmosphere. Halloween was a few days before, I suspect the door to the underworld, the world of spirits and ghosts hasn't been shut properly. Even the players look foggy and blurred.

'Trippier you cunt you're fucking shit Tripper you cunt you fucking cunt fuck off you cunt Tripper you fucking bastard fuck off'

There is someone right behind me shouting at Trippier and his hot beery breath is ruffling my quiff. Normally I would have reached behind and pulled him down for a chat but tonight I don't care. It's a 7.45 kick off. This bloke has been in the pub all day and the alcohol has got to him. He is angry but I don't really know why yet.

Was it 70 minutes? You want me to discuss Spurs three goals? They were sublime, they floated and they put the ball in the net. It all seemed so effortless from this London side. They carved their way through our defence like it wasn't there. Boly slack and in the wrong place, Bennett lacksadaisical and muted in his response. Even Conor in his superman role was hard pressed to stem the flow of quality balls into dangerous areas. Kane was redolent and primed for every move and our defence responded with some eclectic movement. As every Wolves attack starts with a move from the back so the neutral pointless needle threading by Wolves attack was creating some sort of negative feedback straight back to our 25 yard box.

It looked beautiful every attack we made dont get me wrong. We were carving Spurs up into pieces every time we moved. Spurs reacted by moving up a gear. There were some tasty players in their defence who were old school Premier League experience. They had seen it all before, they had the T-shirt and the mug. Experience mate. But their goals were only seperated by that period of confusion we had seen before. Switch off and don't concentrate for a few secons and boom, another goal. The Southbank shuts up shop in the vocalising department. We too are in shock I think. This is the Premier League.

Lamela. The space...the fucking space he had. He floats, everybody floats through our defence. He takes his chance. I think I could have run down there to tackle him.

Moura the Tottenham flyer is heading towards the box and is in flight. He's moving into the air as soon as Trippier hits the cross. We have nearly everybody in the box but no one on Moura. He is effortless in his header. It's barely a glance at it and it's in. No chance, no fucking way. Coady is shouting and I can hear him from up in the Southbank. People are shuffling along the seats to get a beer or have a piss or just go home, who knows man.

Kane. The big wanker. He isn't the player I thought he was for sure.

England Striker, golden boot winner, now petulant dickhead. The elbows, the subtle digs, the conversations with the Referee off the ball. What a creature. I am watching a sole leaf blowing around in the air above me in the Southbank when he scores. Held aloft by the heat from our exhortations and anger. Harry fucking Kane, fuck off. Knobhead.

But something changed on 65-70 minutes. I'm not sure what it was. Maybe a wounded animal is most dangerous when it's cornered. Moutinho and Neves were cancelling each other out. Again they were being bollocked by Premier league experience, ability and a drive to win. Jonny was too busy tracking back to support his team mates. Doherty was wearing too many hats too. It was all confusing and shit. Throw Morgan Gibbs White on. Jesus Christ, as soon as he had the ball seconds after Moutinho trudged off, it was on, here it was at last. A madness, creative, dynamic, all the fucking keywords, all the moves and grooves.

He slinked and dinked around like he fucking grew there. Like this moment was his completely. He had watched this Spurs team throw gorgeous shapes all through the match now it was his time on the dancefloor. He throws his jacket into the crowd like John Travolta in Saturday Night Fever. He throws an angular shape to show everybody he means business and it was off mate. Kicking off.

This was inspiration and this was what this team needed. Some blood and bollocks. Some movement at last. Gibbs White flung himself into every move, grabbed the ball, shifted it from foot to foot and this was Wolves. This was what we wanted to see, this is exactly who we are. We score...Jimmy after a lofted ball from Doherty, I see the net bulge all the way down the pitch. My shout of triumph choked off by a fucking linesmans flag. No fucking way. A lad is watching the game on his phone and he's going crazy.

No way was it offside. No way. I remember an Albion fan I was talking to on a train somewhere last season. He said the Premier League was corrupt and I laughed. He said 'Wait and see', and those words are starting to rattle around my peanut head a little. I'm wondering if he was right and this place is cursed. I look at my feet for a few seconds of peace. Shuffle them on the concrete. Put the heels together and do a Clown walk one step forwards and one step back. I look at the blokes head in front of me. He is bald and his head is smooth as fuck. But he has dandruff on his shoulders. That's mad. Why does he have dandruff if he has no hair?

But everything is moving now, everything is in flux. Tottenham don't look shiny any more, don't look slick. Gibbs White is making shapes they don't know how to deal with. This young man has little to fear from these international players. Morgan has actually won a world cup. Leo Bonatini is doing things too, but I don't know what, I'm too football stupid to define where he plays and what he is doing but all of a sudden there are other shapes, other moves and tactics and we are making huge gaps in the Tottenham defence.

A ball to Jimmy who is tripped up in the penalty area. We look at Mike Dean. Penalty. Fucking hell, fair play. Ruben steps up. I hide behind the fellow in front of me. I've only got one eye on the net. I can't watch penalities. I'm waiting for the net to bulge. Bang. Ruben never dissappoints. He has a second wind now. Gibbs White has given Ruben some room to breathe and to facilitate his art which means all of a sudden Ruben is Ruben again. Moving, looking for that pass.

Which comes. From Gibbs White. I didn't even see it. I expected the ball to be recycled to the wing for another pointless stabbed cross that nobody would be there for. But instead, magic. He threads it through to Helder Costa, it's on for sure, yes, no, yes fucking hell. One on one with the keeper and it is a missed chance. Fucking hell Helder I love you, you massive knobhead, come here, have a cuddle. Fuck. That was a golden chance. But that pass. Jesus Christ that pass. It was magical and worth the ticket money just for that. Beautiful. Art mate. Morgan Gibbs Fucking White eh?

Fuck, it's in the box again. Jonny? What's happening? Jonny on the floor and Mike Dean again points to the penalty spot. Fucking hell. Jimmy grabs the ball. It's his go at the penno. I crouch down again and all of a sudden it's there. We cheer and now the Southbank is getting some clue about what is happening on the pitch. We are having a fucking go mate. We are ascendent, moving, probing, Spurs look shell shocked now and we look divine. But no. Of course the fairy tale has to end and Mike Dean puts the whistle to his mouth. These Spurs bastards got away with it.

What is the conclusion we reach? We learn and we teach while we are playing. It is still early days for our journey for sure. Every game is something new to learn, some skill to master. Our team are pupils playing

Scholars for sure. The quality Spurs have is enviable and deep and yet we play them and we can still keep our heads up high. What football it was we played in segments and moments throughout this match. It is the sexy leg under a thigh high slit skirt, the promising cleavage, the glance under black lashes that flicker. It's there for sure. Even if we lose we still win, we have seldom experienced this quality and this beauty on this Molineux.

We learn and we continue to learn. It's a painful process for sure and I can be sure that Nuno felt every painful moment of the match as we did. He will be analytical and confident that his ideas will flourish at some point. Maybe with a squad member of quality here or there. Maybe a subtle shift of tactical nous like bringing Gibbs White on will change the errant course of a game to something more palatable to us, the paying public. Who knows.

Back in 1981 my Old man has collected me from the Police station. He gave me another fat lip for being arrested. My balls are still hurting, I think the cop damaged something inside me and they will hurt for months afterwards. But I'm in my room and Mom has bought the 'Pink' which I read as I get my album out of the brown rising sun plastic bag it was safe within. Oh man those colours on the sleeve. I put the record carefully on the turn table. Delicate needle placement like I'm injecting a vein and that needle goes in the track. It clicks and it pops. The music wafts around my room a little as I try not to worry about going to court. Breach of the Peace they charged me with. What peace? My balls hurt. I can't eat anything because I have an open wound in my mouth. I've got a headache. I listen to this thing...'Yes – Tales from Topographic Oceans'. By God what a load of shit it is.

I have threatened to tell this story a few times but stopped myself because half the people I know wouldn't know anything or anyone in it. But I'm going to tell it any way as if I don't then it will be lost.

In the 70's and I will say it was probably 1978 we are hanging around outside the Molineux. We can't afford to get in. The Molineux alley wall and toilet block has a Copper stationed in it today. Already I've seen one lad crash to the concrete as the Copper in there uses his trucheon on the lads fingers as he scrabbles his hand over the crumbling brick. He lands in a heap and doesn't move much. His mates carry him off. We stand and stare, we move around the back of the Southbank to the away end. Hang around. There are a load of people on the sculptures by the art block. There is a Copper whacking people by the crumbling wall at the back of the Away support bogs. We hang around. We kick our heels and listen to the crowd inside trying to work out what's happening. I have split my trousers at the crotch trying to get into a match in the week. I sewed them up myself but I have sewn the lining of the pocket into the leg so now everytime I walk the trousers are 'unbalanced' and I have to keep pulling them up.

We hang around with other disparate groups of kids. We wander around and around the ground. Looking for something I suppose but we never knew what. There's a group of lads surrounding another kid. Is he

Tottenham? Has he been ejected from the ground? He looks the same age as us maybe a bit older but he looks very different. He looks strange. He looks weird because he has long sunbleached hair and a very tanned face. He is wearing an old pair of Levis and a pair of Converse basketball boots. He has a T-shirt on. The lads surround him. They are about to give him a kicking and I get close so I can give him one too. But there is something about him that pangs a spark of memory somewhere and I'm staring at him closely. I remember doing this as clear as day. Staring at him, trying to work out where I had seen him before. He speaks.

"I just thought I would have a look around" he said. It was an American accent and then I knew him. I had seen this kid in magazines and on the TV. I even had a picture of this kid on my bedroom wall. Jay Adams. Z-Boy. All the way from Los Angeles. One of the most gifted and natural skateboarders I had ever seen. After Tony Alva he was one of my skateboarding heroes. Those photos in the magazines were crazy. The blue California skies, everybody looked fit and tanned. Skating these beautiful full pipes, these crazy skateparks, they looked so cool to a kid that had to prise his window open in the morning because it was frozen shut. To a kid that experienced skies that were not blue, they were Grey...most of the time.

One of the lads that has surrounded him gets his face right in J-Boys. He is a doughnut from Ashmore Park. I have seen him before. We have had words in the past.

"What the fuck are ya doing around here you cunt, where do you come from". The Ashmore kid is ready to get stuck in but this is the part where he fills his lack of courage with idle words while he tries to garner the nous and madness to nut this American Kid.

I get involved. I grab the kid and say he's with me and I just walk with him down the subway and we never say a word to each other. He walks and I just hold his elbow and get him away from this shit we deal with every day. We walk and we don't talk. We get to Saint Peters Church and I tell him to go back to Arrow. Arrow skatepark is the most crazy skatepark in the UK and it was built in what is now 'The Slade Rooms'. Three floors of ramps, bowls and crazy vertical sections filled with half crazy kids. Jayboy I think was there with the Traknology team doing demos. He must have wandered off into the town, following people that were going to the Molineux. Not knowing the madness and the evilness that could lurk around it for anybody not familiar.

"Thanks man" he said in his California twang and he's off back down to the skatepark and Broad street. I watched him walk off just shambling really still not giving a shit. Just one of lifes experiences. Of course you can watch Z-Boys 'Lords of Dogtown' on a dvd or something. Or watch some YouTube clips of him in that California sun. He died a couple of years ago a ravaged man. The drugs were not kind to him and you could see he struggled. But to a kid in the 70's like me he was a God on a par with Derek Dougan, Wagstaff or John Richards. God Bless you Jay Adams and there's the story of me and him.

Chapter 20

Arse Gollums and I am Absent

So the grief continues...but what grief? I soak up all the angst sometimes. I'm an empathic sponge of a man. Lose to Brighton, lose against Tottenham...fucking Arsenal to come. I've got tickets for the game at the Emirates Stadium or whatever it's called. But I'm not a Superfan of course. I have the tickets but I'm ill. Mad migraines that split the day into weird colours and blurs of light. I don't want an attack like that while I'm ambling aroung Marleybone station fighting off Villa youth who always seem to be there milling around waving their arms. I've got the dogs, I've got the Wyrley Essington canal, I've got my little £4 digital radio, I've got my Poundstretcher headphones where only one ear works. Arsenal away? Nah.

There's a football pitch and some kids are playing. They look like under 11s or something. They chase the ball in a pack with little regards to tactics and strategy. It's just chaos at times. There's a little ginger fat kid running around like a lunatic. There's a few Moms and Dads standing in the muddy touchlines. There is an old bloke with a dog....oh that's me. The radio says we are putting out the same team as the Tottenham game and I'm not amazed. How I waxed lyrical at the thought of zooming into the team this player and that player. Gibbs-White, Vinagre, Dendoncker...all these names I mentioned and it just proves how stupid I am and why I'm not Coaching Wolves.

The zeitgeist of the whole 'Play the same line up' meme from Nuno is this. If your idea is lacking then it must be changed. But is the team lacking? We played some beautiful football against Tottenham and Brighton. It was lovely to watch us instigate our ideas against teams that have been knocking around in the Premier League for a few years. In large periods we looked like we grew there for sure. But if you do drop this player or that one is it perhaps a thing that you don't really trust your initial idea and philosophy so you have to change it?

This means your philosophy lacks something so you try to mix it up, change the recipe. It's like you don't really know what your team is and what it's supposed to do. Same line up mate. Nuno does know best of course. But three defeats on the trot and the old wrinkly hand of doom is gently wiping across our foreheads isn't it? Poking us in the eye occasionally, getting us annoyed and a bit mardy arsed...and to be honest we all follow the recipe and the finished product never looks like it does in the book does it?

I'm listening to the bloke at the other end of the earphone waxing about how nice everything is at the Emirates. My lad texts me and says 'Dad they've got padded seats!'. Well bloody hell. My days. Jesus Christ. Padded seats. The dogs are pulling me over to another dog so they can sniff its arse. One team here has red stripes the other is a luminous green kit like snot. I think the stripey team have scored because they are running after this bean pole of a kid with hair like it was stuck on in a Chinese cheap clown doll factory. The kid is laughing and punching the air. The fat ginger kid is in green which sets of his hair lovely. It reminds me of a Hawkwind gig this kid. He's pissed off and boots a lone tussock on his way back to the center spot. The ref looks like a pedophile. Some parent is effing and blinding at something.

So from the start of our game down there I'm getting the impression that the first ten minutes is Wolves getting their faces in the trough straight away. Taking the game to the Arse then tracking back and letting the Arse get a snout in too before biting them on the lip a bit.

It's all cuddles and nibbles to start with. My ginger player has just got a boot in the knee off somebody and is rolling around. I think he's their midfield General as he hasn't really moved much. A bit like our midfield I think. The static in my ear turns into a voice that explains Wolves are inviting a bit of Arsenal love for most of the game so far. The dude explains our Midfield are farting around a bit too much. What do I know? I'm watching a fat ginger kid crying.

My dog has just had a shit and I've picked it up in the little black plastic bag. It's now swinging at my wrist as the game goes on. Wafting the occasional warm waft of dog cack up to my nostrils if it swings too much.

When I turn my head to look down the pitch the radio signal goes. It must be the electricity pylons above me or something so I have to squint down the pitch without moving my head...so now I look like a pedophile.

But our play is impressive and that's the general consensus from my phone messages from people in the ground, to the radio bloke. He's slathering love for Wolves and trying to be passive and failing. We are doing things, splitting apart the Arsenal shape with shapes of our own. Shapes that Nuno carves every week at Compton. They are a tight band this Wolves team, they know what they are doing. Arsenal have a hard on at the moment don't they? I never liked them. They always had this weird vibe about them. I remember Highbury was a good place to go, atmospheric. I ask me lad what the Arsenal fans and atmosphere is about.

'There ay none Dad'

Oh dear. That Premier League tourist sickness. Clappers, popcorn (ok forget popcorn as I wouldn't mind a bucket to munch on during matches) but you know what I mean. I'm not going to bore you with atmosphere stuff. What's the atmosphere at the Emirates got to do with me? I don't care that they have to sit there week after week being sad and quiet. Fuck Arsenal.

But they always come back from a losing position. That's the first thing I think about as Ivan Cavaleiro smacks the opener in. But I bend down and fuss the dogs in happiness. I don't want to start shouting in joy as I watch the snotnoses boot the ball about then all chase it. I don't want to draw the attention of anybody. I just want to listen to the game and chill out for an hour or so before I have to go back home.

'Whats the score mate?' a bloke asks me.

'One nil to us mate.' I say. I must have shouted or something because the parents are looking at me weird and the dogs are jumping up me and a dog foot pulls the cable from the radio and rips the headplug ear thing out of my lughole at a painful speed. The cable is wrapped around the dogs foot and he's being a tit and running in circles around me binding my legs with two leads. I'm about to fall over. I'm miles away from a limb enducing football ground and event. Why now? In the middle of Willenhall? Fucking hell.

I plug myself back in and the radio limbs have subsided and the dude is talking about Traore then Jimmy Jimenez. It was a superb cut back from him to Cavaleiro who boots the thing into the bag. The importance of Jimmy in our team makes me warm. That final third he is a Godsend. He's sticky. Slide him the ball and it sticks to him while he waits for Cav or Helder to boogie in with a shot or two. Jimmy Jimenez we don't need a twenty goals a season striker when we have you mate that's for sure. I can see some goal scoring nutter being brought in maybe, from some sunny clime or Uncle Jorges cellar. But now Jimmy is what we need. But Arsenal are a jammy load of bastards.

Text. 'Jimenez mate'. I don't know what that means. I can't text back with the dogs being knobheads. They wont sit still. Gizmo wants the ball badly. I can't imagine him running on this pitch. There would be blood. Plus I've only got about thirty pence of credit on this cecrepid phone that freezes a lot and moans at me for not having enough memory. I haven't got much memory left meself mate.

So Gizmo the dog is pulling to get that ball, I suppose we are too. The 'band at the back' or Bennett-Coady-Boly as we know them better are carving out their own defensive jams at the back. The radio bloke is being extrememly lyrical over our Coady. There are powerful words being said for sure and I am proud.

Ginger kid is shouting at one of his team mates and everything is going wrong for team Green. I think the stripeys have scored again...yes. It's that bean pole kid with the Clown hair. Turban kid on the Green Team has the ball and a stripey kid is trying to get it off him. There is a disagreement. The Turban kid is annoyed and drops the ball.

Looking to the sky in the West dark clouds over Molineux. Everything is a bit windy. The dogs are sniffing the air. Ginger kid has just booted someone who is writhing around on the floor. This is a very physical game. It seems there is history here between them. Some sort of school boy angst going on. Maybe they are rival schools maybe? I don't know.

Radio bloke is on about Coady again. I'm a bit jealous. He's my favourite player not yours mate. I remember him coming here years ago, our new midfield maestro who was transformed into this defensive artist. It's 2-1 to the stripeys but the green team are well up for those booming hoofs up the pitch from Ginger kid. Turban kid looks like the number ten. He's obviously the target because he's nearly as tall as me. I think he's supposed to knock the ball onto either their wide men who both look like they need a meal and a reason. The greens number nine is a little sod about three feet tall who can handle the ball (which is practically up to his knees). He whacks it goalwards a few times and his shots have power for sure. But any touch on him and he's over. Punching the grass, shouting at the Ref his team mates, anybody really. Traore is on. I don't know who they took off. I don't know anything stuck here by the side of a kids football pitch with two dysfunctional dogs and a shit radio. I wish I had brought my roll ups.

Arsenal are doing things. Just missed a sitter apparently. Their Manager/Coach is called Biro Onioneye or something. I couldn't quite catch it to be honest. I don't care either. I just want this win and it sounds mad at the ground. I check my phone, new text message...

'We are fucking brilliant'. It bleeps again, another message. 'We are fucking brilliant'. He sent it twice the knobhead. I remember when texts were 10p each and you thought deeply about sending one out. The game is going on for sure. Arsenal moving through our midfield like it's not there? Bloody hell. I don't know, don't look at me, I'm not there. Watford did that a bit didn't they? It's all Arsenal but it sounds like they shit themselves when we get the ball back off them deep in our half and start boosting out some bassline football as everybody starts to attack. It must be scary watching Jimmy and company legging it up towards your goal. Must be scary indeed, especially when Arsenal have put most bodies into our half. Bloody hell, little bloke from the Greens has just whacked one deep into the far corner off a volley. Lovely goal. I want to cheer but it's nothing to do with me.

I feel sorry for the Green team, they look a bit scruffy, a bit sad and dull.

So I support them. Fair play little bloke. He disappears into a scrum of kids congratulating him. Careful. You might kill him. He's only little.

Helder Costa has just made an Arsenal player look like a tit apparently. I bet he's wiggling those hips again the sexy little bugger. He's made so many players look foolish this season it's mad. I love Helder. Every time I see him skill up a doughnut I think back to Fulham last year and those doughnuts waxing awful descriptions of his football. Bloody hell. Helder Costa you beauty. I'm laughing to myself now thinking about him. I love Helder.

The Greens are getting into this game now at two all. Some of the challenges are a bit mad. The Coach of the Greens is silent as he should be, but you can tell he's wound up. The Stripeys Coach is a little fat man with no hair who keeps punching the air when his team win a ball. It's crazy. Traore is on. Beep Beep and off he goes. The radio bloke is apoplectic at a missed chance for us. Are we on 80 minutes or what? My phone clock is wrong, has been for weeks. I keep turning up at places at the wrong time. Story of my life really. I'm always the wrong person at the wrong time.

The Greens lump a ball forward via fat ginger kid. Turban kid. Straight back down to little midget striker who fucking fluffs an open goal. Jesus Christ. His Coach goes a bit mental. The ball is loose, just bounced off the Goalie from the Midgets shot. It bobbles and bounces over several feet and errant stabs towards goal.

A Stripey defender with a weird home hair cut runs forward to clear and hoofs the ball, I mean the little sod just put his foot straight through it...but what's that? Fat Ginger kid has had some sort of epiphany, no longer the midfield engine room he has took a run forward, he's right in the way of the clearance. Ginger kid jumps to intercept the ball. It's coming like a rocket and somehow Ginger kid twists his body in mid air. It's to avoid a ball smacking him in the face. To be honest he doesn't need it, his face already looks like it caught fire and somebody tried to put it out with another fat ginger kid who was on fire.

Ginger kids fat arse connects with the cleared ball, it richochets straight off his butt and past the arm waving ineffectual midget in goal. 3-2 to the Greens. Fat kids mates surround him. All is joy. At the Emirates it's all over and done. A point at Arsenal. It's a massive point for us. How many big teams have we sent back into their funky fresh changing rooms to update their Instagrams with half baked desire to do better next time? Loads mate.

Wolves will be concerned with missed chances and debate. They will be analysing straight away. It's the Nuno way. It's the only way. It's another bloody battle where we are learning and slowly moving up the curve. It's the calm before the storm for our team though. I can feel it. Nuno is driving this whole idea with his intent now. It's an unstoppable force for sure. Him and his backroom team are scary. It's all scary now thinking about the future and what may come. Are we still on board the crazy train? Are we all bearing up ok?

The Referee here in Willenhall has had enough too and blows the whistle. I was a bit pissed off. I wanted to see what Fat kid was going to do next. What drama would unfold. It's the International break now and I think I need it again. All Ginger kids mates are slapping him on the back. It's all good.

Walking back down the towpath I bump into a woman with a Terrier. She's quite nice. I feel quite handsome, I probably have a bogie on my cheek and waxy white stuff at the corners of my mouth. My hair probably looks shit.

My dogs sniff her dog, her dog sniffs mine. She's nice and smiley. We talk about dogs. She notices my Wolves pin badge on my coat.

'You ay one of them Dingle bastards are ya?' she says. The mood has changed and she reins in her dog. She's looking at me suspiciously with one furrowed hairy eyeball. She is sneering and she has lipstick on her teeth.

'Yeah I am' I say.

'Oh God...' she mutters...'Fucking Dingles everywhere lately all coming out the woodwork'.

I laugh and get a bit angsty, she was obviously in disguise as it looked like she had two eyes and the correct number of fingers.

'Suck my dick' I laugh.

'I was thinking about it before I found out you were a Dingle' she laugh-shouts over her shoulder. Fuck. I try to think of an Albion player...

'I loved Jeff Astle' I shout after her. She flicks the V's over her shoulder. I laugh. 'Come on doggies'. It's started to rain a bit.

Chapter 21

Yorkshire Gollums And A Return To The Warnockian Dystopia

I keep dreaming about you Nuno. In these dreams you are trapped down a crevasse and I'm knitting together Wolves scarves to try and make a line long enough to get you out. The crevasse is closing slowly and I'm tying knots as fast as I can. I type this watching a lone Apple on my Apple tree in the garden. It's clinging on for grim death despite the loss of all the leaves and foliage. It's hanging on. Nuno you are not that apple. That Apple is us I suppose, the fans. This is how we feel after a loss. We stare at fucking Apples. We feel lonely again and hardly have the power to hang on.

Nuno. We don't know anything about how tough your job is. How you miss your family and the sand between your toes in your homeland. You have come here to Wolverhampton with an idea for us. An idea that has filled us with joy and happiness you will rarely taste in this football madness. Last season we bled and we wept and we all came through the other side victorious, delirious with joy. The tears Nuno, they flowed my friend.

Now we sit in our factories and our offices or at home with the dog. We saw what happened yesterday and we are sad. We are not you Nuno. We are not strong like you. We are emotional and these emotions rip through us when we play our football. Yesterday we lost to Huddersfield. A place you had probably never heard of before you came here. There is nothing to know about that place Nuno. There is nothing there. But they came to us with our fireworks and our madness with another idea I suppose. The idea that they survive and they fight. There is never an idea stronger than the battle to live and regain the right to play the best teams in England within the framework of this strange concept known as the Premier League. Are we not entertained? Yes, I suppose we are, in a fashion.

We have fought long and hard to get here. You know this. Your battle has lasted for a few seasons. Ours has lasted a lifetime for some. But it's not entertainment really, not for some of us. For some Wolves fans this club defines them. It defines a lacklustre life in a Midlands town that is a bit shit to be honest. It's cold and damp in the Winter. It has it's beauty I suppose, in it's people mostly, who are kind and welcoming....sometimes. Huddersfield have been in the Premier league for a season. They were wise and bitter.

We watched our team learning yesterday. I watched you learning too. But you weren't having a lesson from the Huddersfield Coach. Their Ideas were not better than ours, they were just different. Their identity will always be based on survival and the last seconds in the final round of the match. It is a clawing and ferocious idea they have and yesterday it overcame ours because sometimes that bitterness provokes a stronger idea and it is a potent short lived one. They will soon run out of it and this idea of Huddersfield will crumble.

But what was our idea? Nuno, you wanted to win, you had sat and pored over the data, the dvds, the analysis. You had trained the players in our ideas. It was all so beautiful and proud. Of course it wasn't in pride that we expected to win. It wasn't some lofty notion that we were better than them. It was just that we know our ideas are better and stronger than any body elses. Our ideas are your philosophy. And have we not debated those ideas in long car journeys, on trains late at night, on cold railway platforms? The important thing is that they are being discussed. Previous Coaches would have us looking at the rails below, maybe getting lost on that beautiful desert island and that bronzed flesh of a gorgeous model as she slinked back in her lounger with a cocktail in her hand...she is looking at us. She has sexy eyes just for us, she has a slight smile like she wants to join us. We smile back a little and feel a little of that warm tropical sun on our own pale and broken bodies.

Somebody has farted. The girl and the beach just an animated advert on a shit tube station wall. You want to go home. You stare at your feet again shuffling a cigarette end from foot to foot like a ball.

Our idea is still strong and is still better than Huddersfields. They have scored goals here, at our home, in front of us. Fair thee well Huddersfield. We wave to them as they go back victorious to the wastelands of the North. May their victory give them pleasant thoughts as they look out of their windows upon their Godforsaken landscapes. It is your gift for them.

Our idea is that we are learning and we continue to learn. To assimilate this information like a great intelligence. We must learn and we must experience if we are to improve. So the positive thing? You have understood something important yesterday. Our ideas were not stronger than theirs. Which leads us to the next question we must analyse. Why did our Idea fail? What did we do wrong? And how do we rectify this problem? The variables are astounding of course. A squad of 20+ egos, skill levels, emotions, testosterone. There are emerging talents that need to be handled delicately and with all the attention you may muster. There is the harder edge you must show to the more seasoned within our ranks. There is always planning and thinking about the opponent, another 20+ group of lunatics who will do all they can to grind our ideas into the dust. It must be exhausting and exhilarating. When you sent the team out and they return to the dressing room at full time after that result I would wager you allow yourself a few minutes of abject rage that is incoherent and violent. But then I guess you would want to find out why these things happened and then ideas start to flow and the learning begins.

What do we know Nuno, us, the fans? Nothing of course. Some have a misty idea, some vague notion of the intricacies of running a football team. But really, most of us know nothing. This allows us to be emotive and vocal.

This allows us to wax dark lyrics about a loss or a bad run of form. That this must be changed or that. That this person should replace that person and soon the team becomes a game of magic tiles and we sit there absorbed endlessly clicking the sliding pieces of tile, becoming enraged, starting again, or throwing the fucking thing up the walls. Add to this mix the ominipresent and abstract, stoical and obtuse monad that is FOSUN International and I guess its a fucking crazy environment to live within.

We learn Nuno. For sure we all learn. For us the greatest lesson is that we are a project and not a product. These days are early my friend for sure. These days are just the dawn of our ideas in many ways. We are in uncharted waters, a young squad, a Coach unexperienced of the madness that is English football.

There will be days when this voyage we are on will seem unfinishable. The winds will drop and we will look at the sails hoping to see a ripple while you stand there with your hands behind your back on the bridge, looking at the horizon, having your own prayers with your God. There will be times when the storms that assail us will throw a few overboard as you cling to a mast shouting instructions over the howling winds of this league. We look to you for our leadership now Nuno. There will be some of us on the decks fighting rope and sail, the stinging freezing salt waters, the rage of Poseidon.

There will be those who both me and you know who will be below decks praying to their own puny Gods and shaking a pale fist at their Captain who has brought them on this perilous journey. They shout that we should have sailed this way and that. Perhaps that you navigate us to our dooms...let them whimper Nuno. Let them wail.

We learn and we sail on my friend. On this ship with a carved Wolf on the prow. Its a bit salt stained and worn. One eye looks half asleep. It is missing a fang. But when we eventually come back into port then maybe a fresh lick of gold paint here and there. Some new rope ready for the next voyage.

We are lucky to have you as Captain Nuno. For better or worse there are those of us that recognise that you are indeed our leader and our Coach. We have grown to love you in many ways. Thats us that are older of course and more quick to weep at happy things.

We are I suppose your fans (for better or worse) and for many of us you have epitomised the movement of our club towards a world where we have plans and more ideas, and more victories instead of watching some shitty club score a last minute winner in front of 15,000 loud and proud Wolves fans. I will say this Nuno. Lose some games, it doesn't matter. They are errant learning points. Lose five or six in a row if the education requires it. Thats because learning things is hard and requires study and foregoing some of the finer pleasures in life (like winning streaks in League 1).

For the players some minor castigation. Do you know how lucky you are to play for a Coach like Nuno? To train under him as he sets out to change the face of football in this City? How lucky you are to walk out onto that pitch where great battles have been fought between great men. Their names are writ large in our hearts and now you too have the chance to become one of those greats. If we could only put our aged and experienced hearts within your athletic bodies we would run the world. Fight for Nuno at Cardiff, this match is not a normal one. We fight against the great hairless demon Warnock. It is a battle between the light and the darkness for sure. Do not let Nuno face it alone with only us, the fans.

Of course we know that those 'dark days before Christmas' are a real and solid thing. The promise of gifts to come, of getting legally rat arsed, something on the TV maybe...but outside in the great outdoors, the world of our football team...

Last night I came back from Cardiff and sat heavily down in my chair and peeled my boots off. The Stoney went back on the hanger and put away. I put my ticket in the used ticket old biscuit tin with my badges and other mementos, made a cup of tea. I put my head in my hands, covered up my eyes and just sat there for ten minutes. It was two O'clock in the morning and everybody was alseep even the dogs. Why? One nil ahead and then it seemed every ball loose was collected by a Cardiff player. Wolves players were ineffective all game apart from spells. It's got to the stage now where I don't even get a raised heart beat when we are jinking the ball around the opposition box. I have a feeling it's going to be cleared and it is practically every time. In great chunks of the match I am watching the rain swirl in the floodlights above and the wind is twisting the raindrops into little sparkly....you see? I'm fucking useless after defeats. I am a petulant emotional dickhead.

I am depressed again. Those familiar pangs of 'it's all going to pot again' are swirling around my head like those raindrops above. It's familiar because again it's what we expect as Wolves fans. We have had our hour in the sun last season and now the darkness is coming. There is a fight in the car park after the game, Wolves fans. Arguments. Even Horace is getting angsty and a bit nasty to me. Our emotional investment looks like going to shit again. Nuno is a knobhead. He's not tactical enough. No midfield to speak of. Overpowered in midfield. Some of the players (insert name here) are to blame and social media is full of doughnuts getting their voice heard and getting all that bile out. Am I one of them? No. I don't like to share negative thoughts about the team we love. I keep that to myself for late nights coming back from dark listless stadiums. Palm darkness, when you cover your eyes or shut them and just rub your fingers through your hair with your eyes closed thinking about the incidents and the shit that went on. Jesus Christ.

I watch Helder Costa struggling all game. Nothing is flowing for us. He jinks and dives trying to splash some colour but it is all grey and black of course. He is effortlessly shoved off the ball time and time again. The ball, loose, tumbles into space. It is there for the taking, there for us to salvage and manufacture something out of it.

The Cardiff player runs like a man possessed for it, he knows what he wants. That ball. That bitter hairless bastard Warnock has driven them onto the pitch with his spells again. Cardiff are fuelled by his hate and bile. It drives them forward. Maddened in many repsects by his needs. They are furrowed and resolute. The lack of skill more than made up by their own anger and need. Moutinho goes in too but his leg is limp and ineffective, he pulls it out at the last moment and the Cardiff madness wins the ball again. An attack of sorts is on. Cardiff racing forward tongues lolling out of their mouths, ravenous almost. It's all hate ball, all mind games, all

Warnockian pantomime again.

Jimmy Jimenez is having a fucking howler. Nothing is going right, nothing is flowing. He was a sticky player a few weeks ago. A hero and a correct addition. Now everything seems like work for him. Everything is black. The ball comes through for him and he has a shooting chance for sure? But no, he turns his back to goal and lays the ball off. The ball is cleared. Cardiff move in a dysfunctional zombie like speed back up the pitch to their striker who needs '005 of a second to put his foot through the ball which reaches a speed indeed. Patricio goes the wrong way and the ball happily hits Willy Boly and rebounds off for a corner. That would have been a goal you know.

What other names shall we put in here? All of them? All of our team including Nuno? We are learning as I said before. But how much learning do these players need? In a job of course when we are training there has to be progression even if they are small increments we can hardly see.

Traore is getting a handle on things. Patricio is distributing little of worth, we remember John Ruddy moving the ball to Boly and then building. We see Patricio taking a year and a day before deciding to hoof the ball into midfield where Cardiff collect and it's all dog with two dicks attacking again and I grab onto the bloke next to me in some kind of fear...that Wolves fear ,that shit is going to go wrong again. It does and a big shot from distance flies into the top corner of our net and the Welsh go crazy. I look at my feet. I cant even look up. Fuck. 2-1 to them. Names we can litter our post mortems with but what is the point?

We controlled games for long periods in the previous games. We looked good like we were supposed to be there, like the Premier League was our league, and it would merely provide the backdrop to Nunos art and ideas. But this was finger painting. This was the art your four year old kid brings back from Nursery. It's Mommy and Daddy on a boat on holiday last year, but it looks like somebody has vomited on the paper. Your eyes are glutinous blobs of blue and your hair looks like a tree. 'Lovely' you say and it goes on the fridge, stuck there with a fridge magnet from Great Yarmouth. It has a donkey on it, chewing a carrot. The art will stay there until that young mind forgets and we can put it in the draw with the rest of the crap art they bring home.

There was some glimmers of positivity but these were few and far between. This run of defeats and draws is growing like a tumour. In all of us. It's ok sitting there with our head in our hands moving players in and out of the squad or just fucking them all off and starting again.

I can agree with all of them as that's exactly what defeats like this do to us. It makes us feel worthless and shit. When we feel like that of course we self harm sometimes or we strike out and share a few punches with some fool on the car park because he cussed (insert name here) or said Nuno should be fucked off. We roll around in the shitty Welsh mud and we are done for emotionally.

There are some problems here. Neves and Moutinho are blurring into each other during games so that it seems like there is nobody there at all sometimes. It's just a fog or a mist of intent. Something grey and listless.

Morgan Gibbs White comes on but is a false Messiah. Even he can't turn this watery Wolves team into fine wine. Not yet. There will be no Tottenhamesque madness from him tonight.

I chat about Big Alf and how he would have done a job maybe. The last three games have showed me that we can be bullied by midfielders who are physical and stoic. They trample over us. We have three attackers who couldn't at the moment attack a kebab. Our defence lacks movement and purpose. So we sit and ruffle our hair up in the late hours wondering what we would do and how we would put things right. I am playing magic tiles again.

But of course it's not our job. It's Nunos. So how is our nerve 'Wolf pack'? How are we dealing with this blip? Badly of course. Behaving less like a pack and more like a rabble. I include myself in that description. Angry. Pissed off. But we are at a junction of course, a cross roads maybe. It's the point in the journey when all the written platitudes and memes are swept aside under the brazen points tally of the campaign. We know what happens when these blips in our campaign happen of course. I spoke about it in the last book I wrote. We start to attack ourselves. We turn on those we love with anger and violence, threats and verbal attacks. We wax dark viscious lyrics on social media, to friends and family. We notice fans of our rivals start to leach out of the rotten places they inhabit to gloat and preen in front of us.

Fosun will be watching this run with a worrying eye of course. This is the thing which worries me the most. We the fans are obviously doughnuts, emotional ones. We can't help it, we think with our hearts most of the time and our personal struggles are entwined heavily with the club we love. But Fosun? They have investments here. They have spent money on a team that seems rudderless and lost. Nuno will have the confused eyes of his team upon him and the forensic business eye of Fosun too. Now whose nerve will break first?

Will Nuno be removed? Will there be thoughts about another Coach maybe? Another friend of Uncle Jorges? What will be the zeitgeist? Will we make knee jerk changes under pressure? Will we look at January and the transfer window where we will throw money at the problem, bring in quality? I have my own thoughts of course as I have been up most of the night thinking about it.

For Fosun I say this. Keep your hand on the tiller and concentrate. Loyalty must pay for something. Loyalty and being steadfast. Fosun cannot lose their minds yet, it's not time. In Nuno we have an idea and yes it is still strong, it is unique and it is precious. He is our Leader and our Totem. Would you throw him to the Wolves? Really? What Nuno needs now more than ever is our support and our love. He needs to know that we are with him and will either live or die by what his thoughts and impressions are.

I know football and Wolves is what always occupies his mind. He thinks about it constantly. We can see this. We love him for it. These results are what? Glitches mate. Aberrations in the matrix of Wolves. They are nothing yet...we wait until May to find out how this collecting of points has made us fare but the time for falling is not yet, not now, not this early. This is the time when we actually support, as fans our team and our City, our Coach and our owners and more importantly I suppose, we support Nunos ideas.

In the next few weeks we will maybe see a few more defeats. There may be some big ones too. There may be some defeats that make us weep as we walk back to the car or the bus. There will possibly be more rumbles in the audience at Molineux, some crap in the press. I guess that there is no love lost between our local press and Nuno. They will be coming for him in the next few weeks so be vigilant, be aware. Their silence at the moment is the intake of breath for the diatribes to come. There will be a whole load of crap to come in the run up to Christmas but have faith.

Nuno will understand the problems we have. He will again delve into the footage to see what problems we face. He will be looking to fix those problems as fast as he possibly can. Remember the variables he has to deal with. Have knowledge of what Coaching a Premier League club involves and have patience and faith. As when we have faced the same problems in the past we answered the baying crowd with Grant Holt, Sagbo, Jermaine Pennant. Those times are gone, done and dusted.

Now there is hope and there is a way out and it will come, I'm sure of it. We have to start believing again I suppose, we knew these times would be hard. I watched customers rolling in and out of the spangly beautiful club shop when I was flogging my book outside the Northbank in July this year. They were happy smiling, beaming faces. But I was struck by the happiness not in a jolly warm way. I knew these people would not have a strong heart to see us through the coming months and campaign, I knew they didn't have the experience to get through it. Me? I sat through the Summer with a big furrowed brow thinking through all the variables, all the things that could go wrong. My smiles only lasted as long as the bus ride through town and the smoke bombs, the happiness.

I feel strong of course. My future is woven with Nunos and I will fall or rise with him, live or die in this hellish Premier League. I am loyal to Coaches who I see work hard and have an emotional connection to us. I think perhaps I love Nuno in a way. In many ways he has represented on more than a memetic level a rise in my clubs fortunes. What he says to us is not dogma and not platitudes and empty promises. If he says he is sorting out the problems then that is exactly what he is doing for Nuno doesnt tell untruths. What do I offer you back Nuno? My support always. I sing so loud I cannot speak. I walk distances to grounds that make my crumbling bones cry out. I spend money I do not have so I do not eat for days so I can see our team and your ideas. You will have my love forever come what may.

Love.

Chapter 22

Russian Oil Gollums

But what does our love mean? Tonight is murky to me, these past bad results weigh on me despite all the positive platitudes. It makes us a bit mean I think and that's the philosophy of the Wolf in many respects. Hiding away in the forest when things are getting tough and it's Chelsea tonight at Molineux. They are a slick outfit these Chelseas. They are expensive and shiny with names we can't pronounce (although we are getting better at it).

In the afternoon I have seen Gaz Mastic sitting forlorn by the canal staring into the water which is clear after a few frosts. Gaz is clasping his hands together giving them a dry wash. There is dirt under his fingernails.

'I don't like it Mikey...I'm not sure Nuno is the man for this job' he says.

Oh Gaz. I know man, it's all doom when we see a few errant results. But we look good and we have one over riding principle, instilled by Nuno...no, 'carved' by Nuno in the slick polished conference sized desks of those high and mighty clubs of Premier Land.

Resilience.

We always look like we are in a game. We always look like we might grasp a straw and Jota or Cavaliero or Jimmy will bust a few goal scoring shapes. Hope, I think I've already waxed about that. The night is strangely quite lukewarm and funky. The trip up with my mate Knocker was a strange one hustling through the pre match traffic to Faulkland street car park. Already there are doughnut Londoners milling around. Some have parked their cars. Big Jaguars and the ubiquitus 'Chelsea tractor'. But there is an impatient Wolves fan in one. A young fat man with a crunchy shit beard. He honks his horn a few times and I am tempted to get out and boot a wing mirror off...but no of course not. Let's not let the dim crinkle of hope in our bellies get soured by an altercation before a ball has been kicked. But the stress is palpable. We can feel it.

We stand outside the South Bank and wax for a while before we go in. There are many young Chinese fellows oodling about. A few young Portuguese too. Are we international yet? One of the Portuguese fellas buys a Wolves scraf from the pop up shop outside the turnstiles.

I idly watch people buy stuff with Nunos face on it. There are all sorts. A drunken man stumbles past and he doesnt even look up, he just walks to the stand like he's on a tight rope. Concentrating on something...on getting in I suppose. He disappears through the turnstile. It's all good. That is the first positive thing I've seen tonight. The drunken man is IN. Victory for all drunken football fans.

There have been changes. I'm walking and trying to look at a phone with the team on it. I haven't got my readers on and it's hard especially as the Phones owner is wafting it around my face while I try to focus on it.

Saiss in midfield replacing the suspended Ruben Neves. There is something in Saiss I like and I feel good about his appearance. His selection. Morgam Gibbs White starts too.

Last week Morgan let his colours run all over the pitch. It was a shame he never scored but...what is it with him that makes us so comfortable. He is one of ours of course but I think there is a deeper meme within him. Something different. I suspect he epitomises what we are now. I know he has his England appearences as a badge of honour and the dry pundits have waxed shiny lyrics to him from the comfort of the TV studio. But I don't think that is it. I think Morgan has a deeper and more satisfying aura around him.

He essentially epitomises once again the 'spirit' of this team. To learn from the Master Nuno and his staff, and too foster that typical Wolves spirit, to always fight to always listen and conform to the Coaches ideas. But within that he also has his own ideas too. These ideas are that he will fear no team, fear no player, no situation. His temerity to chase down balls and to look for space in which to move is a beautiful thing to behold. So now I suspect he is in a 'false nine' position? In the attack? I hustle through the turnstile and say hello to people and this is good. This is positive and the concourse is loud. Nobody here sits or stands in small groups whispering doom. It is all upbeat and battling.

These fireworks and lightshows we have. Wow. I stand in my position for the start of the game. What is all this pyro stuff? This insane shouting through the PA system. The flashing madness, the absolute spectacle of it.

Even the Chelsea fans are dumbstruck, open mouthed wondering what the fuck is going on. But there is a message here for other clubs, the big fat men at the FA, the lizards on Match of the Day. This is Fosun saying things. Waxing their own lyrics. Yes Chelsea, you are a big club. You have spent many days in the Premier League, succesful ones. You have a great Coach, great players...but this. Well this is Wolves and we too have things to say. Look at our mad fireworks, see the frenzy of the crowd. Do you remember it too? When Chelsea actually meant something? When you too remembered the past?

Many times already this season I have entered other teams stadiums and been shocked by the lack of atmosphere. Many of them have been funeral like. Manchester United at Old Trafford. Brighton at whatever their stadium is called. Has their stay in these lush environs of the Premier League affected them in some way? Have all these supporters become mere customers?

You see being a customer gives you freedom to slash great negative comments across social media when your team aren't performing. Also 'the customer is always right' and in these great empty stadiums devoid of passion I see customers not supporters and I am thinking of these day tripper football fans milling around the Southbank. There is something in my pocket of this jacket and I pull it out as the lights fling mad photons around the ground. It's a Barnsley ticket from last season. I remember how cold it was. The barman with the burned Iron shape on his jumper in the club we went to before the game. Whacking 'Southbank Resistance' stickers everywhere we could. I digress again, I'm sorry. But Barnsley will never have this. They will never have a Molineux like this or a team, or a Coach. The Ref blows his whistle and we are off.

Saiss is alive hunting and grappling from the start. But then again so is Moutinho who isn't late or shy about getting a leg in here and there. That is a change for sure. I suspect even at his age Moutinho is learning something about this league.

Chelsea players are falling over like drunken men at the slightest touch. At least the play acting isn't extended to writihing around the Molineux pitch like they have been shot. They are pros for sure, Get the decision and move on. Get to your feet. Play on. Their Coach looks like an Italian academic. He points and he shouts. Nuno just stands arms crossed watching every tackle, every play.

Chelsea are playing some beautiful football. But you can tell it's football by committee again. Any exubarance is snuffed out and it's pure formula...but it works. They dance balls through our midfield with aplomb...but our players are there for sure. Right there. A simple tap on the spine to a Chelsea player from Moutinho lets them know he is still there. It makes his pass errant and confused. We collect the ball from his misplaced pass. We move too. Fast movement almost electric as Jimmy forces a throw in....what the fuck? Ryan Bennett chuck in a thirty yard throw. Bloody hell. Where did that aspect come from? All the ball boys have towels! They are wiping the ball down before the throw! What madness of planning is this? We have a chance but Jimmy fumbles under pressure. The ball is farted out for a goal kick. Bloody hell...you think you know a team. What was all that about? I like it though.

Coady is alive and being a predator again. He is covering ground like a bad man. Sniffing at the heels of these footballing play boys...but it's not like we are the ragamuffins of the whole groove. This isn't some David versus Goliath thing. This is a team who can stand right where Chelsea are with the feeling they deserve to be here and fuck your history and how many years you have been in the league.

There is a difference too in our play from the Cardiff game a few days ago. Now we look like we have space to play, space to determine where we move and what we do, there is space to lay down the rythyms straight off the Compton training ground. Here is Saiss again. His distribution is muted because he is keeping very close tabs on those multi million pound Chelsea doughnuts with the funny names and the weird hair.

Chelsea break and shoot. Coady is right near the right hand post. He throws himself at the ball. Patricio is shaping up to cover and to save. Coady connects with the Chelsea shot. It skims off his head into the goal. Coady buries his head in the grass, it is a goal yes. We are 0-1. Coady allows himself a few moments of self pain and agony. Then he is up and directing our madness, shouting pointing, defining defence, neutralising attacks.

What a Captain this is, what a leader. An example even, of how a Captain should be. To forget after a few luxurious moments of negative self assesment in the ignominy of an own goal and then to spring to your feet and throw yourself back into the madness. At halftime I am trying to keep my roll up alight down the side of the Southbank. I am talking to people. A doughnut is having a go at Coady about the goal. I stand over him while he waxes negative waves. I start to stand closer to him, and closer, and closer until he is up against the wall and he stops talking now and just looks up at me with these beer addled eyes that look all sad. I don't say anything at all but his friends are a bit scared, they look at him then back at me. I've got a Conor Coady mug and a signed photo. Nothing epitomises our rise more than Conor Coady. Cuss him and you cuss the team and the idea. There is no debate in this.

"I have my best cups of teas in my Conor Coady mug" I tell him and he smiles because now I've given him an out. A way to salvage the situation. This dude has a spot on his forehead and beads of sweat now. My face is inches away from his...but it's all a laugh all debate...all fools. Coady will have times when the ball slices off a Coady body part. His job is to negate attacks, block the ball, block shots, be the fence, be the barrier.

There are going to be plenty of times when the ball hits him and goes in. Chelsea were lucky. You have to support. You have to fight. You have to dig in shout....I'm telling the dude this but I think I'm getting too angsty again. I back off. Light my roll up. All good. Don't cuss Coady around me.

Our shape remains the same of course. But our efforts are now trurned up to 11 on the dial. We chase hopeless balls. We ignore the Chelsea Referee who looks like his hair has come from a Hoover bag and been glued on by a blind sad man. His yellow card is becoming faded after being dragged from his pocket so often to be waved at numerous Wolves players who commited a sin of daring to obtain the ball from a Chelsea player. How fucking dare we try to put the kibosh on this glorious London team. How dare we tackle Avya Dahnthecut their 100 billion pound half starved dickhead. How dare indeed. The yellow card has come out that often we should have been warned about flashing images.

There are bloody strange decisions all round to be honest. The one linesman has only a passing knowledge of football. Eight or nine times the ball is out of play, over the line. I can see it from here in the Southbank mate. His flag stays lowered. I don't think he can actually see. I entertain the notion it was actually him that glued the Refs hair on. I want to run on and attack them, my angst is real.

The stand has gone quiet and the Chelsea fans are throwing their arms around and singing something about West Brom...you mean North Birmingham FC of course. I want to sing something about their rivals but you know, I cant for the life think of who Chelsea hate, who are their rivals. Because Morgan Gibbs White is 'runnin tings'. This is bassline football. You can feel it in your belly before you actually hear it or see it. I'm flicking the V's at the Chelsea fans but watching the pitch. Moutinho has just gently brushed past a Chelsea player who has fallen down again. It's a crying shame.

Vinagre down our wing is loving this shit. Pirouette and change stance, idly caress the ball and spin again, he's off down the wing and Jimmy is shouting. Wolves don't fucking care do they? Shape is everything. Morgan Gibbs White is cememnting a place just behind Jimmy and Jota. The spearpoint really filling the gap between midfield and the attack. What a fine idea that is. Maybe the one thing nobody ever thought of. This zone is Morgans. It belongs to him. Now he can mix it about a bit. He was given the role in the Sheffield Wednesday cup game and was a little confused by it and now? He knows it intimately.

We pass and move and the ball is a blur. Gibbs White collects. The ball is a soft one, not pin point. There is a tangle in the mangle but Morgan is up for it. Arms wave, knot and weave. The ball is Morgans, he sees Jimmy making a run. Perfect weighted pass. Jimmy collcts in the box and lets one go. Boom. Between the Chelsea goalies legs. 1-1.

My glasses fly in the air again. I fall over the seat in front and I fall over the rear. Somebody pulls me up and I fall down again. I hold my glasses tight. They are my last ones. I fall and I get up again. Singing. Shouting. Arm waving. I fight through the arms and madness to look at the Chelsea fans. Sad faces. Yes. It is nearly done. Nearly finished. From behind we have fought strong and hard. We have stuck to the idea. Is this how you want it Nuno? This shape and idea? Is it everything you expected? We have drawn dividends, split the multi million pound Chelsea defence. Equalised. We are there now for sure. We have to be.

Now nobody in the Wolves side is a bystander. They are all actors on the stage. It's the finale the end of it. You see Chelsea are reticent and shy to flourish. They have been muted by our movement. Of course Chelsea are a brilliant side. Their football is gorgeous and sexy. They move effortlessly but are affected by our efforts and our ideas. We have them too. Moutinho moves and darts between players. Saiss attacks, moves, negates attacks. Gibbs White....oh shit. Chelsea are moving. Their weird haired striker is running fast. Shit, it's a one on one with Patricio. Oh bollocks no. Not a goal from them...but what's this running in from the wing? Ryan Fucking Bennett mate. His legs are a blur. His speed phenomenal. The angles and the dangles,will he get to the Chelsea player. Will he intercept..fucking hell. Bennett tackles. It's clean as fuck I promise you. The ball over the touchline safe. The Chelsea player disconsolate. It was a chance for them but for this man Bennett. Last year a moment captivated me. Neves goal against Derby, the volley and the magic. But we had really already won that game, that campaign. But this tackle. You say 'That tackle by Moore' and fair enough wax all you want about that but this. Well this was something on a par with that. The beauty of that tackle was sublime and understated. Just like Bennett. We are going to fucking win this. We have to now. There is no way God will allow something like that to happen wityhout it becomes a pre cursor to a victory. We are everywhere now and we are inspired. We move and we create.

Again we are mowing down everything in our sight like machine gunners, spraying madness and football all over the pitch. Chelsea may keep the ball well but fucking hell what are you going to do with it? A Ferrari in your garage is just a lump of metal and rubber that looks nice. You have to take it on the road man, you have to drive it. This is what

Wolves are doing. Chelseas brilliant football has become a log jam or a traffic jam I suppose. They have that many exciting elements, stratgies and tactics that for the moment they can't choose what they want to do with it. But us.

Ball practically on the Chelsea touchline. We see everything in the stand, in this Southbank. The ball slides across the goalmouth and there to poke it home the little Wolf himself. Diogo not Diego Jota. He stabs the ball and is off to celebrate. I am punched in my bad neck. I fall over again. My glasses come off. My flat cap is over my eyes. I get a knee in the leg. My shins are smashed. I am singing. We are singing and we sing and we sing. Diogo fucking Jota you beauty, you little sexy bastard, you did it. I love you Diogo.

Well...there is Chelsea done. Their fans file out with great sad visages and I am laughing and waving at them. This is everything isn't it? What power we have if we can brush our the poor results of the last few games and bloom into such delightful reply. It was definitely a reply of sorts. That stoical message from Nuno week after week. There is no individual player. There is no slight message of love for him or for him. It is everybody, all of us. Even us in the stands tonight.

I couldn't sleep when I got home of course. The memories of the goals and the conversations are made all the sweeter by the odd dog fart in the darkness and the warm smell of farty shit. But the darkness always holds light in some way because when things are dark it doesnt mean that the darkness is devoid of everything. The dark implores us to fill it with something and to do that we have to create. That is exactly what Nuno has done. He created. He made new ideas and shapes and they have paid dividends. I close my eyes and I can still see the fireworks and smell the smoke. Onwards.

Chapter 23

Brown Ale Gollums and a Threatening Youth

'Onwards' we say, but where? The stratosphere of course. The Champions league nights and the chaos of navigating finances, family commitments, and...fucking finances. I looked around at some of my mates in the Southbank. Some will afford to go to Europe without any real implications. They are succesful, comfortable and have worked hard. I know some of these lads went without to get a season ticket. The lads who were missed by opportunity and chances, the ones who soldier on regardless still smiling, still happy. They are the ones with the holes in their underpants and thin soles on their trainers. I know this. Thinking that it's ok to deal with looking scruffy for a few months, a few less pints when they are out, putting off getting the exhaust fixed because it's 400 quid for a new one and to be fair I know it's loud but...

What do we do? We sing and look forwards to a dream land of sorts but we are still Wolverhamptonites. We still bear the scars of government policies. We still suffer. We still sing. On the way to Newcastle and St James Park. There is something here of course. Their stadium is still basically where it always was. Right in the heart of the city. Right in the hearts of their people too. Their heads are big. It's something me and a few others have noticed. These Newcastlites speak with strange tongues and often the tone is vehement when they speak of their club. I am outside the 'Town in the Wall' pub in the city center. Here the gargling tones of their accent are strong. Their identity is strong also. I am smoking a roll up and watching people walk around outside doing human things like shopping or something. There is a lad who keeps glancing at me as if he wants to speak. We make eye contact. He speaks. Something about the match and Wolves. I don't know what he's on about half the time but he has unleashed a stream of commentary and madness I barely understand.

I get fragments of it. Little words here and there where 'Nuno' becomes 'Noowanorr' and Wolves becomes 'Wooz' and there are other words and my mind is drifting. I don't often wonder what other teams think of our team as I simply don't care but I am amazed at this dudes accent. His mate comes out and he doesn't like me for some reason. This new dude finishes his pint and flips the pint glass quick like he's going to use it as a weapon to bump me one. But he thinks a little and decides against it. I am glad as my leg is hurting and I don't want to roll around today.

I jump in the lift at the ground. Horace throws me in. I've got a steel rod in my leg he tells the Security doughnut. I am glad. How many floors has that fucking stand got? It takes 15 seconds to get to the top and all of a sudden it's good and wholesome again. There is 'us' walking around drinking, meeting up with mates, talking, laughing. Looking forward to the match. We are on a high. I am glad I am here amongst them as it's a little corner of Wolverhampton now. Still risky as fuck. Still dangerous but it's my dangerous, my danger, my towns.

We mill around and take photos, we mingle and we chat. There is talk of the team and who Nuno has chosen for todays madness. Someone has an inside track and has leaked the team news. I don't like that stuff. What if Rafa Benitez gets his hands on it. Will he adjust his selection, nullify threats based on this social media leak? Small things for sure. But man, everything with this team is planned with an almost insane attention to the finest details.

Walking around the Waterloo road end of the Molineux is exciting. It's as if a huge generator is humming deep underground producing energy and disspitaing it out towards the rest of the world and that power runs into boardrooooms of clubs, into the minds of prospective players. That buzz of the hive is seen in the media too. It's empty as ever, the newspapers the official feed, the online bollocks. All quiet on the Wolvo front but it's not the idle quiet for sure. Things are moving, being put into position. But the Security dude is staring at me just standing there with my belly relaxed hunched over really. I must look like a weirdo. I don't care. I was here before you mate. I haven't a clue why I am thinking of the Northbank while I am shitting myself at the top of the steepest football stadium stand I've ever been in.

St James park is huge. We are perched high up in the one end of the place. It's a cauldron of quiet, a veritable silent bowl...not like the dead that filled Old Trafford of course. The Newcastleites are propagandised. It's a massive catchment area for one club. Fifty thousand will fill it today but as fervent a belief they have it's vocalisation of that belief lacks. It's fucking quiet. 'Nuno had a dream' reverberates off the rafters. We look to the West and the sun is setting and throwing these beams and daggers of light through the translucent sides of the North stand. It's definitely spiritual this place but it's soul is lacking. What fervents have these people been through in the past few years? I have no clue. My mind is occupied by Wolves and Wolves only. But something has happened here for sure. We are playing in all Gold.

There is a strangness to this team. It is a new Nuno shape he has given us to get our heads around. Adama Traore starts. This man is a delight. Already those who lack foresight have denigrated him vocally and on social media. Who are these people? Those who lack knowledge. He collects the ball and he falls over. He has some runs, he falls over again. A tackle on him and he's on the floor. A voice behind me shouts some abuse about him. That's ok. I'm filtering this shit out. If it's not Costa it's Traore and if it's not either of them it's somebody else. Has the Traore experiment failed? I will leave that conclusion for others more skilled than me to define. I support and that is all I am qualified to do really.

Adama has been filled with the junk and poison of playing for Tony Pulis last season. Do you know what that must have done to this young man? He had time at Aston Villa too. His head must be filled with that much bullshit maybe Nuno isn't really being a Coach but a Counsellor too. Trying to even out the kinks in Adamas game, carving away that rough black marble to unveil a world beating player, a marvel and a work of art. So Nuno barely chips a piece away and people are castigating his art as being 'shit'. Have patience. He is still the most electric player on the pitch bar Jota and Gibbs White who is benched for a while after he destroyed Chelsea. Madness.

We are not the slick side of the other night against Chelsea of course. This is a new shape. New tactics but with the same motto. Keep the shape, keep the idea maybe work harder than your opponents too. There is no display of half heartedness from our team. They are quick to second balls, if unlucky at times.

Newcastle have their own shapes, they press high up the field which is silly really. Didn't they see Traore on the teamsheet? There is a flow to the game. Mike Dean the referee does his best to alter that flow by flashing yellow cards everywhere at anything in Gold...again. What is it about these bald headed refs? Are they bitter about their hair? Is this display of ineptitude just a rant at the world at large, or just a general rant at Wolves?

Ruben Vinagre our left back is mostly our 'Left Forward' as he tangles and mangles balls down the wing for the odd cross. He is growing into this. There are fewer worldie jelly leg feints as he tries to confuse Liam Leathertongue or whatever and get some space. Now his game is changing and he is adopting an almost Jonny like physicality when he tries to get the ball into the box. I would love him to come inside a bit more....fucking hell. Jota gets a ball, he chests it down, he's only three yards away from the goalie and volleys it. It comes off the goalies body and it's in. The net sways and waves as the ball impacts. I don't see anymore. It's all arms and legs and madness. I get a punch in the ear, somebody treads on my foot, I go to grab my glasses but fail. They go somewhere. I hug people and we stare at each other and scream wordless joys. 1 fucking 0 my friends...we look to the Newcastle fans to berate and proclaim our magnificence but...they sit and stare.

The pitch is as big as a tablecloth up here. I've had to bring my prescription sunglasses as I've lost my normal ones. I probably look like a tit. I don't care. Elation at the goal soon disspates though.

Newcastle aren't one of those Championship sides like Aston Villa or Barnsley. They have skills too...apart from Rondon of course who is ineffectual pretty much. Coady has the cut of his jib and is muting any move from him. But of course what small tendrils of the goal scoring elations are soon gone and up into the skies of the North East they go. Perez has scored for them. Now their crowd is alive and for a few seconds we see what this place must have been like years ago.

The bloke behind me is shouting about Costa. Bad things. Trouble is with fans buying tickets and reselling them to keep their loyalty points is that doughnuts like fluffy beard and his smackhead mate turn up at games. What do they know about Costa? Nothing. Did they watch him save our season in that season with Lamberk? Have they grown with Helder? No. Helder is learning things and having some sticky moments. It will all turn good of course....I hope.

Nuno isnt an idiot, he will understand the madness of being a highly paid pro footballer. There are no knee jerks here, no concern. Helder will come good but patience is the key. We havent seen the very best of Helder yet. The stands are still a stage for those with loud opinions they enjoy everybody listening to. But us English. We mistrust loud voices. It's in our DNA.

The game has turned into a typical Rafa Benitez game where all of a sudden there are black and white stripy bodies on the floor. Willy Boly has collided with their goal scorer in our box. Perez lies like he is in severe pain but we break as he writhes. The Newcastle crowd aren't happy but who gives a shit.

'Fuck him let him die gooo on Wolves goooo on' somebody shouts. It might be me. The attack is false and empty and play is stopped while somebody goes to check on Perez. Their striker had tried to headbutt Bolys elbow...a vicious assault on Big Willy for sure. But the Ref gets the game on again and everything is now the languid sad violins of the symphony Benitez has his teams play. It looks like Holocuast violin music.

Newcastle are playing foil to the obtuse decisions of Mike Dean. A referees job is to allow football to be played surely? But as soon as the rythym builds from both sides not just Wolves. That fucking yellow card is out again at another Wolves player. Decisions are all over the place. There is no continuity, no real idea of the game just flashing yellows all over the pitch.

Even the Newcastle fans recognise that Dean is playing the leading part here. This week down the canal I watched a little Jack Russell tring to fuck a Labrador. It wasn't happening and we laughed at it's little arse going ten to the dozen as it tried to climb up and get a shag. Mike Dean reminds me of that dog. Wanting to take part when it's obvious to everybody else it just isn't happening.

There were moments in this game for sure, when I was looking out over Newcastle and thinking what a nice place it was. Times when my tongue probed loose teeth. When I shifted weight from one foot to the other. When I took my sunglasses off to clean them on my shirt. Moments you dear reader will understand. I will take the point for the draw of course. We aren't totally brilliant today. The shape isn't moving, isn't having much effect. In my mind I type this of course. Tip tap of the keys and tip tap of the football and the rythym is now one of a precious point...

Of course this is Wolves. This is Nunos Wolves. As our minds wander and fritter away at the game there is still the idea yes, still the same shape. Same subs practically but what is this Nunos Wolves? They kept at it. Everything attack had intent written all over it. Benitez and Newcastle were happy to have the occasional break but were ensconsed in keeping that point. That';s their philosophy. To 'keep' rather than 'get'. That is the difference right there.

The ball is down here by us and we are clicking the passes together. We are into injury time, the dying seconds. Someone dinks the ball through to Jota. The old Jota. Remember him? I haven't talked about him much so far because there wasn't too much to say. He was learning stuff, assimilating Premier League informations. Now he is ascendant again. He believes and takes the ball, digging it out and he's on a run. I notice something else. The bloke that has just come on for Newcastle not a few minutes before isn't looking at Doherty. The Irishman has flung himself all over the pitch for 90+ minutes and now flings himself into the abyss once again. Why? He's not involved in any of the moves ahead of him. Doherty is running forwards and he has left his man. Doherty is a free runner. He tracks Jota like a shadow but twenty five yards away. Jota spangles and clangles with defenders on him like a zombie film. Jota shoots and the ball deflects away from goal straight to Doherty who nods it in. Last minute winner.

This is what we live for. There is insanity and moshy limb moves in the stand. I scream. I don't even care about my glasses. I nearly fall over the front seats. I grab onto someones arm. My plate in my leg smashes against a seat. Elbow in the eyes. My hair is a mess. There are a few seconds of play after the restart but fucking hell. We have won again. Back to back wins in the Premier league, a rare thing. Again? So soon after Chelsea? Why the fuck not?

The Geordies are not happy. There are things said outside and we laugh and continue on our way. I don't care mate, not any more. You haven't been given the God given right to win games you have to fight for them. Your edifices and massive stadiums are nothing without belief and love. That is the difference between us and them when the margins are so thin you can read a newspaper through them. We were evenly matched for sure. But we had something else. Something about Nunoism and playing, working, loving as hard and as good as you possibly can. Sometimes that effort isn't enough as we saw at Huddersfield and Cardiff where hate and fever were the philosophies.

I dunno. It's a long trip back in the car and we wax long about the future and the past with Wolves. I watch the lights and the traffic and slumber half asleep into deeper thoughts about what is happening to us as a team and as a city. Are we doing ok? Us fans? Is it that mad we can't quite take stock of it? It's still early, I get back home and my lad tells me we have won as many games as West Bromwich Albion had all last season and it's still early December. I can't sleep but I am dreaming...how does our song go?

Chapter 24

Eddie Hitler and the Waiting To Die Gollums

Years ago I used to work in Ablow street in Penn Fields building garden sheds. Hammering together pieces of sap and resin wet pine into shed shapes. It was a shit job but I loved the smell of it. Only one bloke was allowed to used the circular table saw. The thing was rattled and held together by odd pieces of hastily tacked welding and screws. Once the blade actually flew off and wedged itself in the joists above the workshop. It was a place of reflection this saw room. We were often found, us workers, stood around waiting for the bloke that operated the saw. He looked like Eddie Howe the Bournemouth Coach.

This individual was a bitter twisted little fucker. When he ate his sandwiches at lunch he always looked like he was chewing a mixture of dogshit and glass. That's how much he was enjoying life. He drove a brand new Ford XR3i and he polished it sometimes and all his tapes were sorted out lovely, in little holders. Phil Collins and fucking Enya for Gods sake. I don't think he actually listened to them but they were there for show. To show how cool he was listening to cool music in his cool car with his surf Tshirts eventhough he had never surfed in his life. I hated him.

This Eddie Howe lookalike was a Villa fan and had a season ticket at Witton Park Stadium or whatever it's called. He had a Villa sticker in the back window. So one day we were stood around the saw table while Eddie Howe was moaning again. He moaned about everything you see, to anybody that was captured by his aura...or waiting for a couple of saw cuts. He was droning and it was very hot that day. The sawdust was making me itch and the resin now soft in the Pine was acrid almost and I could feel myself wanting to smack him over the head with a 2x4 to get him moving.

The saw room was a dimly lit shithole, the same as most saw rooms. Most factories and workshops probably. It was none too clean. I knew there was a Mouse or two in here and some lunchtimes I would leave a crust under the saw table for Mr Mouse to grab hold of and have a yam.

"The fact is..." Eddie Howe was waxing,"You shouldn't have a flourescent light in a saw room, it's illegal." He was telling my mate Bry about the saw and I wasn't really taking much notice. Bry asked him what was important about a fucking light and what kind it is.

Eddie puffed his chest out and started one of his lectures..."A flourescent tube flickers and you can't tell whether or not the saw blade is going around..." Eddie said and went to flick the saw blade...which was actually on. Eddies finger went flying in the air somewhere as he screamed. The blade had took that fucking finger off like a hot knife through lard, like shit through a Goose.

"Me fucking fingaaaaaah!" he screamed. Bry went to help as I stood amazed at the big arc of blood that went flying around. I stood back. I didn't want any on me thanks. Industrial accidents are always weird times. Office staff appeared, Gaffers turned up and attempted to do Gaffer things which were mostly trying to blame everybody else including me, stood there with an eight foot long 2x4 and a stupid half amused look on me face. I was trying not to laugh. People were scurrying around trying to find Eddies finger in the half a foot of sawdust everywhere but to no avail.

"It's like a lucky dip ay it?" I said to Bry but nobody laughed except me.

Eddie got rushed up the Royal Hospital and we cracked on with the day which had been brightened up a lot by the drama in the saw room. Bry wasn't happy, he was a delicate soul.

Next day Bry looked ashen and worn out. I tried to talk to him but he was muted and half there it seemed. Even at lunchtime (it was chip shop day) he just picked at his chips and ate his battered sausage with the same joy he would munch a tramps dick.

The day wore on and I could tell Bry needed to get something off his chest. Late afternoon a lorry arrived and myself and Bry were ordered into the roof space to stack up the lumber from the lorry. I didn't mind it up there, it was quiet and peaceful away from the banging and clanging from the workshop. Sometimes you could have a crafty roll up as long as you chucked the end in a bucket of water they kept up there for fires. Eventually Bry opened up to me. First he looked over his shoulder and pulled me to him close.

Bry had got back home the previous day and did what he always did.

Sat down in his favourite chair by the fire and turned the TV on. He had a Staffy named 'Turtle' a lovely thing all muscle and a daft head. Turtle was not his usual happy self that Bry had got back home. He wouldn't stop sniffing Brys feet.

Bry wondered if he had any of Eddies blood on him. Bry always wore turn up jeans because his legs were short and he couldn't be arsed to sew them up. He turned his turn ups down checking for Eddie blood and lo and behold Eddies severed finger fell out.

Quick as a shot Turtle grabbed hold of it and ran off into the kitchen with it and started cracking and chewing it with a look of happiness only Staffy owners will know. Bry tried to get the finger off him but Turtle wasn't having any of it at all. He growled and he snarled as he ate Eddies finger. Brys face was the saddest thing ever as he recalled the events and I was crying with laughter on the stacks of new wood that summers day in Penn fields. Eddie Howes finger eh? Every time I look at Eddie Howe I think about that finger and the dog eating it.

Nuno had a dream...to build a football team. I've eaten too much cheese or something. I see Eddie Howe the Bournemouth head Coach. He is in a dimly lit cellar somewhere. It has been freshly but badly painted. There is a strip light above him which is flickering...he holds a cattle prod and in front of him are a box of Puppies. There is a voice over a small Bluetooth speaker. It is Colin Wanker..."You know what to do Eddie baby you know what I need" he mutters. There is a lap top and connected to it is a small web cam. Colin is watching. On the Laptop screen we see Colin. He is gently burning his nipples with a tea candle. He looks demonic, his face fills my vision. I hear puppies whimpering. I see Eddie Howe walk slowly towards them...Eddie looks like a bloke that's going to go ballistic with his collection of automatic rifles.

I awake a little. My head is fuzzy. Eddie fucking Howe? Why?. I can hear ambulances up and down the Lichfield road. I turn over trying to get the vision of Eddie Howe out of my head. Softly drifting away. There are happier things to think about apart from Cardiff City, AFC Bournemouth and Neil Warnock burning his own nipples with tea candles...

Molineux is a theatre. Inside are all and sundry, I notice people I know but I am the dreamer and as I wave to people they ignore me (pretty much like real life) but they are all waiting. In front of them is a great red velvet curtain and there is a murmur of voices as people talk in animated fashion as they wait. They are excited.

The lights go down and it is time. There is a blare of trumpets and a cacophony of other instruments. The curtains slowly open and on the stage is a group of musicians. They look beautiful in Gold and Black sparkly tuxedos. In front of them are sheet music stands and hanging from every one of them is a silk banner with a simple 'WW' stitched in gold thread. The audience are applauding. It is a spectacle, all we can hear now is a gentle ryhtym of a snare drum. The lights grow even more dim and then a spotlight smashes into a glaring illumination of a figure coming from the wings. The audience go crazy and are standing up clapping, shouting before the man who has just entered holds his hand out to them for quiet.

They obey instantly. The man is wearing a beautiful Italian silk suit in gold. He is bearded and smiling. It is Nuno himself. He grabs a microphone...

'Ladies and gentlemen thank you...', he says. The snare drum is going 'ratatattatat'. Nuno holds his arm aloft and points to the drummer...

"...Ladies and gentlemen may I introduce to you, on drums, Rui Patricio, fresh from a World tour and the finest drummer in the world", Rui smashes a succession of whip crazy beats and fills before smashing his cymbals. He relaxes into a lazy beat. The audience applaud. Rui winks at the audience.

Nuno points to a sad looking soul to stage left. He is tall and unshaven.

"On Trombone Ladies and gentleman, Matt 'Doc' Doherty" Nuno says. Crowd goes wild and Matt Doherty fills the theatre with a cascading number of Trombone runs which Patricio puntuates with sliding half asleep beats. Now Doherty reduces his volume and is playing a simple melody.

"On Saxophone may I introduce Ryan 'Benno' Bennett", Ryan Bennett steps forward and from his Sax erupts a beautiful array of sensuous notes that seem to lock perfectly with Patricios drums and Dohertys Trombone. Now it sounds like something. Now it has a melody. Nuno taps his hand gently against his leg to keep time. Bennett steps back. Nuno points to another of his band.

"May I introduce...on Trumpet, the dulcet tones of the King of Steeze Mr

Conor (Captain) Coady.". Nuno motions Conor forward and he blasts a riff of such intensity and complexity that even Nuno himself smiles. Crowd go wild, he is a favourite for them obviously. He too relaxes after the applause subsides and takes a step back. Nuno points to a tall beautiful black man who steps forward.

"My friends may I introduce to you Sir William (French Funk) Boly on Bass guitar". Boly starts to play slowly, simple notes and quite refined, almost classical but tempting easily the subtle ministrations of the brass section and the rythym of Patricio, then all of a sudden he unleashes a tirade of slap bass funk riffs which splatter across the theatre. The crowd shout and applaud. Some of the women throw their knickers on the stage and Boly picks up the cleanest pair and mops his sweating brow. He throws them back and there is a massive fight among the women of the audience and one strange man who try to obtain this treasure of sweaty 80% lycra and 20% cotton. The air is filled with fibres as these animals rip the sweat drenched underwear to pieces. Bouncers appear and are punching all and sundry in happy chilled out violence.

"Ladies and Gentlemen.." Nuno continues, "...from the hills of Portugal, the assassin of cool, the killer of many men and the finest bongo player in the world Jonny Otto!". Jonny starts to rumble the bongos, his palms are gentle at first in perfect step with Patricios rythym. But then we hear that palm smacked animal skin start to sing as Jonny layers more beats on top of Patricios shapes before he subsides and the rythym is again quiet and restrained. All five players are now playing an upbeat tempo and are watching Nunos hand intently for direction. From stage right walks a small man. He is carrying a Fender Stratocaster in metaalic gold. He plugs it in. Nuno motions to him.

"Ladies and gentlemen, from the theatres and brothels of Portugal where he learned his trade, the Master of the strat, the Lord of Love Mr Joao Moutinho". Nuno turns away theatrically as Moutinho rips an amazing blues riff before tilting into a complec jazz riff which segues perfectly into the muted brilliance of Bolys bass guitar. Moutinho ends by throwing his guitar in the air and playing it with his teeth. Nuno laughs and shakes his head. As soon as the applause subsides, another figure walks onto the stage from the left. He is a young man, he holds a flute in his hand. Moutinho strikes up a choppy rythym which the rest of the band follow and the young man puts the flute to his lips.

"Ladies and Gentlemen, may I introduce to you the prodigy of the band and perhaps the greatest Jazz flute player to be in my orchestra. Mr Morgan Gibbs White!". Nuno shouts. Gibbs White is indeed young but his fingers are a blur as he lets out of his mind a beautiful melody that floats and enters the ears of all watching, first we think of New Orleans and Carnival...then he changes again and it's shades of golden notes, the ache of blacker minor notes and then again we hear the melodious refrains of Gibbs White for the moment standing back and taking his place with the rest of the band.

Another figure and another member. This one is also young, he is assured and cool. He winks at Nuno as he comes on. Nuno smiles. The young man is carrying a black Gibson SG and erupts into a sound that resembled other more famous guitarists but with a true flavour of his own that weaved through the funk melody of Moutinho and Boly as bursts of staccato brass which swung from this way to that before he points the guitar at the audience like a gun and springs a tirade of rock riffs then classical flamenco. Nuno smiles even wider..."Ladies and gentlemen, on lead guitar Mr Ruben Neves!"...

I turn over and move the dogs out of the way in bed. My pillows are too stuffy and crap. I bang my elbow on the side table. The dogs have most of the room and I try to weave my legs around them so I am comfy.

I must look like a man that has just jumped out of a tower block window. Arms and legs are like a swastika...I think about getting up but I am drifting...thinking about the game tomorrow. Eddie fucking Howe. My mate Ian hates him, says he's a fraud of a manager. I don't know about that, I never read about other Managers. But I remember Howe of course...when we played them last.

His team are a horrific bunch of expensive doughnuts who can play. But they don't know why. I see Colin Wanker on the lap top screen. His huge misshapen nipple looking like a rats nose. He touches the candle to it. The few hairs around it catch fire. Colin groans. I smell his burned hairs and I am drifting. Trying to get away from that cellar deep under Eddie Howes house...I can hear music again. It is a Hammond organ, it's breathy notes are subtle at first but there are some misplaced notes. The musician is trying to play too many at one time. The band try to keep up with him and then all of a sudden. They blend and the stabs at the keys become a caress and his fingers fly, pulling out a riff of such soul and deep love that as the audience initially put their hands over their ears now they smiled and began to tap their feet...Nuno has his head bowed and then he raises it as the notes proliferated. This is what he needs. This is what Nuno wants. The notes blend and they mix and there is a new sound there, it is funky and soulful. Jazzy at times, and often an errant finger produces another strange note but it all goes together. "Ladies and Gentlemen...on Hammond organ straight from the sunny climes of Portugal...my good friend Mr Helder Costa!".

The crowd scream a little now. The energy is rising and still we are a little way from the start of the show...but it is there for sure. This band know what they are doing. They are tight. From the wings walks a small man. He is small but he is big. He looks assured and confident. He has a Jazz harp and his fingers fly across the strings...they are a blur in fact. Nuno spreads his arms out wide. "Ladies and gentlemen on Jazz Harp Mr Diogo (Not Diego) Jota!!!".

The crowd are amazed at Jotas flurry of notes. They are on their feet. They fucking love Jazz Harp. The rythyms are loud and mad. Nuno tries to calm them down. This is not the start! These are the introductions! But Jota catches a finger in a string! An injury! Jota looks crestfallen. He will play no further part in this concert. Disconsolate he walks off the stage and the audience applaud him any way.

Nuno looks to the wings and from the darkness comes Ivan Cavaleiro hurriedly putting on his gold suit holding an Oboe in one hand and a Fish Finger sandwich in the other. He wasn't expecting to play! What is this madness?

Nuno waits while Cavaleiro finishes his sandwich. The band are giggling and Nuno sends them a furious look and they shut up. Cavaliero is trying to button his suit jacket but his fingers slip with buttery fish finger love. Nuno hurries over and helps him. Cavaleiro thank Nuno with a bashful look and puts the Oboe to his lips. The band play and Ivan sensuous lilts notes here and there among them. His fish finger smeared fingers glitter and slide over the mechanics of his oboe and there is a sound of course. Hues of soft lazy jazz weaving here and there, appearing all of a sudden with Helder Costas riffs.

Now the band are playing. For all of these introductions they have had to hold back on their playing. They have only played together for a short time and their have been some bad gigs when the audience tramped sloly disconsolate out of this theatre with sad unhappy faces. Sometimes the notes were too muted, the rythym too complicated. There was no groove. But the last few concerts have been excellent. Now what? This band sounds hot, they sound tight. It sounds like music of old.

We remember that music, us that are going slightly deaf. We may not understand the complexity of the task and the music but we understand the soul of it for sure. They sound like a band Sinatra would have behind him. Strangely a Sinatra like figure slowly walks onto the stage holding a microphone. It is Jimmy Jimenez! The crowd go crazy, more not to clean knickers are thrown on stage. Jimmy doesn't pick them up but he laughs. Nuno does too.

"Ladies and Gentlemen may I introduce to you, straight from the land of the Inca..and on vocals the smooth tones of Mexico...Mr Jimmy Jimenez!" Nuno shouts. The band are now playing a loud upbeat tune and the audience despite the no standing rule are up on their feet and dancing. The flash of lights on the polished brass instruments. The shapes the string players are flowing. Jimmy does a little shuffle and Nuno conducting thrusts his arm out three times and the musicians go BRAP BRAP BRAP, a pause and Jimmy croons out by himself such a voice, such a delight "Nuno...had a dreeeeeam, hey! To build a football team (that's right) with Chinese owners aaaaand a wooooonderkid from Pooooorto". Jimmy nods to a small Chinese man in a balcony seat who is slurping happlily on a Kia Ora orange drink. It is Jeff Shi and he lifts his carton of pop up to Jimmy in acknowledgement...

One of the dogs have farted. That earthy shit smell wakes me up. Another bloody ambulance flying up the Lichfield road. For fucks sake I have to go to the footy later. I can't be tired. Ive got a small triangle of duvet. The top corner. The dogs are hogging it. I try to pull it out a little and my hand pulls off and I punch myself in the eye. I try to make myself as small as I can so I can fit my body underneath. But my knee is getting cold. I want to dream about the rest of the concert! It's mad. I love it. I start to drift....

Eddie is holding a puppy in his hands,. It's a little Staffie puppy and it is wagging it's tail at Eddie. Eddie doesn't care. He has 4000 volts he wants to put into it. The other puppies in the Aldi cardboard box are whimpering. The light flickers like a strobe light. Eddie isn't even listening to Colin anymore but he can hear him. His tinny voice through the speaker...

"Do it Eddie! It's never fair, they spent millions and what are we? What are we Eddie? We are the little men, we are the downtrodden, it's Wolves, we hate Wolves Eddie! Stick the fucking prod on it! MAKE IT SCREAM!!!" Colin shouts. Eddie looks at the puppy who is sticking it's tongue out. It wants to lick Eddie. You see puppies only think the best of people. Eddie moves the cattle prod closer to it's nose. The blue arc of the electricity within it is ethereal and harsh...

The sound of breaking glass! Upstairs! Eddie turns around and looks at Colin on the laptop screen but Colin is drawing new eyebrows on his head with his own excrement. There are heavy footsteps down the wooden steps. Eddie lowers the prod and turns as the cellar doors smash inwards. It is Nuno. He is wearing a bikers jacket and a small gold and black neck scarf, jeans and boots. He is carrying a baseball bat with barbed wire wrapped around it.

Nuno smashes Eddie over the head with the bat and Eddie falls sobbing onto the dirty floor. Nuno reaches down and picks up the puppy, placing it safe inside his jacket, The puppy licks Nunos beard and Nuno gently strokes his head. On the laptop screen Colin is screaming at the camera. Nuno goes over and switches it off.

There will be time for Colin Wanker to get his just desserts. Nuno puts the box of puppies under his arm and turns to leave the cellar. But he looks at the hunched figure of Eddie on the floor before he goes. Nuno spits on him and walks up the stairs. The puppy is licking his nose and Nuno laughs...

I awake. One of my dogs is licking my nose. He wants a custard cream. I look at the clock and it's 7 am. Time to get up really. Have a cup of tea. Walk the dogs, get ready for the match against Bournemouth. I lift the duvet and the dog gets in between my legs and I'm warm again. I just lie there for a bit. I'm a bit excited. Molineux, Nuno, our team...I'm sure I had a weird dream about it but I can't remember what it is exactly...something about Jazz, baseball bats, puppies...

Of course I'd like to do some sort of proper report on the Bournemouth match but it was impossible. The football here has become a proper journey now, a quest I suppose. I expected Wolves to try and jam their fingers in the cracks in the great cliff face that is the Premier League. We win 2-0 and Cavaleiro finishes off the day with an injury time goal. It's cathartic for sure. I am starting to feel like we are getting some rub of the green at last. I feel like things are OK and I don't have to worry any more. I feel quite normal in fact.

After the game I am idly watching two Wolves fans having a go at each other. I know the one bloke, we have had words before. He doesn't come to games often and I think he scrams a ticket here and there. He is arguing with a young Wolves lad who doesn't seem to care much about the size of the older dude or the foul invective coming out of his mouth. As I walk past I'm not expecting them to share punches but I am a little bothered about the argument they were having. It's always about the team, always about certain players and each others opinions on players. People seem so aggravated lately and it's bloody Christmas. Where is the brotherly love? The joy? We have just beaten Eddie Hitlers Ice Cream Gollums. It's funny isn't it? Everybody should be laughing. But here they are arguing and threatening each other in a crowd of people trying to get past, trying to get home or to the pub.

Chapter 24

The Offended Gollums and the Crumbling Edifice of Kloppa Castle

It's a bloody big cliff, like one of those mad Limestone ones in Yosemite National park that rise out of the eart like ...my teeth really. Another one fell out this week. But I digress. It's a bloody big cliff. Are we dangling by a finger? Nah mate. We are trying to run up the fucking thing. Sometimes we get a hand or foothold, sometimes we are in a scrabbling slide and are saved by our rope only to fling ourselves back up it.

The Bournemouth game was a thing because they had spent much money, they had players that could slide that ball around in silky lush shapes. But so did we. But there was a difference of course. We had discipline and shape. They had shape and discipline but looked like they couldn't be arsed.

Underneath Pool Hayes Bridge down the Canal I sheltered with the dogs out of a passing shower. It was that cold December rain again. There's always a drop that goes right down your neck and back. Even the dogs look pissed off. Christmas is soon and all the jollity that goes with it. I can't remember what matches we played over last Xmas. So I roll a fag and watch a Heron doing bird things on the other side.

I try to remind myself to have a look in Nuno Volume 1 'The Chinese Revolution at Wolverhampton Wanderers' only £7 on Amazon...I might put the price up so nobody buys it. My heart and soul went into that book last season.

Tonight is the Liverpool match and they are flying high. Jurgen Klopp their Coach has built a team for sure. Many entrants of much expensiveness arrived flashing their shit expensive watches, driving their shit expensive cars. Are the players shit? No, of course not. They are exotic and athletic, intelligent. They are going to give Manchester City a run for their money in that other climb going on above us, on the cliff face of megaball.

So Liverpool are that. People I know are looking forwards to the match. I suppose I am too, but not as much as some of the other matches of course. Someone once said Wolverhampton is like Liverpool should have been. I don't quite understand that, it's like a Zen Buddhist Riddle.

I suppose I will be standing somewhere rattling the riddle around my head looking like a forlorn abandoned dog outside a shop and it will come to me and I will just shout out "aggghhuuhh" and people will think about calling the Police.

They beat us 2-0 of course. I say of course because Liverpool at the moment have a bloody big hard on and it's a hard on that took three years to get into full fettle. Klopp isn't a lunatic, of course he knows what he is doing. He proved that at Dortmund. He might look like an extra in a 70's

German Piss porn flick but underneath that faintly weird persona he has is a dude who knows his stuff. I think his persona accurately describes his team and indeed the city they come from. It looks kind of cool and trendy on the inside but on the outside it smells faintly of piss and vocal angst. But they have it for sure, whatever 'it' is. There are many fireworks pre game and a DJ playing some tunes to the synchronised flashing of the floodlights. More fireworks, more pyro, smoke everywhere. Some dirty bastard in front of me has dropped his arse and the stink, the smoke from the pyro...Jesus Christ.

My eyes are stinging with the essence of beery fart for it is that time of the year. When we tip gallons of alcohol down our necks and wax extreme lyrics of love or hate depending on who we are interacting with. Sky Football have designated this match a Friday match. It's when the factories, building sites, warehouses and offices vomit out their pale and demoralised employees into the madness of a half day and a trip to the pub, mates, enemies, too much alcohol...yes. It's Black Eye Friday.

Somebody is rolling around the floor in the subway. I think at first they are ill then notice a drunken play of sorts, in one act. He's a bit close to the 'homeless' dude with the Staffy who sits there looking all forlorn as drunken fans splosh pound coins in his hands and drunken women fuss his dog. Perhaps he will make enough cash to change his car that he gets into after every match. His car is better than mine of course. But alcohol...

I should have partook of course. Gone a bit insane with everybody else but I'm concentrating too much. I don't want to lose a grip on what's happening at Wolves. I'm over anaylysing not the tactics Nuno employs or the individual performances, breakthroughs etc but the philosophy of the whole Wolves idea. How it all intermingles with the owner group Fosun. How we think about it, what we think and all the madness that goes with it. I suppose as well, what the fuck is happening? Not in a negative way of course, but the nuts and bolts of how the whole club is run. What new ideas will they have? Considering this whole Nuno-Fosun-Wolves axis, the beer farts, the casual drunken violence, the odd Scouser waxing lyrics outside the ground.

Funny lot Scousers. I never really had an opinion of them, and I still don't. Only that they tend to moan a lot about how people think of them. I suppose in many ways the time I have spent up there was doing other activities with which I shared a love with the odd scousers I bumped into and had a laugh with.

But there is something in Liverpool that has a melancholy about it, a relentless melancholy I suppose. I don't hate them like some fans. In Costa coffee before the game a little dwarf bald headed Scouser about sixty years old ladled out harsh accented opinion that we were 'The Wolves firm'.

Fair enough we are a hefty bunch of friends, we often scowl and look miserable...but not violent. I write poems and draw for fucks sake. I want to shout into his face 'I'm an Author mate! I write fucking books ya know! Why do you think I want to roll around the floor with people at my age?'. But I don't. Of course I don't. I don't care about Liverpool. I don't care about Klopp either. There is a hole within me when Liverpool is mentioned. The same as Wigan, Barnsley, all those places. They don't mean anything to me. Just stepping stones my friends, that's all.

Mo Salah scores their first. His hair looks like a seventies porn stars bush to be honest. It could do with a good trim or something. He has one of those screwed up faces that will live on past his playing career when the money is running out.

He seemes to hop skip and jump around the box with aplomb. They are very good these Liverpools. I show my appreciation by jeering at their fans at the bottom of the Steve Bull stand. They have come from as far afield as Bilston, Wednesfield and Sandwell to see their team. I have noticed many Liverpool shirts being worn in my town. Shirts that have not seen the light for many years, but now with Liverpools success they are being clawed out of musty wardrobes and slung onto hunched backs. What a decrepid bunch of cunts. Manchester United and Liverpool hate each other but they are mirror images of their fanbases.

I think there maybe 100 proper Scouse gits in the bottom of the Stevie Bull. But despite the goal. You know what? We looked good. We looked like we played them every week. We did not look out of place at all. In fact we took the piss out of them a few times. Boly twisting up Salah with some jinked footwork despite Willy Boly being fourteen foot tall. Salah looked like a child next to him. Boly didn't put a foot wrong all game for me. But then again none of the team did either. They all have a look on their face that scares me a little. They are learning things fast. They are assimilating information fast. Experience too is just a platform to expound new ideas they have to get their heads around. Ruben Neves is learning. See his furrowed brow? He isn't under any pressure. That furrow is not through fear. It is through concentration. He is studying what is in front of him and learning from it. The three seconds on the ball in the Championship is now one solitary second, if that. Now he has to shift his footballing brain into another gear. There is no time here to pick and place the perfect pass, although in this game he does just that on a few occasions. Now he has maybe under a second to pick the pass and player. The gap between one and three seconds is not big. But here in the Premier league it is a chasm of time of course.

Traore has also shifted gears. Every game I see him in he is improving. Gone is the over muscled drag racing runs and now they are replaced with a sort of calm quality, where he is learning to think as well as explode. There are a few occasions he is sublime to watch and he seems a much more mature player. Tonight I am very proud of him. Next season he is going to be a gigantic player for us. I am sure. There is movement upwards in his ability and technique. He is still raw of course, still a project. But man the prospects of this man running things next year amazes me. But then I have a pang of regret that he might not be here next season. Things are changing. Is he a luxury?

But what of the others in our team? Well we were us of course. The same team we have seen all through the campaign. We are bloody good you know. There was no lack of respect from Liverpool at all. Fair enough there was the same amount of insane refereeing decisions from the obligatory bald headed lunatic in charge of the whole thing, and some Liverpool players were extremely sensitive when it came to players touching them whereupon they would crash to the ground like someone had bumped them in the knee cap with a bat.

Jonny Otto our left back amazes me every week. He does so much it's amazing. I think I am beginning to like him a bit. He is full on Staffordshire Bull Terrier but with a human brain. What was he to Liverpool? A great match, every was quite easy at times for him. He is what he is our Jonny, sometimes his defensive side overcomes his attacking strengths. But what do I know? I'm still amazed from the pyrotechnics. I intimated a few pages ago that the whole pyro show was a bravura chest pushing out load of old bollocks from Fosun.

Who knows what madness infects their heads when they are perusing the catalogue of explosions and funky sky sparks the pyro company sends out. I of course was not that dazzled. I had lost my only pair of glasses at Newcastle and now I have to wear my prescription shades...I think I look pretty cool...or blind. I'm not sure. I realise that they aren't actually spectacles but they are normal shades. I can hardly see anything. Why do I keep losing things?

In my after match rambling and checking my notes I havent written anything about Coady. Liverpool were his boyhood team. He should have been glowing after this match, I hope he was anyway. Onionskins mate. What do I mean by that? Dodging the Liverpool fooligans lurching around the ringroad by the coach station I let that thought rattle around a bit.

Onionskins. See through. Thin. That was the difference between us and them that's all. The difference was very bloody thin. They had just enough quality for sure to ease past us a little and win the game...but we were there my friends. We were right on the money for a lot of the show.

My mate Knocker wants to run a few Liverpool fans over as we drive off through the madness of the traffic. Every is fucking Conan the Barbarian once they get behind a wheel but Knocker is Conan most of the time any way. He tries to take a few knees out. Somebody shouts but we are gone, through onto the Licky road and in the middle of Heath Town before we know it. Yes. We were not battered here for this game. That quality Liverpool have is bolstered by a few years farting around putting the pieces into position, getting the players Klopp wants. We are infants really, striplings or seedlings. We are just getting started.

Chapter 25

The Tarquin Gollums Away and No I'm Not Going

Awake. With a face like a snotty sleeve, like a crooked haircut, like an old man staring at the sea...in the distance Nuno looks at Fulham FC.

I'm not going. It's Boxing day in the UK. The day after Xmas. You see it's the only day I really give in to my darker and more hedonistic persona. This means I'm up at 10 am drinking Jack Daniels and imbibing in other intoxicants.

A day off to Fulham to watch us play the Tarquins is not on the agenda. Of course others will go and I applaud them. But I'm not. Instead there are Chocolates and turkey to be demolished and attacked. I can't really deal with another day in London. The place depresses me. I have never understood how people can say the place is dynamic and creative, fast paced etc. All the bollocks we read and believe at times. Fulham last year was a great laugh. I was very drunk. Horace shouting at the Tarquins to shut up...and they did made me laugh long and loud. But today It's all about finding an illegal stream on the laptop. Putting the headphones on and making sure everything is to hand.

Watching us in the Southbank is a weird but pleasurable experince of course. You never really get to grips with how we spread the ball around and what spaces we make. It's the first time I've watched Wolves on the laptop for a while. I think I need it to be honest. I'm a shit pundit for sure. Most of the interlocking tactics and madness escape me sometimes. I'm still shocked by the beautiful football we are playing. This means my mind is in the right place to see how we actually look. I'm 'watching' instead of 'seeing'.

(Strawberry Cream Quality Street)

Sorted mate. The stream is lovely and clear, not too knobbly and gappy. I don't know who is commentating and I don't care. Their Coach is Ranieri who has been brought in to shore up Fulhams defence. Ryan Sessignon is 18 years old...again. These doughnuts can't stop waffling on about his age.

(Half a glass of Jack Daniels straight and another Strawberry cream Quality street and a twiglet)

Fulham are on it of course. They move the ball around sexily. 110 million pounds worth a dysfunctional sexy of course. Moutinho and Saiss are our midfield madness today. Saiss is tall and angular and his play is the same. He sniffs trouble out everywhere. There is no over running our midfield today of course. Not with him around. He is a nibbler like Jonny Otto who is also plying his trade today.

Moutinho is a cuddlier shorter aspect of our midfield but those lovely weighted balls to our onrushing attack of Traore-Jimmy and Costa are perfectly matched by Saiss. The commentators are having a go at our defence. Conor Coady a midfielder from Huddersfield. Ryan Bennett unloved free transfer from Norwich. William Boly unknown French prospect. What? They have dealt admirably with the best teams in the Premier League. We have smashed teams on our defence over this first half of the season.

I'm not spouting propoganda here you know, they actually have. Do some remember this aspect of our squad? I don't think they have. Instead we get little asides from these vocal commentators in the stands around us that so and so is hit. We hear this crap especially at the odd game when these empty kettles scrounge a ticket. It's stupid. I want to reach over and shake them by their necks. But I don't. I just hope that the players keep their ears closed to fucking idiots that struggle to point their dick in the right direction when they have a piss. I'm jiggling the lap top thinking about it.

Saiss has just dumped a Fulham player on his arse. The Referee says something to his back. You see Saiss doesn't give a shit what you think. I am liking Saiss more and more as the season goes on. Saiss waves a hand in reply to the Ref. It isn't worth a word mate. Let the Fulham player know that you are around that's all. It's football, a kind of stylised combat I suppose.

Of course Costa is getting some heat, a few missed chances, a few mistimed passes. But there is no sadness here about Costa. I love the way he gamboles into space. I love everything he does pretty much. He is everywhere probing and moving, waiting for the rhythm to erupt. The Tarquins wave their clappers at something.

What a fucking bereft place Fulham is. If only they could assimilate some atmosphere into that place it could be a good day out I suppose. The TV Producers are reducing the volume to the various Wolves fans songs which often has the words 'fuck off' etc within the verses. This makes the whole show somewhat strange, as if the atmosphere of North London has permeated the show like a bad beer fart. Now all we hear is Fulhams fucking clappers. The cardboard folded, branded and sponsored abominations that Fulham fans love. Was it last year when Wolves introduced them to Molineux and most of them were thrown at people? Clappers. Jesus Christ.

(Jack Daniels and a mini Scotch egg, a slice of Turkey and a pickled onion)

Mitrovic their striker is doing things. He's a tall lad built like a brick shithouse with a crap tattoo on his neck and hair like a Rottweiller. Him and Coady are going at it a bit. In fact it would be quite heated I suppose but Coady is a total pro. All that matters to him is keep Mitrovic out of the whole show. They tangle and mangle themselves as Mitrovich is sent on another looping run at our defence.

Fulham don't get the ball much but when they do it's all snot and grit as they move fast into our half and our shape is pulled this way and that. When a ball does get crossed into our box from a Fulham attack then it's a all Willy Boly. This man is massive for us. Every sniff of goal Fulham have is negated by Boly twisting and flying high above these mere mortals below him as he clears the danger. Fulhams defence is very shit. It's a wonder we aren't three nil up ya know.

(two mini Scotch eggs and a caramel thing..slurp of Jack Daniels)

Jonny Otto and Doherty are being put under pressure again but not that hard approach Huddersfield and Watford had when everything was pressure and movement. This is a lot more sublime and softer almost. Maybe Doherty is still under some funk about defending. He is not letting Ryan Bennett feel too lonely. Fulham do move fast but so do we. We have loads of possession, we ping the ball around lovely, it's all funkadelic or the Jack Daniels is kicking in because its the end of the first half and I'm a bit drunk to be honest and it's early afternoon. Mid day kick off wasn't it. So it's one oclock and I'm already too loud and obnoxious. I notice the dogs have pissed off somewhere and I laugh and fill my glass up again and have a look around for some more food.

(four mini sausages, a mini kebab and three slurps of Jack Daniels)

Second half and I prop the laptop back on me lap and watch the start of the second half. I am feeling warm and remember the last time I went to Fulham. We lost of course and it seemed like that climb out of the championship was becoming long and arduous. But drinking in the pubs with good friends made me feel good and wholesome. It seems like an age ago now. Morgan Gibbs White is trying to splash some movement around. Traore is getting better. He's getting leaner I think too. He is so raw it makes my eyes water sometimes. He is getting not stronger but more intelligent for sure. Now he is looking around him more, seeing opportunities and space, moving into it. He is still that supercar that makes you look a prat as you hoof the accelerator and the back slides out again. He has to learn that softly and gently are also words he should use. Transfer the essence of those words into his football. Nuno knows this of course. I wish I could watch Nuno and his staff work with him. I am probing a crumb of something in my beard and the camnera goes to Nuno who is doing the same thing. Fulham score. Bollocks. That kid Sessignon who's only 18 apparently. That kids been 18 for years and years surely...i might actually celebrate his 19th for the poor bastard. He is in yards of space when the ball comes to his and he hits a half hard shot at goal which comes off Coady and plops into the goal. Bollocks.

Jimmy controls the ball in the edges of the Fulham box and he is acrobatic...he tries a bicycle kick that goes over. What an Xmas present that would have been. Match of the day being replayed endlessly as we watched...did this happen in the first half? What half are we actually in?

(Jack Daniels...no food)

Drunk. With a face like a Tramps cough, like a cheap sandwich, like a deflated paddling pool.

Wolves of course aren't that bothered. The shape is everything. Hold on Traore got subbed I think...ten minutes ago? I have another slurp of Jack Daniels and shout something incoherent. I'm confused who came on for him...was it Costa? I am sure he played the first half...I think I am a bit drunk to be honest. The shape...well I watch it and I recognise it. We stay the same. We can put another fresh pair of legs on and the shape doesn't change. The commentator says Nuno needs a plan B. It's the same bullshit throw away comment people make when they ask for a 20 goals a season striker. It's sad and depressing commentary purely because they are grown men that refuse to comprehend what the actual fuck is happening here. Nuno doesn't react to things because he is the fucking reaction to everything and everything is the plan at the end of the day. We stay compact and flawless pretty much...ok Gibbs White is off and Cavaleiro is on. That's good too. Stick to the plan.

Horace (whom went to the game) tells me after the game that he chatted to a steward at halftime and they said they had made the pitch narrower. Ah then. Ok. Alright then. Why would they do that? To stop our forays down the wing? Vinagre comes on for Jonny. Ruben (Lets twist again) Vinagre is young and beautiful. He only on five minutes and he iis communicating with Cavaleiro beautifully. Those quick balls to feet. The telepathy between this players is increasing in dribs and drabs.

Nuno is chewing the finger of his glove as he watches the game. Ranieri has closed ranks. Fulham sit much deeper now as we press. Typical Ranieri, he gambles this man. He thinks he has those three points in the bag and all he has to do is protect it. Of course we press higher. They want to get us on the break. But Saiss has other ideas, so does Moutinho and so does Costa.

(another Slack Spaniels and a weird piece of Turkey)

So Fulham are doing this whole five man defence thing and we are trying to find a hole through it. It's tough bollocks, it's a full shift and half an hour afterwards too for sure. Costa knuckles a ball into the box. It's touchine madness from what I can see through my imbibed Slack Spaniels and frothing Turkey. The ball shudders and it shakes as the wrestling match goes on in front of the Fulham goal. Saiss turns up and pokes the fucking thing in the net. Thank God for that.

I get up and do a victory dance, The dogs are barking. I nearly fall over. Family are shouting at me, I've interruppted their film. I don't care. It's last minute heroics again. No matter what happens during a game we can gather enough froth to spunk the ball in. Is it lucky? We had 80% possession at times during the second half. A much better balance for sure, I am happy. My head is whizzing around and I can't focus on the screen but there...see Mitrovic having a go from a long punted goal kick. He's onto it, he trundles the ball towards the ungaurded Wolves goal. Coady is forensic and watching the feet of Mitrovic...Coady achingly a few feet away from a tackle and there the ball goes. But Coady changes from the forensic to the physical and he puts his head down and charges towards the ball. I sit up. Glass in hand and watch it go towards goal...but of course Conor gets it. He always does. That's why he is our Captain and leader. He hooks the ball clear and we breathe or should I say drink...the last of the Slack Spaniels goes down my neck and it's all done.

Drunken errant post mortems are a thing here. I sit and nestle dogs in a warm glow. It's a point isn't it? We still grow every week, every game. We are growing and I don't think we are going to stop. For sure there are elements we need to look at and improve but really? I will let others deal with that madness but agree...we need to get that killer thing going. That rythym we need to get back back and start to love again. We are playing those Tottenhams at Wembley tomorrow. First trip there in 30 years or so? I don't care about Wembley and I don't care about Tottenham either. I just want to see my team improve and by God they are doing that every week so far.

Chapter 26

Hotspurt Gollums and Another Day Out In Nowhereland

Awake. With a face like a Latvian fry up. Like a free Tesco doughnut. Like a grope off a wooden hand...in the distance Nuno is looking at Wembley Stadium...

When Tottenham came down to Molineux it all looked very slick and sexy from them. All these England players, that Song bloke from Korea. They beat us fair and square and man didn't they look good? But again we didn't look much different to them. Same class, same beautiful movement, it's just that them gits that put the ball in the net a few times and we kind of lacked the luck I suppose.

This is the return fixture and I have a feeling about it. A strange feeling. Normally of course we have a little trepidation when we are playing these 'top teams'. Trepidation. Funny word. I always have the idea that we are going to beat every team we play. I think that's still having those foggy and misty memories of playing the Liverpools and the Tottenhams and the Manchesters way back when the only flares in stadiums were the trouser kind.

It's London again and 'that' stadium. London to me is Nowhereland or Nevereverland. I don't like it. I don't like many of the people that come from here and I don't like many of the teams either. I don't mind Brentford, they are hilarious.

Wembley is a strange place too. Many fans will have happy memories of it and I will admit I have had a few positive thoughts about that godawful place of late. We rarely lose there. The last time I came down here was for the Sherpa Van final. Walking through the crowds I see someone still has the souvenier Wolves flat cap most of us wore that day. I think they were a fiver. We are all jolly. We are all singing a bit. We don't really have any respect for these teams any more in this mission, this campaign. Mine is wrought by memory but younger fans have this season to base their thoughts on. We are looking good. We are still there. We still brandish Nunos ideas as our totems.

Keep your shape, keep playing the way Nuno says, keep your heads, everything is OK. This is where the ideas of Nuno bleed off the pitch and into the stands, over the advertising hoardings and up the concrete steps, along the rows of seats, up our trouser legs and into our hearts. We don't ever give up now. We know the idea is strong, it has legs to last 90+ minutes.

The concourses of this place are huge and vacuous and there are many sour faced staff doing the things they do. The pat down is cursory at the turnstiles. The faces of the staff sad and depressed. That's London for you. I suppose it's great for most people who visit but not great to live here. Wembley inside is huge but empty.

I'm tempted to add the emptiness of the Olympic stadium and Old Trafford to that list, maybe Saint James Park too. But Wembley is just a hole in the Psychogeography of Wembley as an area. Spurs fans wander here and there and they don't look happy for some reason even if the last two games they played they have scored over 10 goals or something. Spurs are emphatic and on a roll for sure.

A woman cleaner brushes a bit close to my feet as I stand in the dim concourse chatting. Somebody shows me a phone with the teamsheet for today. Dendoncker in place of Saiss/Moutinho. The 'Donk' has only played for us in defence but he's a handy midfielder too. I lack the footballing brain to analyse what Nuno wants from Donk. I don't want to say anything. But Nuno and Ian Cathro our 'dude who knows this shit' have obviously learned something from the last time we played them. I imagine Donk will be breathing down the neck of one of Spurs electric midfielders. Donk will at some point have this doughnut firmly in his armpit. Nice and safe...out of trouble.

Our songs are beautiful as we kick off. The start is muted. There are no fireworks here and no light show. It's like an orgy in a cold bus station for sure. Extreme backwards and forwards action at the start. Donk is fully in there and he has his Spurs midfielder under wraps for most of the time. But Spurs are fucking electric. Boom here and there, simple touches into space, moving snake like through gaps we have in our shape. But this is quality footballing.

Of course Spurs will move and groove around the pitch. Pinocchio or whatever his name is has had three years to build his idea at Tottenham. This is a mature footballing opponent. Poch looks like he collects his trimmed fingernails so Witches don't get them and make spells. He has an intial idea fair enough. But so do we. Patricio barely gets his quiff flat in a few lithe leaps to keep a few distance shots out of the way.

BBC Wolverhampton are blocking the moves...BBC? Bennett-Boly-Coady. Highly mobile these lot mate, our defence. When attacks from Spurs do materialise the BBC are there hassling the narrative. Breaking up moves in the initial stages. So there is time for Doherty and the Hitman Jonny Otto to move back and skirmish with any attempts to ping that ball wide.

Jonny is doing his 'touchy' thing again where he prods and caresses any Spurs player with the ball. These touches are saying 'Here's Jonny!' as the player has a slight look at Jonny their hearts sink. Jonny is the thief in the night mate, the monster under your bed or the shadow your dressing gown casts from the dim 50 watt landing light that looks like an ogre.

Harry Kane always looks like he has a secret, a sordid one. It's almost like he is ashamed to be alive for some reason. He won the Golden boot in Russia and his golden fucking boot now lashes a shot from 25-30 yards out and it's just out of the fingertip reach of Patricio and it floats in the back of the net. 1-0 to them.

I'm not even sad. That's the strangest thing. Under Lambert or at times Jackett our former Coaches I would have been depressed and shitty. Now?

I couldn't give a shit. Our players run back to their own half and wait hands on hips or discreetly stretching and staying warm while a mosh pit of congratulatory Spurs players confuffle and entwine themselves in each other. We wait for them. We wait and we watch. Ruben Neves is ultra Stoic. He watches too but all the while he is talking to Donk. Donk turns and says something to Coady. Coady is demonstrating some movement, some description to Boly who nods. Otto is saying something to Boly. Patricio is shouting to Coady. Neves watches. Donk is listening to the bench now. Carlos the assistant Coach and Nunos number 2 is animated and his hands and arms draw the pictures to go with his words. Nuno has his arms crossed watching, his tongue darts in and out of his mouth to gently probe his moustache. His eyes are everywhere analysing and observing. Traore is given words from Jimmy...everything is communication.

I'm remembering Austria all those months ago watching the live feed of our training game in the mountains. There was no commentary just Coady...our midfielder from Huddersfield and now our main man in defence, Coady shouts and commands. That Scouse accent cutting through the feed like a razor.

Shape and idea mate. We don't change. Traore is getting very slick. He is our best player for me. I know that is a broad and emotive statement. I have watched much football over my long years on this Earth. I see Traore and he scares me. He frightens me because there is the idea of Nuno in the flesh. Adama is now the project as Coady once was. Traore (I hope) will be the most exciting player we have ever seen at Molineux once he has shook off the maddisms of Pulis and Lambert his former Managers. Each of our players have two or three Spurs players around them as soon as they get hold of the ball. You see as soon as we have it we threaten.

Spurs players are blind to the fact we are pulling them out of position. This is the Adama thing. He gets the ball then the scrotums of the Spurs players contract and they are on him. Space for Jimmy. Space even for Cavaleiro which we infiltrate instantly. This is the idea. We are 1-0 down and we still move.

There is a definite change to Spurs in the second half. They are tired, you can tell. Not physically but mentally. Pinocchio looks the same. They all look shell shocked. We did this same thing to Chelsea the other week. Why? I don't quite know. But something happens to these teams, these expensive assemblages of talent. We wear them down with our absolute discipline and effort to win to defend, to attack again and again.

Nobody dips a head. We are a team, that's the difference here, that is the fulcrum to a corner kick for us after a Cavaleiro run into space and a hastily cleared ball. The Corner kick goes in. Boly. King William of Boly. Nobody is looking at him waiting there. How much did this Spurs defence cost? I don't know and don't care because Boly strides in crashing through the green turf and the Spurs defence. He's like Godzilla wading through the seas of Japan to cause some intense mischief to cardboard skyscrapers. There should have been lightening and smoke somewhere while he strode forward.

The ball is weightless and everpresent for the head of Boly. He connects with it and there you have it. Crowd goes wild. I fall, get a knee to the lip, some monster hugs me and my glasses are off...again. They are my last pair. I've destroyed three pairs so far this season. The monster falls onto my bad leg. Pain. My glasses are somewhere. My friends are grabbing, pulling, shouting. The happiness? I can't describe this. Are we channelling last years joys? Is there no end to this crazy train ride? I'm barely hanging on here. But it's not important is it? This equaliser...it's still even stevens. Nothing to get excited about surely? But this is Wolves. This is the Nunos Wolves. This is just the start of the madness. I think I've broken my leg again.

We defend and we move. Cameos of footballing brilliance. Moutinho has space. They should close him down but no. He has space then he can create, he can channel the moves learned on Comptions cold grounds to this place. He spills balls from here to there, from him to that bloke. It's all about the tempo I think. That is the idea. The tempo is accurate and relentless. Have I finally found Nuno? Have I finally understood the philosophy? Is it this tempo we play all through the games we have watched that has driven us to the top half of the Premier League? I think maybe I have some dim idea.

Spaces within the Spurs box are at a premium though. Again we cannot denigrate this Tottenham team. They are very good. But they can't keep a beat up, cant tap out the staccatto movements we have. Now our players are slowly coming to terms with this Premier League. I think the problem is concentration. To beat us you have to be either whipped into a frenzy of madness ala Colin Wankerism or have a unique groove like Liverpool have manufactured over the past few years of Kloppism. But this Nunoism? Jimmy collects the ball at the Spurs box. All it needed was a slightly open stance of a Spurs defender. Space that measures mere inches and that is all that Jimmy needs. He has to kick short and sweet. The pace of the ball is like a snooker shot. Poke. Between the legs, an unsighted (perhaps) goalkeeper who throws himself to his right to palm the ball away. But it is gone of course. Into the net. Jimmy reels away. He has scored at Wembley. This kid from Mexico.

The Wanderers number 9. Thank you Jimmy. 38 Million for you? I will chip in a few hundred quid for sure. Now my fat lips bleeds as I get an elbow in it. A body flies past me into the row in front. For a moment I nearly follow it. Horace dead legs me with his knee. Now I can't even scream in delight but I crouch down and huddle myself out of the limbage and I am laughing looking at the concrete underneath me. Thank you Jimmy.

Now it's all us. Spurs have dropped out of the running. They clutch their chests in horror of it. That this team should be throwing delicious shapes across this pitch at the home of English football. Costa moves and Doherty moves too. Ruben Neves spins around the ball and sees Doherty in space and forward. Now Spurs are just onlookers, just a mere audience. Doherty touches and caresses the ball to Costa and he is off. Gone. Away. Ball at his feet he moves towards goal leaving flailing Spurs expensiveness devoid of any thoughts. Costa is off. Only him and the goalie. We don't breathe. We don't think. We just will Costa on. My Helder. How they cuss you sometimes. Not in front of me of course. I remember you playing for Lambert when you saved our season. How you played under that fucking clown I will never know. But you did. A player so young and so full of ability and all they could do was try and destroy you. Your injury. A few of us knew how bad it was even if the club remained tight lipped. We knew. We say your pain at the start of last season. We now see you learning more and more under Nuno. We see you understanding what it means to play in this league. We know that sometimes that ankle might grinch a little, we see that there are great sides we play against when even you can't seem to force a way through. But Helder we love you always.

Helder with a Spurs doughnut at his elbow slides the ball into the net. It is 3-1 to us. Home of English football. This vacuous fucking empty space with nothing in it. In London too, a place with so many people in it that people just become things, objects.

Poch has had three years to assemble his team. Three years to construct a footballing side that can play and can compete. What has Nuno had? Three Months? Walking back to the car I am scared. I'm asking Horace whether or not I should start saving for European trips. Get a little tin and put the odd pound coin or fiver in. Be disciplined and not dip in it for something. Should I start saving? We are already a year ahead of plan. This is supposed to be our Championship promotion year and we are slicing and dicing huge teams in front of us. At the start of this season we were supposed to consolidate our position in the Premier League and now it seems we are creeping higher and higher up the table. What will may bring? What madness have we in store for this second half of the season? I lie awake all night thinking about it. Thinking about Nuno being happy as he ran onto the pitch at the final whistle to congratulate his team and offer solace to theirs. It's all academic. I won't be going to Europe although that book would be funny to write. Perhaps some of our players won't either. But right now I think there is only me thinking that as everybody else here is making plans to go. I wonder what Nuno will be thinking? Next game probably.

Chapter 27

Return of the Owl

It's never easy losing a match after the cocaine and three hookers display of the Tottenham game. My word we looked lovely. Of course we have to come back to ground level eventually, you wake up with a sore arse, a sore head, a nosebleed, possibly a dead body (or two) and the Police banging on the hotel door. Alas for being a football fan. Alas for loving a football club. Gently slap the half undressed blonde on the bed..

'Do you want a cup of tea and a bacon sandwich bab?'

Molineux can be an unforgiving place as a fan. We expect our home to be a fortress of sorts, a veritable stanchion of our immutability, a pantheon of our love for Nuno and that love…oh man that love is strong…it can do no wrong…but it's never like that. Molineux is a place that often tends to galvanise and inspire other teams to play a belter of a game. Nine matches of defeats? Next match playing Wolves at Molineux? No problem.

'Sell Neves he's shit, get the money now, buy better'

What discordant and harsh poetry these voices are. I hear many of them and that's ok. I don't get aggravated any more by it. I'm aware of their angst but not of the intellectual thinking behind any of it. Knocker points out the young bloke who said it and I watch the fella wipe his nose on his sleeve and now there is a silvery film of snot on it to join the already hardened snot already there. I think that explains things. Sell Neves yes, buy a hankie with the money maybe. It's not hard to just pop to the bogs in the Royal London and nick some bog roll, put it in your pocket for later maybe?

Social media is alive with sadness, but that's ok, because social media isn't real. It's a bullshit made up place for lunatics like me and you. It gives us a platform or a stage. No wonder the reptiles of the Press are lunatics...unimaginative ones. They are the dregs or the residue of what 'social media' used to be many moons ago. No wonder Nuno hates them, they are not real.

I mean Social Media isn't all doom and gloom. If it wasn't for social media we would be ranting at drunken men down the canal about the result. Or throwing Fray Bentos pies around Poundstretcher on the Licky Road. It was easier in the 70's of course. We would all run out the back of the Southbank, across the car park behind Molineux Hotel. We would be throwing darts and pieces of asbestos roof, the odd brick. Shouting. Getting it all out of the system. Now we have to plod home under the black skies wondering if there are any Quality street left when you get back. Not wanting to pick up your device for a few days knowing that the vitriol will be real and you are sad enough any way and it's January, and it's cold, and shit, wank. Fuck off.

Roy Hodgson the Owl is a good coach, Crystal Palace a well set up team. They like to play that expansive football that tumbles beautifully from end to end. There is a kind of beauty to it anyway, if it's that kind you look at from a distance anyway. Ayew and that doughnut Millyjellyvest score and they wander back down the motorway, winners, victorious blah. They have been in the Premier League for five years now and the win isn't shiny and new in any way. It's that same old stolid mashed potato, a few carrots, a bit of stringy beef football. It looks ok, but once you break the skin of the turgid Hodgson gravy that's it. School meals bollocks. And they win. I don't know how happy the Palace Ultras were, they were stuck up in the armpit of the Northbank making a stink I suppose.

"Zaha looks like he has got a shrunken head doesn't he? He looks like that fucknut out the film...Beetlejuice wor it? The little head hahahahaha"

So what's the crack here? Look at the statistics of course. They must say something, offer some explanation maybe? We are shit against teams that stop us playing the game we like to play. That's what they say. That's the empirical look at it. But what about the metaphysical part? Are we poor tactically? It's not the shithousery of Barnsley and Preston last season for sure. These teams are scared of us and have maybe took a few minutes to watch our games and get ready to play against us with a plan and an idea of their own. Plus we are indeed a scalp. For what reason I don't know. But how many teams played against us this season and last and displayed an almost cup final fervour to win? Loads of them.

Players that shone in their games against us are seen as absent in the next they play. These teams that beat us often get dicked in the next few games. Take Villa last year. Their victory broke them. Cardiff seem to play with a tube in their veins that pumps some exotic Warnockian mental drug into their bloodstreams that makes them fly around our players in a madness that verges on insanity. Warnock is the Reverend Jim Jones of the Premier League and his players gobble his evil fruit juices and potions on demand. Hodgson probably gently cries in the corner of his dressing room and that's what upsets these players of his, that is what provokes them to beat us. The thought of him gently sobbing. He probably never got over Managing North Birmingham United to be honest. The smell of that place still haunts him in his sleep. He must make a go of this. He has stood at the abyss mate.

"Hodgson has a face like a dumped quilt stuck in a hedgerow"

Is it the fact that we have played so many games over the Crimbo period? Well no, so have Crystal Palace. Did we look tired? Nah. We looked ok to be honest. I was expecting some sort of win, 1-0 would have done me, a penalty maybe, or a bundled over the line scrum that ended up over the goal line. Is it about lack of plans?

Nuno is stoical for sure but is that a shortfall? I don't think it is to be honest. Do you want to change your style for every game against an opponent that has a prickly system to play against? I'm not sure that's the way forward to be honest. I mean you can only stick so many plans and tactics in a players head until it explodes all over their expensive cream rug in front of their ubiquitous 100″ plasma hardon LCD mega telly.

What's the point of changing your ideas to accommodate another teams? Does that mean your nascent infant idea that is being slowly nurtured into a world beating one is crap? Not fit for purpose? Nuno puts out his sides as a mission statement, as the foundation of his and Fosuns philosophy.

Now if you want to change it because Hodgson the fucking Owl wants to put pressure on the full backs to stop them playing then what? Are Hodgsons ideas stronger than Nunos? In the short term yes. At the moment perhaps we are operating a light and tetchy version of the Nuno idea. Maybe the constituent parts struggle to adapt to what Nuno wants rather than embracing it fully and running their tits off to win. Who knows?

Hodgsons ideas are what they are, same as Nunos. But the Owl has had five years to build his up, no matter how flimsy the thing is. They are entering a period of success after their initial games. They have a belief for sure. They knock the ball around beautifully again. But we looked unsure and lacked confidence.

Our players didn't look the same as they did against Spurs and ok, that's cool. Something has happened. Maybe it's being away from their families for Xmas. Maybe they miss the barbecues or whatever on the beach in their homelands. But I don't think that's the reason either. I mean these dudes are paid big cash to play football for us. They play out of their heads for us. They fight to their last breath sometimes. Witness Saiss at the end of most games we play. He's knackered. Same goes for Doherty with that face like he's wondering whether he has left his car keys in the car outside…he's knackered that much I could cry for him. He throws everything into the mix.

I think there are a number of things about this loss I should rumble around my head. It's a bloody young idea this whole Nuno-Wolves thing. Only really a couple of seasons old. Foundations are being laid for sure but we are looking at the artists impression of the whole edifice before the bloody thing has been finished. I know people look at me angrily when I say the words 'learning curve' or 'early days'. But it's true.

We are still getting to grips with each other, still trying to feel what each other are about. We are still babies making baby steps (apart from leaping around after the Spurs result). But that packing out the midfield thing is giving us pain and we have to embrace it to a certain degree because we are making other teams change their ideas and philosophy without changing ours. I suppose that gives us an advantage straight away simply for the fact the greatest teams never change their system for another no matter what teams they are playing against and what the rewards may be. You see the football we play is the most important thing we have, sometimes it's the only thing we have.

Nuno has an idea yes. He has a dream too and it's one we share. Do we want to luxuriate in the depressing clamber for points this early in our development while sacrificing the philosophy of Nunoism?

I think not. In trying to find Nuno we have to at least understand the larger and more broader strokes of the whole art before we start to fill in the details. These details are something we will see being put into place over the next few years I suspect, the next few transfer windows. We shift the players on that have no real part to play ie Douglas, Afobe, perhaps Bonatini and we replace them with players that correspond and believe in the idea and that can galvanise those abstract tactical talks into bonafide glorious victories.

I've never met Nuno or any of the team apart from Conor Coady (praise be upon him). Finding Nunoism or Nuno is a bloody hard task to work out but I think one way you can find him or his philosophy is via the ideas he puts out there on the pitch. After the Spurs match at the Press Conference some reporter asks Nuno about his family. Nunos face drops for a second before he smiles disarmingly and he brushes away the question to talk about 'football'. But before the smile there is an abyss of violence there within those eyes.

Here is Nuno. Here is the madness of Nuno. With him there are no blurred lines, no airy vacuous prophecies, no lies just his idea and his football. Does he have to find solutions to our midfield aggravations? To those teams whacking on a few big whippy necks to trample our beautiful Moutinho and Neves?

I don't think he does to be honest. I will take a few more of these defeats (if) in the future the idea and the philosophy pays off. I don't want him to change the system we play. It's lovely thank you very much. I love watching Costa/Traore/Jimmy/Cav rampaging around. I love everything about this whole Nuno thing, this whole playing and smashing apart teams in the final third. If Fosun and Nuno have invested time and energy plus wads of cash to this idea then I think as Wolves supporters we should invest a little patience in the whole project. Take these defeats straight on the chin and get straight back in there for more of the same. Keep the idea sacrosanct, it works (sometimes) and it looks lovely thank you very much.

As the season gets into it's second half we are looking very good thank you. Everything is going to plan in a broad sense. Everything is cool. Of course I haven't got much of a clue what's going on anywhere. I'm just a fan, a number like most other people. But I do recognise something going on here. Something that is going to get very big. Of course we too may have a part to play. You know, us doughnuts, but I don't know yet what that part is. We just support, but that means throwing all your cash onto the roulette table of premier league madness again and again.

Sometimes that little ball ends up in the right hole and you shout in victory and collect those delicious chips into your arms while you ogle the various lady friends you may be able to afford now you've won big… sometimes the ball jumps out of your slot and everybody groans in pantomime sadness and you end up walking down the canal back home in the cold dark, penniless.

Carry on Nuno. Don't change a thing. Don't listen to the doubters and the master tacticians, don't engage with Reporters who pry too much, who try to make you into a football 'personality'. These people are not important. What is important is your football and your madness. Because at the end of the day you are at the right place to formulate your dominations. We are as mad as you. Truly.

Chapter 28

The Lizards and the Ghosts of Aston Villa

The Lizards are coming. I can smell them strongly in the ether. The media. The men who whisper into phones. The men who sniff and snuffle under doors. I did warn people about it last season. That they would come for us. I am surprised it has taken this long. Their Iphones are buzzing and they smell the blood of something. They are here and in force. Their little expensive winkle picker shoes are trembling and their shit stopper drainpipe trousers are shivering.

Questions about Nunos family. Transfers, delicate times for Wolves, when one wants some semblence of civility and thought from people as negotiations continue over Abraham. None of that of course. All we have is threat, and vitriol maybe. Even from Aston Villas Coach who decides to throw a few bitter shapes himself, communicating his thoughts to the player and everybody fucking else by providing the same bitter alms his predessesor and Chairman did against us last year, about this time too. Why it concerns Aston Villa I haven't a clue.

This is a triumvate of debate between Abraham, Chelsea and Wolves. You might as well ask the bloke who jet washes Abrahams car than ask Aston fucking Villa. It's nothing to do with them. Nothing. He just parks his arse there for the moment. If we get him on loan then he will be parking his arse here instead of there. Does that make sense? I hope he scores loads of goals for us if he comes. All power to his elbow. More places up the table and the more cash we get so we can buy a 60 goals a season lunatic from somewhere else we haven't heard of. Aston Villa will be shagged without him. Hilarious. Serves you right for running to the FA with your lies. If he comes then he comes, if he doesn't he doesn't.

Lizards man. You could tell on the match of the day edits that Wolves are getting the shitty end of the stick in televised highlight edits. Tottenham has all the possession didnt they? Did Wolves even play that day? The funniest part was Gary Linekers screwed up fig face. He looks like he drives a BMW.

Honestly it fucking killed him to talk about Wolves. It was agonising and I sat here and laughed my aching balls off. Brilliant TV. It fucking kills him, we kill him. The more we win the more he dies a little inside and that shrivelled head will eventually revolve around on its neck as he spews luminous green vomit over Alan and the Murphy bloke.

If you see a post on Social Media that posts obvious bullshit then call it out. Confront these bastards with the truth. They hate nothing more than having the spotlight turned on them. They shrivel. You see the more we attack them back the more people begin seeing the sports media lizards for what they really are.

But not all are Lizards. Many years ago Steve Gordos and David Instone used to write reports about Wolves matches for the Express and Star, there were many other writers too of course who covered footy for the E&S over the years. I met Steve this summer at a Kenny Hibbet signing and to be honest I was more interested in Mr Gordos than Kenny. Sorry Ken. Steve Gordos was a great writer of footy related stuff...this is all relative of course, but I found his writing to be concise and had a rythym all of it's own. So I want to give Steve Gordos my love tonight and hope his groove is still strong.

Chapter 29

Return of the Offended Gollums and the FA Cup Something Round

Awake with a face like a pickled eye, like an unknown sausage, like a Gnats fart...in the distance Nuno welcomes Liverpool to Molineux in the FA Cup. The magics gone? In the FA Cup? Not here. Of course we have the added love of the FA cup due to the fact we are still in many ways an Old Gold and Black club. We remember those heady days of actually winning the bloody thing on a few occasions. New fans can walk around the Molineux museum and look at the photos, see the shirts, see the faces.

I worked at an Engineering place shortly after my 17th birthday. Years ago mate, when things were first starting to turn colour and stereo. This place was in Pelham street Merridale just a few minutes walk from Molineux. In those days the factories were just starting to recover a little from Thatchers meddling with the system. In the few factories and workshops left there was still an old school way of doing things and I fondly remember the old chaps who worked there still.

Many of them were getting on, few years from retirement. They had eaten their lunch in the same place since 1947. They had the same sandwich in most cases. Some had Cheese sandwiches. Some ate the odd tomato sandwich. They drank from the same mug they had been given since that time too and most of the mugs hadn't been washed for years. Having a cup of tea there meant trying not to notice the grinding dust like a skin over the none too brewed liquid as well.

It was a great place simply for the fact that tales of the Wolves were always a big thing at break times. Discussions would range from that weekends match to how John Barnwell was doing, how good was Paul Bradshaw. All the standard crap. Of course whenever we moaned and groaned about a match they old 'uns would smack their lips, put their mugs down or the paper. They would fix you with a watery eye as if looking at you to see if you would understand the nuances of what they were about to tell you. It would always be contrasting a player of today with one of yesterday. Of course us young 'uns were stupid. I mean that sincerely. Of course we thought we knew everything at that age. We went to the match for a punch up, a drink, and to watch the Wolves. It was all pretty new to us this football bollocks even if we had been going there a few years.

The watery eyes would fix you, they would appraise you and they would utter a few names. Stan Cullis. Billy Wright and Bert Williams. These people, these names had an effect on these old bastards that we couldn't quite fathom. They were mentioned in hushed tones, with reverance like they were holy things. Of course we would laugh and joke.

'Them were the olden days mate, football is different now'

...and of course they would slowly shake their heads. Pick up their mug of grinding dust smothered tea with a few bits of steel in them. They would shake their heads and pick up the paper and mutter. I never understood it then, but I do now you see.

Molineux has a minutes applause for Bill Slater. Most of the crowd don't undertsand it, him or that team. But they clap because it's respect. I clap because even if I never knew or saw Bill play I now understand it at least. The old blokes would talk about his exploits of course. For England and for Wolves. But the most over riding aspect of what Bill was about to these men was respect and honour. He was a man that they recognised as one of their own. Luck or skill had Bill in a Wolves team led by that colossus of a Manger Stan Cullis. Bill would have recognised Stan Cullis as a man that would lead and would forge a team out of nothing. Cullis was a hard man to please and the fact that Bill played most of his playing years at Wolves is a testament to how Bill led his sporting career.

We clap and we remember. I also remembered the old blokes I worked with back in those days and if I don't miss them I certainly remember them.

We have Liverpool. Bill would have loved this particular scrap I'm sure of it. Jurgen Klopp would not have been liked by Stan and Bill. Klopp would not have been liked by the old chaps sipping tea either. They would not have liked his team. I can see them now grumbling about the Firminhios or whatever. The Ogris and the Mo Salads or whatever their names are.

In the Liverpool team they would probably have picked out Milner as somebody they recognise or at least his style of play. But they would have dismissed him of course with a wave of the newspaper clutched in nicotine stained fingers grey with cutting oil and muck. But they would have pointed at you and said..

'He wouldn't have made our reserves in those days'

They would have been right too I suppose. Liverpool are fielding a 'weakened team' or maybe a 'B team' or a 'string of reserves and kids' but it's all bollocks and propoganda. You see this team of Klopps cost something like 200 million squid while our strongest team has been assembled at something like the costy of 70 million. But that's all quantitative crap isn't it?

What is going to be the difference? Shape mate. All of a sudden I feel the tendrils of Ian Cathro as Dendonker our Belgian utility bloke is inserted into the latin love fest of Moutinho and Neves in midfield. I'm looking at a phone with the team on as we make our way over to 'the other side' of the Southbank for this match.

Not in our normal seats of course but stuck among people that have arrived at the amazing Nuno show a bit late. They don't know the songs. They shudder a bit when someone shouts about 'fucking scouser bastards' and maybe cringe. But this is what WE live for of course. But Cathro has watched Liverpool down here. He has probably sussed them out by now and him and Nuno have probably had long talks under the watchful eye of Billy Wright outside about these Liverpools and how they love to throw their shapes.

So we have a midfield of three a forward line of two (Jimmy and Jota). We have Jonny Otto and Ruben Vinagre flinging the wingys and the normal BBC defence. But who's that in goal? John Ruddy of course. He's been taken out of his box and given a bit of a rub over with the duster and is flung into the fray. I love John Ruddy of course. I have waxed much lyrical content over him since he came here from Norwich. Patricio has been given a day off. That's cool. John Ruddy is a safe pair of hands for me. That save against Hull last year where he palmed it from underneath his body was pure steez.

I abuse the half and half scarf sellers around the subway. They are a disgrace and a shame. There are other ways to make money other than selling these fucking abominations.

'Get ya scarf' he says in heavy Scouse.

'You want fucking setting fire to mate' I reply.

It's not the first time I have threatened to set alight a seller of these things. I did the same at Queens Park Rangers last season. It was probably the same bloke to be honest. There's probably a factory in the Wirral producing fucking millions of these scarves and trinkets. They employ Crackheads to sell them because...if you think about it, what self respect does a Crackhead have?

We play fast as usual of course after the fireworks have subsided and the smoke is stinging the eyes of the Liverpool fans at the bottom of the Steve

Bull. I notice there are a few up in the Notrthbank armpit too. They make little noise which is strange. I have noticed this vocal wail that comes from them at points during the match. It's a slow low moan that weaves it's way into my ears. It sounds like there is a funeral going on. People pulling their hair out in mourning. These wails reach a crescendo of sorts and I recognise the tune. It is 'Fields of Athenry' which I think is about agriculture or something but now it is sung and wailed across my Molineux. I think it is a dirge like song and I suspect that even the Liverpool fans don't like singing it because we have only played about twenty minutes and they look sad already. I think they know what's going to happen.

I notice a Liverpool fan or two have sneaked into the Southbank. Normally they would get a kicking and be thrown down the stairs but ya know...magic of the cup and all that bollocks. Plus they look the sorriest pair of bastards I have ever seen. One has a half and half scarf on. He looks drunk to me. He's dancing on the steps. Wolves fans just look at him and I suspect they feel glad they are not like him. I want to kick him down them to be honest but I'm in civilised company so I have to behave.

The thing is I like Liverpool. I like the people from there for the most part. I enjoyed watching them play football in the 80's and 90's. I say enjoyed...I mean I watched them because there was nothing else on. In those days the only fun you had in a chair was the telly.

The trouble with not having any massively negative opinion about Liverpool is that they simply become a team who plays nice football that enjoy watching if there is nothing else on. They are enjoyable but ultimately defunct. Any joy that happens on the pitch between those Maroon clad Liverpools is rapidly sucked away by the depressing reaction from their fanbase.

I enjoy watching them now. If I hold my hand up to my face so I don't see their fans. They move the ball around skillfully and if you were just a football fan or a neutral I can see this being a jolly good footy match to ogle. I see they have that little dude on that looks eight years old. He moves well, falls over a lot too.

Klopp is having an animated conversation with the fourth official. It's all wavy arms and jerky legs from him. He folds his arms then starts again at him. It's moaning for sure. No goals have been scored and I know we have won this game already. You see I look for Nuno and he is sitting down in the dugout laughing with somebody.

There is the game in a nutshell for me. Nuno and Klopp are playing a Chess game and Kloppy has lost the plot already. It's dramatics and acting, its smoke and mirrors. Maybe Kloppy the Clown has his eyes on a bigger prize...like the Premier League title and this game is just all filler and no killer.

What Klopps players think as they watch this I haven't a clue...but if it was me I would be feeling a little miffed our leader is more intent of frying the fourth officals earhole rather than directing the 'Holy Smokes Scouse Football extravaganza' on the pitch.

The first half we make shapes, Liverpool make shapes too. It's an even looking thing before Jimmy pops up and slots one in for us. Crowd goes wild. 1-0 up mate. FA Cup magic and all that shizz. Our limbs are making a few day trippers feel unsafe. Ogri or whatever his name is evens things up at the start of the second half so 1-1.

I mean this isn't a match report. It was on the telly, it's probably on Iplayer by now. Go and watch that or read a report about it somewhere. Shapes wise we are not the equal of Liverpool for sure but we are winning regardless of the score. They move the ball faster than us. But they don't move it was sexily. Maybe one pass in five we complete is a beautiful thing that makes you gasp and roar whereas Liverpool can put five great passes together, But you see what I did?

We make 'beautiful' passes occasionally where Liverpools are merely 'great'. Here's the difference. Art versus manufacturing. A game can spin on beauty and art if it's in the right place at the right time. Wolves thunder and move when in attack but the ball is often spilled or dragged back to another stolid Liverpool attack. But it's really porridge football. Will they win the title these Liverpools? I don't think they will ya know. It will be close of course but Manchester City are far more beautiful than Liverpool in what they do, and it's beauty that wins games and championships not the Grey monadic spreadsheet football of this current Liverpool team. They may have hope but it will be dashed...probably when we play them on the last game of the season. Us clinching victory over Liverpool while they need a win to get a point lead over Manchester City. Coming out of that ground in May will be hilarious if it happens, I am looking forward to it and day dreaming as...

Yes it's him again. Ol' Ruben has decided to inch forward a bit. Maybe it's that Dendoncker thing. That extra man in there. But Ruben Neves wants to have a look at Liverpools box so his saunters over for a look. The ball falls to him and it's like that Derby goal again but with much less pathos. There is a hush for sure as we know who Ruben Neves is, we know him well. The crowd yells 'Shoooot' as the ball tumbles in front of him and that's exactly what he does. He puts his foot through it and it arrows into the net past Minestrone or whatever their goal keepers called. Is he the one on the leaked sex tape with those Scouse girls? I don't know. All these quiffs are starting to look the same to me.

Net bulge. Crowd goes wild. I look at the Liverpool fan in the row in front of me and he's that wrecked I don't think he knew what had happened. Ruben fucking Neves you beauty. You grabbed this game by the scruff of it's neck and give it a good shake for sure.

The Reptiles in the media won't be happy and this fills me with love for Ruben and love for Nuno too. I love the fact those fat bastards at their newspaper 'hot desks' will be punching their balls in anger. You see they have tried to frame a narrative with Liverpool and my friends these Lizards have shot their bolt very early indeed for my liking. I know Journalists fritter loyalties around according to who they suspect will make the running this season. I see this and you do too. But the thing is if you have to denigrate our team and the way we play after this victory then you are just like Klopp arguing with the fourth official.

They have all lost the plot and it's only January. The media have invested practically everything in Liverpool winning the league. Of course it's in the absence of form from the London clubs like Manchester United, Tottenham and Chelsea that has lead the press to nail their oft changing colours to the Liverpool mast. So it was the fault of 'the wind' according to Kloppo the Clown, or the man flu or whatever airy and vacuous excuse the doughnut grasps hold of in the glare of the camera lights at the post match press conference.

Outside the ground on the way back home I am laughing my tits off despite being in a bit of pain. I chat to a Scouse who has nothing but nice things to say about Nuno and our team. He would like Neves at Liverpool. Moutinho too, Willy Boly. I say nice things back but I don't mean them. I say things about Mo Salad or whatever his name is. He's the only one I can remember at the moment...the rest of them float out of my head as soon as the final whistle is blown. I wish the dude a good journey back and he tells me he lives in Fordhouses down the Stafford Road. I laugh and he doesn't know why. I wonder if he scrabbled long in that musty smelling wardrobe he has to find his shirt.

Nobody will love us for this of course. Many neutrals will love the fact that this was a 'giant killing FA cup game' but my friends with other colours...you are doing us a disservice. We are a team and we are on a journey...maybe that journey will end up at Wembley in May who knows. Heading back to the car I'm just thinking about Ruben Neves again. A lot of Liverpool fans thought they were buying him in the close season. Picking players from other clubs like it was a mail order catalogue. Tough shit ay it. I am laughing all the way down the Licky road.

Chapter 30

The Great Blue Tomb

Of course this whole Manchester City thing. Now normally I would rage after a 3-0 defeat like this by waxing some extremely negative bars about how Manchester depresses me, how their team pisses me off. I would make analogies here and there about the game and finally make some psuedo philosophical points about how Nuno and Fosun have got a plan blah and blah about this and referee blah about that. However and whatever.

Down the canal this morning my attention was drawn to a human turd under Pool Hayes bridge. I stood there for maybe three minutes looking at it wondering who had shit it, why?, how? and all the questions I normally roll around my poor head after a football match like that. I know when people need to have a cack then they need to go but there were bushes either side of the bridge they could have crapped in. But here? Where people walk?

At the Eat-your-head stadium last night I had similar thoughts. Why? I know Manchester City are a vanity club. I know they are a 'Big Six' club. They have Laporte, 'Bacon' Sane, DeBruyne who looks like he videos himself licking dogs arses...I mean they even have Jesus for Gods sake.

But it all looked and tasted like shit and for once it wasn't an observation borne by defeat, it was just how it was and how it happened...and to be honest last night was one of those times when I looked at this magnificent stadium full of Manchester City fans the same way I looked at that turd this morning...just asking why?

Queueing up before the game outside you had to negotiate road blocks, barriers, fences, Greater Manchester Police. There were signs and notices all in bright red warning stylee. Do this and don't do that, go there, don't go here. It was like walking into a death camp. In true Wolverhampton style we didn't like it, there were a few words exchanged with the ShowSec staff who were on duty in place of normal Stewards. Always a recipe for that pure Wolves humour that is unmatched anywhere around the world. But it was a forced humour of course. The whole pyschology of the place battered the senses from getting off the Metro outside the stadium until we were out of the whole sorry place.

It shouldn't be like this surely? I know they have security concerns and a history with terrorist attcks, but how far do you have to pander to these stupid bastards who blow themselves up? So turn a day that should have been a delight for all, a cracking display of open beautiful football, a probable loss of course but the chance of a win...into something that was distinctly inhuman, algorithmic, crowd management fascist bollocks.

The Stadium is beautiful of course. Like a Pringle shape with these sexy curves, ok seats, good spaces in the concourse (compared to other grounds) we were vocal once inside the place and away from the goonage and body searches outside. Familiar faces, beautiful faces, ugly ones, but you love them too. We sing in there and we are loud as per normal. Our songs echo off the roof and around the pitch because...well, we are the only ones enjoying ourselves.

What is going on? Why is there this silence? There was nothing here for us. This was an empty place. There were some empty blocks of seats around the stadium where people in Blue and white should have been sitting and cheering their team but these were few and far between. This was nearly a full house for sure. But nobody was saying anything. There was no happiness here, no joy. These people didn't look like football fans. They looked as if they had been herded in off the street with cattle prods by the ShowSec fascists and told to sit down and clap. I suppose those rare days when Prince Sultan the IV of Buramaba or whatever his face is turns up the crowd are told to clap politely and prostrate themselves before his might magnificence as he waves his soft hand and surveys his greatest toy...Manchester City FC.

'See how my fine players move the ball, see him? I forget his name but he cost me 110 million pounds, see how good he is, see how he passes to that other fellow who cost me 85 million pounds' he says and will nod at the assembled security goons who will then spring into life battering the home crowd into cheering or something. 'Smack' and 'whack' the riot sticks go as they are provoked into singing the praises of their team. Well...that didn't happen of course so the result was huge periods of an almost eerie silence as City stroked and groped the ball around our box looking for a way through that would eventually come.

Laporte, Bacon Sane, and Jesus waxing delicious shapes down the left wing and boom they were 1-0 up.

The early goal. Bollocks. I expected a huge roar from the home fans but what we heard was just an increase in the background noise really. Like the central heating thermostat had just kicked the gas boiler into action. It was a whooosh and a few clicks.

Now I know I write, that's my thing but really with this City team on the up and a chance of another Championship I expect to be writing things like 'Cacophony of noise' maybe a 'festival of decibels' or some other shit like that. But I will put my hand on my heart and say truthfully that Birmingham City made more noise in the bottom of the Steve Bull stand last season. I was mortified. Not by the goal. But by the lack of madness that should have been on display.

When we score I fall over the seats, get my glasses smashed. There was none of this. But I will share this one observation. At the time the goal was scored I watched three Manchester City fans walking up to their seats in the stand to the left of me and they never even turned around to look at the pitch. They just continued to walk, heads down, it didn't register for them. There was no reaction.

What is this new sorcery? This new angst? I couldn't fucking believe it. The same way I couldn't believe the amount of half and half scarves people had on. This is a whole new thing for me this particular tragedy of knitting your teams colours to another teams. Almost as bad was watching people buy them. As I walked past the hawkers of these monstrosities I intimated that they needed burning and the people selling them too. It got a bit nasty, I will be honest. But fucking hell troops. Have we sold our souls so much that all the rivalry and dislike have been obliterated at the altar of making a couple of quid out of everything? I've threatened these doughnuts so many times with arson and a firey death I bet there heads shrink into their shoulders when they see me coming.

It's this tribal madness that makes a football game enjoyable. Getting one over on your rivals a few times in a season, going into work the next day to denigrate your 'other' team supporting Co-Workers. Sometimes you get it in the neck too. Sometimes it all spills over into friendly fisticuffs and...well you know the rest. That is what football is about. That's why we love it.

Now of course, up here in the rarified atmosphere of the Premier League I am noticing that this has gone away, this crazy madness about your team. These poor bastards have been marginalised so much that just going to the match has become some sort of negative thing instead of joyful. It's become a job for these Manchester City fans to drag themselves in and show some emotion. Do you remember Maine Road in days of yore? You've heard the stories, if not seek out some poor old bastard Wolves fan like me and we will tell you how inside that ground it was a whole slew of crazy madness, emotion, feelings, songs, tribalism. Now? At this place....this is a Tomb.

Earlier this season I wrote about 'The Great Red Tomb' pretty much in the same vein as this blabbering. The lack of atmosphere, the actual inability of all the pumping soundtracks and video screen madness to provoke anything but the rare emotive song that kind of threatened to grow into a raging voluminous racket but in fact slid down the complicated roof, down the steps and just lay breathless and half dead on the crap pitch like dying baghead. We have seen this atmosphere before haven't we? Arsenal, West Ham, Tottenham, Manchester United, Liverpool away fans...the list is growing. What's going on? Is this the prize we have fought so long for last season. Is this the payment for those trips up and down the country singing Nuno songs and laughing? These tomb like expensive grounds with absolutely nothing within them?

Boly has slid into a ball winning tackle. What say you Willy Boly? I thought it was a fairly innocuous thing to be honest. If Boly had decided to snap Man Citys Silva then Silva would have been snapped. Boly goes in. He wins the ball, Silva basically runs into the tackle, he pirouettes, he is dead surely? But no.

I've had enough painful leg moments to know that when you are hurt, it hurts. Silva is acting. The linesman flags like he's owning up to losing that twenty quid note somebody just found. His fucking arm nearly falls off he is that violent with his flag. The City bench erupt in a faux angry mob justice things all wavy arms and shouty bollocks. The City players surround the Referee. It's a done thing isn't it? Red card and Prince Boly tramps off into the bowels of the sky blue Tomb. Was it a red? Not for me,

I will be honest. Of course as soon as the tackle is made the crowd becomes alive crying for restitution, for justice, for what? Who knows, but they are on their feet. At least it's some fucking emotion. It's a wonder there aren't a few fatalities as the pooled blood in their lower legs cut off from sitting down all match suddenly rushes into their hearts to explode them. Apoplectic? Not fucking half mate. I want to throw something at somebody. Maybe throw somebody at somebody even. Shitheads.

I'm getting a definite Aston Villa away feeling here. Like the Gods have turned their backs on us. You see we move the ball well too. We have chances all through the game. Shapes are changed. I know Nuno will not like this, I know that he will know Manchester City were there for the taking but this is Nuno the Pure. He knows this shit goes on in football. The 'fouls' where the opposition react like they've been shot. The snarky Referees on the payroll of the big six, the bullshit and shadows of on the pitch politicking...but I think Nuno knew at the end of the game that playing the same game as these 'cardboard clubs' is not a way forward.

You see you can have the full deck of shitty reactions to 'fouls', you can get the odd penalty by swan diving in the opponents area. You can get key opposition players sent off with dramatics. But what does that make any victory?

Of course reading a League table in ten or twenty years time will be an abstract empirical experience. Oh yeah Manchester City won 3 goals to 0 against Wolverhampton Wanderers. But what is the zeitgeist of a win like this? Of a campaign and a philosophy like this? Well you see it in the crowd, in the faces of the home fans. They are sad. They smile of course in the ground but outside? On the metro back to Picadilly Gardens? They are not smiling, they are not happy. They are sad because they know that they are the plaything of an Oil Prince. The stadium might as well be made out of cardboard and cheap paper.

They know that they win games mostly by assembling a team that costs more than the gross domestic product of a small European country. They know that if enough of them stand and remonstrate over a small harmless tackle that the Referee will reach perhaps for a red instead of a yellow, maybe give a penalty...which happens as Sterling tumbles over like some lightweight prick after Benno breathes on him.

Do we want this sadness? Do we want to win like this? No platitudes will be written for this Manchester City team, there will be no great volumes written about the art of their football. There are no greats within this City team, no brilliant personalities, no romantic days. The passion has gone, this team is not Manchester City, it is merely a toy of a Prince, a plaything, a gold plated Lamborghini, the most expensive of watches. This team is devoid of love, there is an absence of it that permeates the stands around it and leaks out into the streets surrounding it too. In direct contrast to Manchester United I say this. Old Trafford is a Tomb of course, a great Red one but at least it has ghosts within it moving between the seats and through the concourses. This Blue Tomb has nothing like that.

Nuno I think, after the post match press conference was bold in his humility again. He said beautiful correct things about the match. Nuno is learning, and I think this was less a match where the team learned and moreso where Nuno himself took a lesson or two. I suspect he made a choice in his own head last night. You either win beautifully or you don't win at all. Now thank God he will go back to Molineux and prepare more shapes and ideas, he will look at players that can produce art and beauty but with honour and respect instead of clambering for points to engage the whims of an owner that will never ever understand what English football is about.

Are we over the idea of using Manchester City as a template for our future success? I think we are over it, it has died like those songs the City fans murmured. It has died like the Oasis songs on the video screens, it has died like the two fucking doughnut presenters who did a half time 'analysis' for everybody accompanied by voluminous boos from the travelling Wolves fans.

If I came away from that place with an idea last night it was this one. Our Molineux is the most precious place in the world for me. The passion there is a remnant of how it used to be all those years ago. It has been battered by all seater stadiums and the razzamatazz of flashy TV bollocks.Burned by pyrotechnic displays. Dragged out of bed by Cops at four in the morning. It has been clubbed over the head by security concerns, by over priced food and drink, by modernity in all it's plasticity, it's 'likes', it's 'favourites', and fakeness. But I would rather have Molineux than this Manchester thing on any day.

Now the Premier League is nothing to me, it is just a stepping stone to greater things, to Europe possibly and maybe even the world. We face stadium redevelopment on unheard of levels, we will see players come and go, we will see Nunos ideas flourish. But if Fosun EVER try to turn my club into a pastiche of whatever this Manchester City idea is I will be walking up to Molineux and into those offices and I will show them (bad leg or not) what Resistance actually means.

OK reading that make was a mission in self discovery. What have I discovered? I can be a petulant whining bitch when my team loses a game. I bet I've pissed off half of Manchester. Well...fuck it.

Chapter 31

Crisptown Versus Wolftown

In the Hogshead before the Leicester game I am choking a beer down. There are beautiful people around me. Dave is here from Australia. A few other Australians too. We are a big club down there and these dudes around me now are also big dudes. Not in a physical sense but you see they live underneath the earth for one. How they have managed to cling to the earths surface for years is beyond me. That's why their handshakes are firm. It's gripping on.

Laughs aside. These lads have supported Wolves in Australia among expats whose allegiances are coloured in primary shades of Red, Blue, Green, White and some teams had stripes in their kit too. These shades have been very succesful in their campaigns over the years where we have been a bit shit. We have been up and down these divisions for that long I feel like a Yoyo. God knows what these fellas have had to put up with over the years we have been dangling about.

Nuno wants to put things right now. Dendoncker is in the team again. He is that interface I was talking about between our defence and midfield. I like this place for him and I like him. He is a neck with skill. Young Belgian man, tall and muscular, that lean youth thing going on but you can see he's putting on man muscle now. That's all tactile ligaments and the musculature to pull all that springy muscle in the right places.

Doherty has been dropped from the game to the bench. People around me are discussing it. The fact he had three Manchester City doughnuts on his case for 90 minutes last week has no bearing on this decision I think. I think it's tactical. Jonny Otto is replacing him. I think Jonny likes it over there in Dohertys spot. Jonny is more assassin than ever lately. I am enjoying watching him. I am enjoying everything at the moment. You see I had two or three good Brandies before I left the house and now I'm on my second pint.

I'm sure losing Boly last week lost us the match against Manchester City. I'm sure of it. It was one of those challenges that looked worse than it was. The inquest has been fraught of course. But Boly is not with us tonight. But man we could have won that game. Instead of Boly today we have Saiss. He is softly spoken but rock hard. He doesn't take any shit at all. But he will face a nightmare today I'm sure.

We have our fireworks, which to be honest look a bit shit in the daylight. I've found my spare glasses and after squinting at the last three matches I have attended then this shit seems like HDTV or something. I can see Coadys face rallying the troops. He is shouting and cajoling. We seem up for this. Moutinho is looking around at the team. I always notice him doing this, like hes making sure everybody is here and ready.

Patricio stalks the goalmouth occasionally slapping his sides and things. Tapping a goal post then running over and tapping the other on. He takes a swig of water. He's that handsome he could be drinking from a coconut on a white beach in front of an Azure sea...if he keeps a clean sheet I'll buy him a fucking coconut.

Leicester fans are their normal weird selves singing about when they were Champions but they are very quiet and I don't hear the rest of it and I'm watching us start the game with a bit of love to be honest. There is much stroking of the ball to and fro between our team. There is much movement. We lose possession and we are at them like little staffies on a rat. Nibble and chomp. Have the occasional dig, a little push, an errant foot. Nothing dramatic of course but just enough to tittilate the holder of the ball into spilling it or maybe not seeing a run or a player in the open. So it's attrition from us when they have the ball. We move into them constantly splitting the play up. When we have the ball it's like a fucking hand grenade has gone off.

All of a sudden Jimmy Jimenez and Diogo Jota are throwing casual defence splitting shapes here and there. Vinagre starts, he's a handful too. Everything looks good and bloody hell. Jotas just scored. Incisive. He didn't mess about. This is the Jota we know from the description on his packet. The old Jota? Nah, but the one we have seen slowly building up some momentum and some gravitas as the games this season have progressed. He is starting to become what we knew he always was. A bloody good player and a bloke that can bung in a goal that looks lovely.

We are winning and from the off the game is ping ponging up and down the pitch like a plasterers arm. I'm glad I'm in the Southbank so I don't have to twist my neck too much. Intense.

Dendoncker looks good where Nuno has put him. He is physical and stoic when he has the ball. He understands football. He sniffs out danger while defending and is not backwards coming forwards when there is an attack on either. He can ping things around with impunity shrugging off the attentions of the various blue shirts around him.

People boo Barnes every time he touches the ball. This is funny. We never forget those stripey knobheads down the road. But we do laugh at them now. Donk gets the ball off somebody who collapses under the weight of the challenge. We are going for this. It's a mad game. Even the Leicester fans are making some strange noise now. They are louder at least than when we played them at their place.

OK Benno has just scored a header for us. 2-0 to us. I'm laughing, it's hilarious for some reason and I don't know why to be honest. I've got one of those feelings again like everything is about to go tits up in the most Las Vegas sense. The first half is still ping pong. Rui Patricio has a mare at one point with Jeremy Vardy or whatever his name is. England striker. Rui is on that tropical beach when he tries to collect an easy back pass before it bobbles of his ankle and his feet are sinking into that soft white sand. Vardy is on him like a rat at a potato having a nibble and a suck before before the ball gets to safety. Fucking hell Rui. No Coconuts for you if you don't get your arse in gear.

We are ok I'm sure but that bloody feeling again. I go for a couple of halftime roll ups and a chat with Dave. He's worth a book by himself that bloke. We talk about the old days with no segregation at grounds. The battles under the southbank. It's threatening to be one of those hooligan conversations and this book is too. I change the subject and talk about when I lost my big toenail surfing when I got stung by a Weaver fish. Somebody is quietly being sick up the wall at the back of the Southbank. It sounds weird and I don't want to look but I wonder if it's the lad from the Sheffield Wednesday game but no it's some monster with a NafNaf coat on.

Second half we are doing more shapes but they are shapes when we are asleep and tucked up in bed. Leicester score two goals in quick succession and they are level in the time it takes for this abnormal fart smell to dissipate from our row in the Southbank. This is the second match this has happened. Somebody needs to go to the Doctors and have that rotted ferret that's died in their colon pulled out and given a decent burial. Jesus Christ you could have cut a slice of that bloody thing. Oh my days. The stink. My eyes were watering at this point and were just about clearing when Jota is unleashed by Neves and boom. 3-2. Imagine it. Instead of two rows in front I was a row at the back. I was in the gold and black tumble dryer again. The Wolftown mosh pit. I scream out Jotas name before I get a mouthful of armpit. Somebody treads on my foot. I get kneed in the balls...

Surely it can't get any crazier? Remember the 4-3 game all those years ago when people pissed off when we were 3-0 down against Leicester? I barely remember it but I do remember laughing then and I'm laughing now. It takes ages to settle. Perhaps five or ten minutes have elapsed from my goal scoring mirth before Jonny aggravates someone too much for the Referees liking and they get a free kick in a dangerous area. Fuck off. No way. Who writes these mad football stories? It's just a league match, the chance of three points but now everything is important and everything of importance too. They smash one in and it seems the massive defender neck City have just floats unimpeded into the box and sticks his big head on it. 3-3.

There are defensive aggravations here I can sense it. Not a slight sense of dysfunction because the defence are missing the physicality and height of Boly but perhaps it has just upset the zeitgeist a little. We are more than capable of dealing with threats like these. Maddison I think puts the ball in perfectly. It's a beautiful ball and I love watching him play. But he's the enemy. Like Barnes really their player on loan at Albion who City called back prior to this game. He's shit and they take him off. I wave.

The game of course is threatening to implode in on itself. The individual parts of it, the players are becoming less important perhaps and are dissolving into a sort of madness where yes there are chances from both sides as they battle for the ball. I think the last ten minutes of this match was probably the most important I've seen this year. There is a definite cause and effect in view. We pass and they pass. There have been substitutions on both sides but these new players adopt almost instantly the same rythyms as every other player without any form of major imposition. Nobody is changing anything. It's still entertainment but it is winding down to a conclusion. A point each. A day of goals and at least something. But we are rarely winning at home. We are starved somewhat of joy at home.

But there are passes between Neves and everybody else which are a joy to watch. All of a sudden it seems Ruben is not content to see another pass drop into the stream or the raging torrent of this football only to be carried away by it. Ruben Neves now himself has a choice even within this maelstrom of madness. That choice is to shout out and change the way things are or settle your head into the torrent and drown with a single point. So there has to be a transformation of the game from that winding down abyss like capture of a point or to throw your head back and take the bull by it's horns and leap. We are not content to draw. We want to win. I may be rolling my going home roll up ready for the final whistle but I have one eye on the match....then two eyes.

So Jimmy is running, Jota is running. Forward ever forwards. Outpacing the City defence. It's madness mate, it's march of the mentals. This team are crazy, my team, my lads. It is injury time, we are seconds away from the final whislte. Who will be the Hero when all seems on a knife edge? Who will have the courage to step forwards? Who will have clear eyes? Ruben deftly caresses and strokes the ball a full forty something yards to the feet of an onrushing Jimenez who has run all afternoon. Here and there, chasing constantly, running into space, collecting the ball. Laying it off but always here and there in a kind of madness of intent. How is he still running? But run he does. The Neves ball is as beautiful as can be. It has crept between three City players who look at it going past them like an old flame who doesn't recognise them. The ball is gone for them. It has sparkly Neves fairy dust on it as it electrically crackles to Jimmy.

The easiest thing of course would be for Jimmy to lay his foot into the middle of it and wang the fucking thing past that red nosed git Schmicheal, or Shamichael or whatever his name is. But of course that wouldn't be part of this story surely? I grab hold of Aussie Dave next to me and it's Neves quiet. You know the one, you were probably there last season. But this time it's Jimmy. There is a harmony in this team for sure. As the discordant blast of the shot that never came was smothered by a quieter more academic pass to Jota in space. An unselfish act and one that was harmonious and correct for the philosophies here today. Jota shot, the ball careered off red nose and was there, in the back of the goal.

Limbs? The thrashings of joy and pain, the cataclysym of knee cap smashing against bone, concrete and flesh. My half made roll up goes all over the head of the bloke in front of me, you know he is bald? Not now, he has fine tobacco hair and a rizla stuck on his ear. The din of shin against hard edges. The knuckle in the ear as we sing and shout. The net is settling into it's normal restful state, I glance up for a second through the bodies and the joy and there is Nuno running down the touchline. I shout louder as I expect him to carry on running and at the last moment dive into the adulations in the crowe. Us, joyful and crazed.

We tend to suffer more when we think too deeply about the things that may happen during a match than what actually happens within it. Moments like these catalyse thoughts we have had. Those negative thoughts we have built up inside of us in the days before the game. These thoughts are heavy and have a life of their own. This was a game Leicester could have won of course. The negative feelings we tend to have can close our minds to all thoughts of victory and these closing moments and the Jota goal unleash all these feelings from us. That's why we shout and scream. That is why we coalesce into this mass of joy as Nuno kneels down on the pitch to embrace his Jota, his 'Little Wolf'.

Nuno will be booked by the Referee for entering the field of play. But what is this minor infraction, this meddling of the forces of law and order, rules and bullshit on such a joyous moment? Nothing that's what. We must not repress emotion in these games we play, to fight without feeling, devoid of expressions that reflect a last minute winning goal. Nuno wanted to enjoy this moment with a member of his team. How do you keep such a joy in? How do we repress this chaotic love we have for last minute winners? Do we have to just stand there and politely applaud?

Nuno. He did this without thought to his future and what the repercussions would be. There were no hopes or fears within this display of emotion from Nuno but it was firmly planted in this moment, this brief excerpt of time. It was satisfaction with his hard work and that of his players which meant more importantly...at this time there was nothing more Nuno wanted than to celebrate a joyous occasion with his player, his little Wolf. This moment was not for anybody else except him and Jota.

It is what it is of course. Later that night I am laughing at Match of the

Day turning the volume right down on the atmosphere. Propaganda again. I know that we have them on the back foot now. You see we create chances and create beautiful football and it is a resistance of sorts to the darkness within the punditry and the hate whenever we win a game and creep further upwards or consolidate more and more our position in the League. It is an artist that gives shape to an idea. Jota and Jimmy conceptualised the ideas Nuno had given them and made it concrete and real in that final move. It wasn't the fact that we got three points that made Nuno run down that pitch, it was the act of creating something real from a simple metaphysical idea or two on a whiteboard or a pre match talk. It was Nunoism mate.

There is probably more to talk about regarding this outwelling of emotion. But I have come closer now to understanding Nuno and I suppose 'finding' him and in turn understanding this football which day by day becomes less about individual players and more about turning ideas into reality.

Chapter 32

Destruction of the Alf Garnett Gollums and Shit Is Getting Real

Intense. How do you talk about that match. I've just watched my team dismantle a Premier league ever present. West Ham United. West Ham are a team I have always thought highly of. I was arrested many moons ago for having a physical disagreement with a few West Ham lads and we got thrown in the same Police van. Of course we waxed lyrical about the game we had just watched where Bully got Julian Dicks in a headlock and threw him off the pitch. There was much angst and hilarity in that match and I was highly amused. Much hilarity in the van too as we 'bantered' and rocked as we got took down to Birmingham New Road nick. Getting bailed later we shared the same taxi back into town (but they paid for it).

The other day I watched a videocast thing on YouTube where some hipster doughnut was talking to Robert Plant about this and that. It was called 'The House of Strombone' and was a typical new cash jingly jangly podcast kind of a thing with the interviewer dressed like some kind of corporate hipster. You know the type, corporate haircut, dressed like a techno Nazi in the obligatory Vans shoes, black T-Shirt and loads of fucking beads, LOADS of beads, like they were needed because they were talking to our Planty. I don't understand people wearing beads, men anyway.

The conversation rocked to and fro and ticked all the boxes. Groupies, stories, Led Zeppelin, you know, all the stuff that's been frolicked over by countless pricks in front of Planty for fuck knows how many years. Roberto, by 10 minutes in is extremely pissed off. It's too fucking hot in there you can tell. Planty is getting itchy...

'What have you been doing lately Robert?' The beaded doughnut asks..

'I've been watching a lot of soccer' Planty replies with that smile he has and the bead doughnut changes tack quick. Planty was giving this bloke an out, a way to rescue what is turning out to be a car crash of an interview. So the interview rapidly became work for our Planty. It was watercolouring it's way into a mish mash of pointless grey shite. I've got a point to this so bear with me.

I think the interviewer would have learned about Planty more if he would have allowed him to talk about the Wolves. Because Robert Plant the person would have come out of the filters he has to put up to deal with the madness of his life, we would have seen him truly as he is. That's would have been more interesting surely? Within the framework of his teams success over these past seasons washed with the absolute pain of the previous years we would have watched Planty unfold a little...

I was sure (as I watched Moutinho) last night that our team and the Philosophies of Nuno have given us all some sort of canvas for our own selves. The way we act, talk, interact and discuss issues that surround our lives. I suspect that this Nunoism has become a vessel for looking at the world a little differently, probably allowing us to be a little more open instead of being introspective. I wonder of course if I could extrapolate this new philosophy with pro football players and the madness of football club management with perhaps a wider impact and say Nuno and our team have changed us, as people?

Doherty grabs hold of the ball from Moutinho and he is off down the wing. He runs into a West Ham player and deftly moves his body like a ballet dancer and is past him, he leaves the West Ham man gasping for air, his fingers seek to grab Doherty, to pull him off balance but Matt is gone like the wind. There one moment and gone the next. Doherty continues and is forced to go a little wide by the next obstacle. Another West Ham defender. Doherty strokes the ball. A lovers touch for sure. Who new that this granite faced stoic that is Matt Doherty would open his heart to such artistry and madness? This Irishman that has been cast from the same mold as those vocal but obtuse fellow countrymen as Roy Keane and Mick McCarthy but instead of invective and propagandising like them he weaves his own brush into intricate designs like those on show last night. He bangs a cross in but for once there is no one there for it. But he will do it again and again throughout this football match. That is the philosophy you see. Shape and pattern, compact ideas, short scenarios of total dominance under washed by the foundation of diligence and toil.

Little Jonny Otto is around and about. He is learning too. Ability wise he will have been the same as when he came from Spain. The consummate professional. Train hard and play hard. He slotted straight into the team after a few games. But now his game too is flowering into something great and beautiful. As with Doherty I suspect he has learned something while he has been here. Maybe all great players need a framework or a philosophy to puke your guts out for when you tremble off the pitch after 90+ minutes of ragging up and down the pitch. Maybe he too has seen Nunoism in it's most naked form out on the pitch at Compton and has decided to join in with the whole madness of the Crazy Nuno train. At times he would pop up right in a danger area and zip in a cross or a pass. The simple elements of football, the pass, the defence of the ball, the tracking back of players become less like dotted lines and marker pen slashes and more like some strange type of ethereal trick where Jonny just appears in the right place at the right time. How much is he again? Snap their hand off Fosun, slather his agent and those involved in his possible transfer with tall blonde hookers in stilletos, some cocaine and some mad karaoke. I love the way Jonny touches players as he tracks them and I have a little laugh to myself as I watch him prod and poke.

Coady goes down with a crack on the nose I think. I'm not looking at him sitting there in the box being attended too by Wolves physios. Conor Coady is my spirit player, I understand everything that goes on during games by watching him. If he is hurt I will be angry and annoyed and I don't want that. I don't want today spoiled by horrible things. The journey up here was cool and refined, it was peaceful. I have been in a chilled out state ever since the Leicester game. Something has clicked inside me and I don't know what it is but I like it. I read about our team on Social Media and read about them on websites that keep crashing my laptop. I am enjoying being a Wolves fan again.

We have the best injury record in the Premier League apparently. These dudes with the plasters and magic spray are experts, beautiful experts. I am sure Coady is in good hands but I'm still concerned. You see all this lovely football comes from the back. It starts at Patricio and finishes with Jota. Coady is the instigator of most of our moves forward, he picks out a player here and there with all the skill he has but the most important aspect of his play isn't the accuracy of his passes or his defensive work. It's his vision. Playing a ball to one of his team mates isn't (for the most part) his skillset. Most people can ping a ball thirty yards to a player in space. The important aspect is his almost metaphysical ability to look forward at the players in front of him and rapidly investigate moves like a Chess player. It's all part of the plan, it's a Gold and Black Jihad now, a Holy war for sure. No Gods but Nuno.

Last night Coady played a few balls that had people around me cussing a little under their breath. They lacked vision to be honest. A risky initial ball played to Neves who had a West Ham player not four yards off him. Contrast this with Moutinho who had acres of space. The Occams razor or the simplest pass would have been with the ball to Moutinho. He had space, time to move and then...three West Ham players would have been on him like a shot cutting off most of the ways he would have played the ball, which would have gone back to Ryan Bennett. Instead Ruben Neves.

Ruben collects and pulls two of the West Ham players off Moutinho who moves forward and through them. Moutinho now has space and knows that Ruben Neves will put the ball on him pinpointy style the way he does. Now instead of defending the ball he can attack with it. Which he does. It's almost magical to see if you just spend a little time pulling apart every little jink and pass our team perform and soon it becomes like a complex Mandlebrocht set of ever complex patterns repeating themselves but containing the simple basic blocks they started with in the first place. Coady gets up after treatment. Thank fuck for that.

So the whole kwan that Nuno has instilled here allows Jimenez a brace of goals in front of the home crowd. They are talking about 30 million quid or so to buy him and get him permanently. Would you pay it? I for one would slap that money in their hands so hard they would laugh uncomfortably and have a sneaking suspicion they had been done. Of course they have been fiddled. Jimmy is a sixty million pound player for me. We would get him at half price. You see I have watched many 60 million pound players this season and they lack shit trust me. We could but Jonny too, 18 million squid. Bargain. Money changes hands again but what's the zeitgeist that has these players performing such beautiful shapes? Nunoism mate. That's all and everything.

I feel bad for West Ham as they slither from the pitch under a few choice words from their fans. It's the first team I feel bad for in these crazy last few seasons. They have players with ability and skills and nothing to play for. The same things I said about Manchester City the other week. It's all jangly lights and posh haircuts. Apart from Snotgrass who looks like he collapsed on top of a council worker strimming a verge. What he's doing in this team I haven't a clue but maybe that's a job for the West Ham fans to deal with...I see they are pissing off early to maybe debate that point. I wave to them as they file out. It is a sad wave because their next few years are going to be a little mad and crazy like we had in the dark days. There will be no philosophy from the dildo brothers or Karen Brady for them. Now homeless, they will merely exist until some miracle happens there and it is a shame. I always think of those lads in the Police van with me as we laughed about the punches thrown and the way we got nicked.

"Oh Nuno Santo runs down the wing for me"

Maybe there are other things that happened in the match that I could have talked about. The crap Referee again, the penalty decisions, the fouls unpunished. But you know my thoughts on that, you can read some of the posts I've done about previous games so I wont bore you with them. For me I am content and happy, not with the victory but the way we 'victored'. It was the first time for many many years I have watched my team take apart an equally good team and walk away with three points and a full agreement with somebody I chatted with today down the canal.

"Mikey, it ay always about winning, it's about how you win"

He was right of course. That winning has an important kind of a lesson for all of us. The beaded knobhead interviewer who was waxing with Robert Plant could have learned more about him by letting him talk about football because now we can all measure ourselves against what we are watching at Molineux. By talking about the things that people love allows them to open up like some derenaged flower willing to talk in more eloquent terms than they normally would. I think the love of our team and our Coach can help define what we are and how we go about our lives maybe, there, on that pitch is everything we need to know about ourselves and others, how we fight back against having no ideas, no clue. How we find that foundation is through this team and the way Nuno drives them ever forwards to flourish and expand their own skillsets.

But like Nuno in that press conference the other day. We must not allow the bullshit and the grey faces of others let us forget the most important points. It's not about individuals, it's about 'the team', its about the idea, it's about shape, compactness, hard work and always progression, driving forward. It's about not really having words to describe what it is we are actually watching but walking up the steps of the Southbank smiling your tits off and laughing with your friends. It's about letting this whole Nuno madness kill us and bring us back to life again in some new way, some new shape. Mad times.

Chapter 33

Spirit Of Radio and The Toffee Gollums

Awake with a face like a stolen arsehole, like a Nans elbow, like a bus to nowhereland. Weird. Thats how I feel at the moment. I've just finished listening to Everton V Wolves on a crap Disney Radio with a gurning Micky Mouse ogling the waves. It crackled and it popped but me and Shaky Ray took turns in holding the bloody thing in the air to get the commentary. It was raining a bit so we hid under Pool Hayes bridge again. I like it under here as last season I had many happy moments underneath it as I talked to various lunatics who wanted to talk Wolves.

There's probably a book in it to be honest. Just tales under the bridge. Like Wind in the Willows except lunatics who followed their team. Shaky Ray looks like a Mole albeit one addicted to Heroin. He has a habit of peerring into noting with a beady eye as he concentrates on the match. He is getting his addled brain to picture the words. Make little dramas from a sparse and sometimes abstract commentary. What brain cells he has left any way. He has been addicted to Heroin for twelve years, he buys a ten bag a day, he works in a warehouse in Bilston as a Forklift driver. I have known him for a few years. Big Wolves fan.

I'm not there because I couldn't really afford the day out by myself. It's three matches I've missed now and I'm getting shades of last season flapping around with my leg in a cast as I trundled to a few home games in my wheelchair.

Our team have just smashed this Premier League ever present by three goals to one. At full time me and Ray did a little dance of joy as he swigged a can of Polish beer. My dogs started barking and running around too and before we knew it we were tangled in dogs, loose beer, and joy. Shaky Ray got his baccy out which was dry and crumpled (just like him) so we could have a roll up. He smokes 'Drum' which is a harsh baccy to be fair. Its like Tear Gas to be honest.

We both rolled a cigarette and I was glad of the heat from the lit end. It was cold. I wished I was up there in Scouseland singing and dancing, having a great time. But alas. At the side of the bridge is a discarded sleeping bag and the detritus one expects from people who sleep rough down here. I am sad at this. We are supposed to be a caring Christian nation or something. It's cold. I don't know how these people can sleep in these temperatures.

Weird. We are dismantling teams now. This Messianic message of football Nuno has brought to this team is flowing like a raging river at times. We are locked into a madness and driven forward by our Coach. We are dismantling and breaking teams apart. There is a feeling if you like, a kind of mad zeitgeist going on again. Last season of course it was with people who had struggled with Wolves all through the years beforehand. We were old hands, combat experienced. Now of course a few arseholes have started to appear onto the stands. These people are new people. Or old new people I suppose. They didn't like to go to games against Barnsley and Rotherham. But they do want shiny new Premier League teams yes. But they have appeared late of course. They have turned up with the same fucking chip on their shoulder they had the last time we played these teams and the narrative is the same.

"Costa ya fucking shit get out of our team"

Always Helder. It's like they smell blood or something. His ankle was smashed to bits. It's remarkable he can run and jink around people. He is a dream for me of course. I see his battles to get fit. As well as getting over his smashed up bones he now has to take on board a whole load of other madness. How to unlock a Premier League quality defence. He does this quite a lot, getting his run perfect, sliding in a challenge, boosting a perfect ball across the goal mouth. So for me the whole ethos of returning after an injury and learning these new football shapes amazes me. But we keep hearing the odd voice wailing at away games and sometimes home too. Where the platform these twats who have bought tickets is dirtied and sullied by inane shite, by blather and vexed remonstrations about how a player is getting on during the game. It makes me sick. But everything is rosy isn't it? Everything is good? Weird.

Back home later on I watch the game highlights on the Intertube. It keeps stuttering and jerking around because the bandwidth is cack. I watch Conor Coady in slow motion go up into the air to clear a cross. He has an Everton man straight onto him but Conor is somewhere else. He doesn't even look at the neck on top of him flailing arms and digging in feet to try and put him off. The camera zooms in a little and you look straight into Coadys eyes and there is something there that isn't weird or strange at all. To be honest it scared me a little. It scared me because I had seen those eyes before. It was belief in his ability and nothing was going to stop him clearing that ball. Nothing at all. His eyes were on it mate. The ball was his. For a split second Coadys eyes flickered off the ball. It was a Wolves midfielder. I think it was Moutinho or Neves. The midfielder was perhaps ten yards off him but now Conor knew he was there and where he would move. Eyes back on the ball and he connected despite the Evertonian madness smashing into him. He connects and the ball is headed straight to the feet of our midfield man. Safe ball, a good ball, well cleared. Our Captain this bloke is. We are proud of him. We attack instantly and the madness is real again as we all steam up the pitch going dink, donk, prod, smooth, avoid, pass and we are in their box challenging and fighting to get that ball into the net.

Neves has seconds now. This is the difference in this game. He has that extra time to put into force all those footballing cogs and gears that live inside Rubens head. These gears move and groove as he looks. Then the ball is 'inserted' into play again. We attack and that's the narrative here. Attack. Constantly and when we don't have the ball we defend with numbers. Everything is fluid and dynamic. Everton flap around. They don't know what to make of this at all.

Somebody has thrown a bag of household rubbish in the canal. It's a black bag full of Toilet Duck bottles, nappies and a few other things. There is a packet of bacon and cheese crispy pancakes and my stomach tightens. I love them. Everything is frozen into place here because well...the canal is frozen ay it? I think about pancakes and Danny Batth who we have just sold to Stoke for 4 million squid.

I am going to miss Danny. Not for his football which was a bit flat footed sometimes. Wolves in the Lambert and Saunders tenure ruined him a bit for me. But the double relelgation. We dropped like a stone with a team of malcontents and waste men. He came in from the dreary endless 'B' roster and into a team that at that time was demoralised and defeated. He dragged us up by the boot straps. All of us. We had hope again that this local lad would propel us towards some sort of netherworld where we could be proud again. For all his faults he gave us our hearts back and our love. I wont forget you Danny Batth...but I will forget that Villa game.

How have things changed? We buy Jonny Otto in the January transfer window. This Spanish lad amazes me. We have brought him from Barcelona. Their fans are sad to see him go and wax great plaintive Spanish lyrics on social media. But I already know this mans quality. He is quite short and stocky. But he chews up attacks with a skill that belies his obvious physicality. 'Jotto' as I call him is always lurking around somewhere on that pitch. I've talked about how he slightly touches attackers to let them know he is there. This subtle touch will take the mind of an opposition footballer away from the ball. His mind wont be fully on it. This means a misplaced pass or an errant cross.

This means Jonnys slight massages as he chases the ball mean maybe

20% of the opposition attackers mind will be on Jonny. It's the Jotto fear factor. Jotto chips away at attacks with the hand of an artist. This is what Spanish football is about. Subtlety and caress, with the occasional smash into the shins just to let them know who he is.

Earlier that morning before the match I am helping my mate fetch an engine for his car. I have to explain that we budget Motorists are quite happy to lug an engine from a smashed up car in a scrap yard in the Black Country to a lock up garage so we can replace the shagged 200k miles engine with a funky 60k one. Spend a day fitting it and away you go. The garage quoted him 2.5k for the work. We bought the engine for £200. As I walk around the yard I see an old friend and we exchange pleasantries and weird handshakes. He is laughing and drags me over to his van to see something. He opens the back and there on the floor bound in brown shiny parcel tape is another mate 'Nine Volt Bob' a strange individual. I don't know why they call him 9 Volt. Even though his head is quite covered in the stuff he has half an eye and half a mouth loose. He notices it's me and smiles.

"Hello Mikey.." he says from his half a mouth. "...Ay ya going to the footy today? Everton ay it?"

I tell him I can't afford it and we exchange muffled platitudes before my other mate slams the door on him. Bob bought a car, a big slinky new Audi on credit which he then sold to "My other mate" who woke up one morning to discover that it had been repossesed because Bob hadn't kept up the payments. 'Other mate' wasn't happy and had kidnapped Bob to get his 4k back. Bob's Missus is running around trying to get 'Other mates' money because she thinks something will happen to Bob. But Bob will just spend the day in the back of a van in a scrap yard in Darlo. It's not like 'Other mate' will kill him or anything. Maybe burn a toe with a lighter a bit. I'm laughing thinking about Bob...he owes me ten quid for my Nuno book. Nine Volt Bob fucking hell mate.

Dendoncker is loving life in the team at the moment isn't he? He is busting shapes all over the place as I watch the highlights...sorry for zipping from one subject to another. Yes, Donk.

He's a big built Belgian lad who played in the world cup the other year. Now his purchasement has kind of gone under the radar a bit with all the other doughnuts that flowed in and out of the team over the past year. I watched his debut at Sheffield Wednesday and was very impressed. Now of course Nuno has looked into his mighty tome of footballing philosophies and decidd that yes, he can do a job in our midfield for these few games coming up.

What does Donk bring? A bit of steel. A bit of leg in the midfield. Where a few games we were over run a bit, now these opposition midfielders run into Donk. I bet it hurts too. He's a big lad. Still a bit rangey in terms of physical attributes but he is filling a role here. Donk collects a ball flying around in the Everton box and smashes a volley in. I think it's Jotto who has to get out of the way. I can't exactly see who it is because like I said before...the stream is a bit shit. But that big thick Belgian leg is pure intent to be honest. It's a good job whoever that Wolves player was in the way got out of the trajectory or there would have been some ball sting going on and we all know what that's like.

Watching it I start to wish I was there but there is a weirdness in Liverpool I can't get on with. I like the place for sure. I don't mind the people. I just don't like being 'in it'. If that makes sense. Liverpool for me has a narrative that is defined by it's reactions rather than it's emotions.

I watch and I am happy. I get a text saying we are pretty much safe now and I am relieved but not as much as I should be. No way has this campaign so far been a battle or a fight. We haven't been shit housing points off other teams. We look like we deserve to be there. At the moment we are in 7th place. Below us are names ya know. Big teams who are failing to halt the flow and the idea of this Nunoist way this Holy War of Nunoism. This endless and relentless pressure from the first second to the last. There will be more of this Premier league madness for us next season now. More of these strange grounds that are silent for most of the time.

"Nuno...oh Nuno Santo runs down the wing for me"

I wonder how much Nuno realises how he has saved us. I wonder if (as strong as he is) he actually understands how he has dragged us by the scruff of our necks from the doldrums we were enmeshed within and pulled us into the light of this spangly madness of winning games at places like Everton?

Now I know there have been games against Shrewsbury. Those league one minnows and 'insert angles here' footballing team who have drawn us in the FA cup. I didn't get to any of these games so you will have to fill in the gaps in this book I'm afraid. Of course...I couldn't really afford it again. I'm not a rich man. I can't afford to delight myself with these luxurious away days every week. In fact I don't think I will be able to afford any of these mad games any time soon. That's my current zeitgeist. Which is a bit shit really when you have to write about it. But then again what do you write about Shrewsbury in the FA cup fourth round?

I hear the mad tales about the day of course. We drew 2-2 and there was some aggro on occasions as the fans made their way to the ground. But what do you expect from Shrewsbury? Nothing happens there. Nothing. It's a place people go to die, like Bournemouth. How am I going to wax mighty lyrics about Shrewsbury? I mean...at least when we played Ajax in that pre season friendly at Walsalls ground there was some kind of angle to grab onto. But Shrewsbury is boring. Their team is boring. Of course they had this great giant killing theme going on (as you do) about how they had a chance or an effort or I dunno...something.

When they play the rematch at Molineux I'm not going to that either. But I will be there of course. Watching the game or bits of it from the bridge over the subway with one or two other Wolves fans. It's like old times. There is even a Cop at one point who comes along and tells all four of us to piss off and move along and we all laugh at him and he wanders off to aggravate somebody else. But you know it's lovely out here when everybody is inside the stadium. It's quiet outside and the Molinuex which nestles in the arm of the 'High hill' with Saint Peters Church on top is a jewel. I can hear the crowd noises out here and it's good. I see some football through the gap between the Southbank and the Steve Bull stand. I don't know what's happening inside really but it is a trip into the past. Watching the games up here. Walking around outside until they open the gates ten minutes before full time. You would run into the stand then to watch ten minutes of Wolves football.

It was all we had in those days and it's a little strange I haven't seemed to progress much from the early and mid seventies to now. Fifty three years old and I can't get in. I'm laughing to myself out here. I have already written about the Spurs fella that got his nose broke by the art block sculptures and I walk over there to lean up those great white triangles and watch the game from there. You still can't see much but at least the triangly thing keeps the wind off. It's always cold up here in the Winter for some reason and my leg is grinding away with some painful shapes.

There are goals and there is much shouting and singing at times but I feel detached for sure. I don't think I have anything to do with Wolves out here. Like the club is nothing to do with me. I see this in the people that are walking to work through the subway. Or going home from a shift somewhere. They walk with their heads down a little. This environment isn't theirs I suppose. I think it isn't mine either mate, not tonight.

FA cup matches are extra expenses. Extra money that has to be found. Extra time too. Can us humble fans afford this? I'm not moaning about it as I pull up my coat around my ears for a bit and peer into the Molineux to see what's occuring. I ask another fella what's going on as he has a phone in his hand. He gives me a psuedo commentary of what's occurred and I'm only half listening. Glory days for some. For others it's just another day. Thing is we are safe now...that's good. That's a weight off our shoulders for sure. Now I know the 'magic' of the FA cup is a thing. I know it will be great to go to Wembley stadium and watch our team play. I know this...but I don't feel it. I think you should hit every FA cup match to be given the moral right to walk up to Wembley in May. You've earned it for sure. But I haven't. All I want is us to be safe in the Premier League. To build a squad that will play in Europe. Dare we say that loudly now? With our position in the league?

Last season I was quite vociferous to the BBC and Premier League TV as they interviewed me that yes, there will be a European expedition in the near future for Wolves. I opined about walking arm in arm down some European city with some mates singing and dancing while the locals watched bemused. Wolverhampton in Europe. Everybody will go of course. There will be flights full of fans, beer drunk, songs, reports in the national press all the crap that goes with an English team in Europe. But it's not my battle any more I feel.

I won't be going to Europe with the Wolves because I don't belong there with them. I am just a doughnut and an average bloke. I am Nine Volt Bob bound up in the back of a van with parcel tape because he owes somebody money. I'm Shaky Ray holding a decrepid Disney radio in the air by a frozen canal while the snow blew down so he could get a signal. I'm Shaky Jake working down drains so he can pay his rent. I'm Gaz Mastic who delivers crates of out of date beer to people for a few quid a day. I'm a zero hours fan to be honest. I will now get to games that I can afford and not the ones I can't. These games are now not my games. I struggled with the Wolves over the years but now I don't have to help, I don't have to struggle any more because my team are all big and grown up. I will leave that to the new hip Wolves fans who search out hipster pubs in cities and towns pregame so they can drink their fruity beers. I will leave that to people who are connected to the club in some other way that isn't concerned with being a simple fan.

I suppose once upon a time there was a Tavern...but it's not there any more, there aren't any glasses to raise because you are on CCTV and the bouncers will kick you out for singing and dancing. We can't while away the hours anymore because we haven't got the time mate, I'm at work at nine, up at 5am tomorrow too, got to take the hours as they have taken next weeks off me because of profit margins and monthly figures.

It's cold up there on that hill and before full time I'm the only bloke left up there. Even those stalwarts on top of the bridge have pissed off to do something else instead. Something is going on in there for sure...but at the moment it's nothing to do with me and I wander off to grab a lift back home before it gets crazy on the roads. Mad times. I'm such a miserable bastard sometimes. Jesus Christ.

Chapter 34

Olly the Wickerman and We Break Manchester United Again

Awake. With a face like a fake Toblerone, like a punch in the bumhole, like a forbidden eyebrow...

It's one of those days. Those FA cup days ya know. When your dreams you have kept quiet since the early rounds starts to nibble away at your mind at inopportune times. It's not worry, it's that Nihilistic darkness that seems to grow as your expectations do. The semis will be at Wembley. We have a resurgent Manchester United down the Molineux with that confused Scandinavian fuck nugget Ole Soldskars or whatever his name is. He's got a face like he's looking at a magnet and wondering what strange magic this is.

I've got history with Manchester United and the people that support them. I remember their laughter you see. The snide comments from 'the Manchester side' of the family up North. Tempered you see, by the half smile and anger of the Wolverhampton side who has had to take all the 'Yanited' bollocks for many countless years. Soulskar has the look of a manager that has been day dreaming about getting back to his hard drive that night and not the football his team is about to play. He looks furtive as fuck on the telly later on. He doesn't know what he's doing you can tell. Yanited are now coached by Committee, a Politburo of Yanited Lizardry that ooze and slime their way through the plush soulless corridors of The Great Red Tomb...or Old Trafford as it's better known.

These Lizards are preening themselves in the hot sun of Yanited latest successes. But what do I see? I look at the team who denigrated their former Boss Jose Mourinho. Hounded him out of their club. Aided I daresay by lizard whispers from men in tight expensive suits. Perhaps these men have beards too, tight trousers, shitstopper trousers. I bet these men also have curly pointed shoes. The whispers in the ears of these Yanited players must have paid dividends because now THEY have the power. Of course the Lizards don't know how to Coach a team of radically dysfunctional narcississtic lunatics such as Pogba et al. Of course not. Now they have an Aunt Sally of a Coach...a former player (tick box), Champions League winner (tick box), former Old Purple nose acolyte (tick box). Of course Ollie will be the fall guy, the wicker man that burns on the skyline of Manchester when everything goes tits up.

At kick off I've been whacked in the head about eight or nine times by the flags Fosun has planted in our seats. I'm not waving a fucking flag...five seconds later I'm waving a fucking flag. I see the Steve Bull stand upper haven't been given no sexy gold, silver or black flags. That's because they are a very generous lot these Steve Bull stand regulars and they share things like flags, pies, bottles and even money with the less fortunate away sections below. God Bless the Steve Bull stand.

There are the lights and the flame boxes at pitchside. I can just about see Alan Shearers shiny bald head in the BBC Commentary box up the end of the stand. There is music. There is a flag in my ear. There is shouty man on the PA doing shouty man things. People are talking to me. I have a flag stuck in my eye. An elbow bongs me in the ear as something happens that I cant see because theres a transparent golden hue over everything all of a sudden as my mate Knocker holds his flag over my face. This is madness. The stand is shaking with the volume of songs being sung in this insanity of a stand. This Southbank is everything about this night. The late kick off. Thinking going up town for a beer at 3 O'Clock in the afternoon 'might be a bit early' but being there anyway and now after ten pints, a beefburger, probably twenty fags, and that might have been cocaine you snorted in the Royal London bogs but you weren't sure but now you are in a queue outside the Southbank with a hard raining falling, a stormy wind that blows up your back (and your front) everything is curly. The Steward searching everybody asks you to open your coat and that last vestige of heat you retained is gone into the air. You can't find the slot for the ticket thing, it's the wrong end of the ticket. Bollocks. You are trapped. You try to concentrate. Nuno had a dream. The ticket goes in the right end and the right way up. You are leaning on the turnstile so it just opens and you fall into the Southbank. It is time...for a Carling or that Cider that tastes like pop. Someone stumbles past you with blood streaming from their nose. You go 'oooh' and 'ugh' and 'bloody hell did you see his nose?'. I love this stand and I will miss it. It's really a home for me.

Nuno has set everything up. Saiss at the back in place of Benno who is suspended. Doherty wondering whether he has left his keys in his car again. Matt Doherty has the look of a man trapped in some sort of existential dread, like a man that has gazed deep into the abyss of our existence, a man...perhaps that has looked in the face of God...and lo and behold Moutinho jogs past and wizards the ball from Pogbas foot. Pogba doesn't care. He plays every match looking like a bloke being dragged around a Garden Center on a Saturday afternoon instead of playing beautiful football. It is sad for them they have splurged big dollar on this ineffective demoralising Clown. But it's not my problem. He's not our player thank God. He will probably go to another team in the close season. Maybe an Italian or Spanish one, but they may not put up with his bullshit there.

Conor Coady. What a beautiful player. He's laughing again at something. His movement is sublime and tactile and at others they are enforced and delivered with aggression that is controlled and organised, perhaps relentless too. He's our Captain in more ways than one. Nuno understands the need for a presence on the pitch.

An effective totem if you like for this philosophy Nuno has. Maybe we can even say he is the medium by which Nuno represents himself on the pitch? Whatever philosophical bollocks I can come up with can wait though as Coady dips the ball off some Yanited thing and the ball is recycled quickly to the front using Neves as the channeller, to Moutinho who dips a ball through red shirts to Raul and Jimmy has a half chance or maybe a quarter chance. Jimmy is also relentless. The ball can hit him anywhere and at whatever speed. Knee height, chest height, hits the shoulder, bounces off a Yanited defender, whatever. He is alive to it. He controls and he disseminates the ball here or there. To build the attack, to be academic about the shape and the way Nuno wishes him to play. To collect, to spread the ball, a half chance presented and Jimmy will stab the ball goalwards. But others feed and wait for his brilliance and they know how this man will play. Boly collects and grumbles the ball off a Yanited player. I think it's Hererrarah or something. He's a miserable looking sod. Bolys big leg busts him out of the way like a kid playing football with his Dad in the garden and Dads had four Carlings and thinks it's a real match and his kid is slide tackled into a pile of cat shit. The Herrera bloke gets up moaning at the Ref. There is a lot of that, chatting and bollocks. It's the ghost of purple nose for sure. We can hear his Scottish lilt if you listen closely, it's a drunken sad wailing.

Moutinho is here again nibbling away at things in midfield. This bloke never stops does he? But watch him and you can see the hard work for sure. But you can also see guile and vision. He knows what's going to happen before Yanited players do and he's chasing and moving in lovely arcs across the pitch. Collecting and probing, moving here and popping up there out of nowhere. Grabbing hold of possession. Again recycling, recon for sure. Searching out holes here and there so he can send maybe Jota ahead and into space or Jimmy who will hold it, waiting for his muckers to flood in.

Jota.The Little Wolf. Moving and running into gaps but also being playmaker at times letting someone, maybe Jonny Otto ahead of him and into some rich space. A few weeks ago many fans on Social Media were calling for Jota to be dropped. I laughed then and I laugh now. Diogo Jota is a bloke you will fight for six hours and still not gain an upper hand. My littlest Staffie Gizmo is Jota personified. He will have a go at anything, even horses. So if I extrapolate stadium insults from pricks who don't understand football our fans would have dropped Neves, sold Diogo, dropped Patricio, sold Coady (because he doesn't understand the sweeper role...no shit, that was said to me) and that Jimenez (ay strong enough). Fucking great isn't it? I'm glad these twats are safely out of the way in the stands.

At half time I stay in my seat and chill out for a bit. I'm still not thinking about Wembley yet...well a little bit. I know we are going to stuff Yanited tonight. You can tell. We knew when the draw was made a few weeks ago. We break teams. We have broke them in the past with a team of misfiring lunatics Coached by Mad Mick bless his heart. We break them for sure and Yanited look a bit broken.

Their fans who have come from as far afield as Tamworth, Cannock and Telford are silent for the majority of the game. I suspect they are sad because their team isn't shiny and new anymore. That maybe too, they have to go back home and gaze at the signed Nicky Butt Yanited shirt they bought at an auction once. They were a bit drunk and at the time bidding £1,200 for it seemed a great thing to do. Everybody was cheering in the pub as he stood up and bid. It was great. The laughing, carrying it home stumbling through the wastes of Tamworth, propping it against the wall, drunkenly exhorting the legacy of Nicky Butt to his wife who is ready to stab him. But Nicky Butts photo at the bottom of the frame is strange, the eyes seem to follow him around...

The family didn't eat for a few days...but Nicky Butt...they probably can't remember what he looked like now or what games he played in. Now they are standing at the bottom of the Steve Bull with a lukewarm pie donated from above trickling down their necks. Ollie at the wheel...Jesus Christ. It drones on and on. When the Dad collapses at work and dies that Nicky Butt framed shirt will go on ebay and they might make £100 on it.

Saiss is doing things. He loves it down that end playing Bennos role. Romain is throwing all sorts of niggly shapes into Yanited attacks. This normally ends up with a Yanited player on the floor holding a limb. It must be like having a fight with a rotary washing line playing against him. People just get tangled up in Saissness before crumbling into an incoherent mess on the floor. Sometimes they win a free kick and then Romain looks disgusted at the decision, like it's the biggest miscarriage of justice he's ever seen on a pitch. Other times he jogs on nonplussed knowing he just dug a stud in some football stars soft bits. The names Romain Saiss mate. Don't forget it.

I still haven't heard the famous Yanited away support sing. The Red Tomb has permeated their being. It sits above them like a Crimson mausoleum, looms. The ball is bobbling around the United box. Wolves are playing towards the Southbank this half. We draw in attacks with our songs and madness. We pull our team closer and closer to us time after time like our singing has some strange metaphysical attraction to our Wolves. It would be interesting to see how many goals are scored up this end as opposed to the Northbank. But yes, we draw them in for sure. Moutinho collects and he sees things we don't. He sees dead people...OK maybe not dead people but Moutinho extrapolates shapes from his mind and sees immobile United defenders who to be honest have the trims of dead people for sure. Bloody horrible.

Moutinho yeah, he has already moved between them even as he collects the ball. The move in his mind is already done and dusted before he moves a muscle. This is Matrix level shit and Mountinho is Neo doing the bullet time thing and boom. He's gone through them like shit through a Goose. He lays off to Jimmy I think and a shot, a deflection, the ball hits Jimmy at waist level. He is going to what? ...goal? Fucking hell. How did he...hang on. A flag in the armpit. An elbow in the nose, my glasses are gone. My face is shoved into a non too clean armpit (again) from a big man. I see my glasses, I fall back. I bend to pick them up laughing. A knee does my ear in. I am trod on. All I want to do is look at the Yanited fans and give them the what fors but I am grabbed and loved by people who smell of beer and happiness.

I don't care. 1-0 to us. A goal. Our singing made that and I shout but nothing is coming out but a feeble crackle. I have blown my voice already. Raul you fucking beauty. It was similar to his Tottenham goal. A hard stab of the foot/shin whatever and goalwards it went fooling the Yanited goalie who has been very good so far...but not now.

Limbage mate. Extreme limbage. There were people in the air I shit you not. This is when we are alive. Now we know the game is ours. We take full control of the whole game. We knock the ball about with a skillset that borders on the magical at times. Neves having a pop at goal from 30 yards. Doherty skilling up down the wing. Jonny Otto popping up making a nuisance of himself but away from the individual skills an almost metronomic tick tock of movement that just looped endlessly on the pitch. This is football. This is total football. It's just like watching Brazil, honestly. I know we sang it many times in the past with that ironic Wolverhampton humour but now? This is Brazillian football, it flows and it has a rythym all of it's own that confuses and demoralises the opposition. I think as well that maybe the fact this Wolves team enjoys playing together can also demoralise teams.

We smile and we fight again and again as the game progresses. It's about six minutes later and Jota is unleashed and picked out by a ball from midfield and Jota is versus Shaw who flaps and twangs away before Jota sends him on his arse. It's a tight angle, Jota controls, the simplest of controls and on his left foot bollocks the ball past the outstretched hand of the Yanited goalie. 2-0 to us. Que sera sera..whatever will be will be...we're going to Wem-berly. Horace is talking about booking Hotels and what a day we will have. He's already planned it out but hasn't said anything about it. But inside his 'oh I'm not bothered about the Cup blah blah blah' he has envisioned himself there already. The semis and then the big day out. Conor Coady lifting the Cup...fucking hell. Every one of us has done this haven't we? I can't hear the words FA Cup without seeing gold and black ribbons on each handle. I don't want to go. I am not making any strides to get a ticket. If one pops up I will go but I'm not breaking my back for one, no way.

Are we in the real world? Outside the ground after the match we are singing walking down the road. The last time I remember that was the Sherpa Van times. Bully, Mutch and Dennison. People laughing and shouting happy, good times. My mate Danny said to me in the Southbank 'Mikey we deserve this, we stood here when we sang, Que sera sera, what ever will be will be, we're going to Shrewsbury, Que sera sera" he shouted over the noise. Fuck yeah we do deserve it. We have done our time for sure and now this is us walking out of the Prison gates with our belonging in a green plastic bag and the sun is shining and it's a little bright, we have to squint to see properly but we are happy and we are content.

Chapter 35

The Destruction of the Great Red Machine (Part 3)

Well I did say Ollie Bummer Skyslice or whatever his name is would become some sort of 70s cinematic effigy...or something last time we played them. Oh dear, it's all going to shit for him isn't it? But what do you expect when you come across this team of ours right now, at this moment?

Nuno hasn't had to mallet any of these Wolves players into the team at all. After last nights win against Manchester United I hear that Fulham have been splunged straight back into the glorious madness of the Championship. Relegation my friends. Now there is a team that have been malleted into position so much they tend to let opposition players just run into their box and score. Amazing. It must be all the dents in their heads from Ranieri who got shifted for Scott Parker who looks like a Thunderbird puppet and by all intents has the fucking football coaching skills of one. Nah mate Nuno has molded our team, with words and teaching, philosophy that is debated with every kick on Compton Park.

I will miss the great piss ups in London before that game but I will not miss the sterility and forced jollity of their ground, which although quaint has a sort of favourite Aunt thing about it. Of course you love them but you don't want them hanging around too much. So last night I laughed at them and I laughed at Ollie whatever his face is as he watched pink unicorns and pretty bubbles float around him while he watched the team he 'coaches' get their bumholes well and truly fingered by our Portuguese and Mexican contingent, as well as a shout out to everybody else in the team that isn't Portuguese or Mexican.

I didn't go of course. I made the excuse that there was nobody here to look after my dogs but really I wanted somebody else to go with my ticket. They haven't seen a match at Molineux this season eventhough they watched us rattle out of the Premiership and down the leagues like a kebab through a pisshead. I wanted them to go, experience it and love it. Me? I've seen loads of games this season, not every one I know but enough thank you. I'm still getting over Benno at Bristol City last season to be honest. In fact I'm still not over Rob Hindmarches equaliser at the shit years ago. In fact I think I'm getting over all of last season at some strange slow pace. In fact, I don't think I will ever get over the madness of supporting Wolves. Ever.

You see when we actually achieved Premier League footy for next year (2019-2020) I took my foot off the gas. The points were in the bag mate, we are there and the great Gold and Black machine marches on. I actually remember sitting down in my chair and holding my head in my hands thankful and let the stress leak out of me in a series of long foul farts that had nothing to do with the football and more to do with a discounted dodgy smelling Ginsters steak bake from Tesco One-Stop on the Licky Road.

Strangely enough when I went down to Tesco before the match to buy a cold coffee, some Lindt chocolate and an Avocado...I saw Gaz Mastic in there buying some Rizlas. He says hello by the way. He keeps asking me for royalties from when I mentioned him in the last book. I had to buy him a four pack of Carling black label, I mean it's not even beer that stuff. But then again this is a book not quite like a book if you get my drift. It's just insane rambling about Wolves.

I am that bloke you never met before in the pub who leans on you as he's had five pints, he mutters and slurs in your ear about his medical problems, some Wolves stuff from the past, his car, his dog, his wife hates him, Steve Bull, the Sherpa van final, fucking hell I'm sorry. I do wish sometimes I could wear a tight suit, curly winklepickers, a quiff and nice teeth. Walk around looking at my phone a lot like those doughnuts at Compton the other week.

I'm not saying what I was doing there at Compton because I promised to be quiet about it. It was a secret. I'm a fucking Elite Superfan don't forget.

At Compton we are met by Paul Richards the 'Wellbeing Manager' or Liason dude, Me and Horace shook his hand and he nearly ripped my arm off. Big Alpha Male grip, a backwards and forwards motion to show you he will be a tricky one to grumble with. That eye like a Copper who is seeing the cut of your jib. Horace is beautiful and smart. I am wearing an old Czech Army jacket with the arms only having a tenuous connection to the rest of it. It's got more holes than Poundstretcher car park. I am wearing an old Motorhead T-shirt. My jeans have a pawprint on the knee which at first resembling mud soon (within) the heated opulance of Wolves

Training facility I realised was dog shit. It has earthy dogshit tones that tickle my nostrils as I relax on the comfy settee. There are two beautiful media dudes sitting there when we get comfy and before you know it they move away somewhere else. It's either the smell of dog shit or Horace just staring at them in the way Horace does. We are here to see Conor Coady and I look like a tramp or a Groundsman.

Paul Richards and Horace are man spreading at each other in the reception and talking about fitness subjects I have no idea of. Running and heart rates. Stuff like that. The Woman from Sky Sports News walks past us to the coffee machine. She has stilletos on and a big bum. I smile at her and she starts to smile then notices I am a tramp with a huge gap in his front teeth and dogshit on his knee. I've got a smile like an abandoned graveyard. She looks like she wants to be sick now. I try not to smile at any one and wish I could hide in the bogs until Coady turns up.

There is a zeitgeist here. You see I'm not saying much because I'm listening to people around me and soaking in the polished skirting board groove, the nice art photos of Wolves greats, the receptionist is lovely (she used to live by me but the posh end).

Players wander around in and out from training or creeping around in expensive sports footwear I've never heard of. You see the team have just finished training and are ambling back before Nuno does his Friday Press Conference. Tim Spiers turns up. Our Express and Star man is only mildly scruffier than me. He looks like a Maths Teacher. His shoes look like Cornish pasties.

I want to go in the press conference too but Paul Richards shakes his head. No. Spoilsport. I would have sat quiet for sure or Richards would have grabbed me by the head and dragged me outside. Then there would have been a big upset. Eccentric Author in Compton Assault shock. Or some bollocks like that. I wanted a roll up. No way you can smoke a fag outside, not when players are milling about. I wonder if there is a quiet corner...but Coady is out. I'm not going to say about what went on. Only that Coady is a beautiful well mannered young man, affable and funny, witty, an absolute pleasure. He has great teeth. I try not to smile. Horace smiles, he has great teeth too. Everybody has great fucking teeth here. No NHS bollocks mate. Private health care. Money teeth.

But I digress. The thing about Compton was an underlying groove I thought at first was a kind of aloof and polished thing...apart from Conor of course. But there were a lot of sharks in there. You can tell the sharks. They have beards and aren't fat. Tight trouser lizards always checking shit on their phones, always have their collars up. Always side glancing around. It scared me a bit. I'm an empathic sod at the best of times but here this sharkery was spinning around the room like the smell of shit on my jeans. It was palpable. That's the word. It didn't seem like Wolves. Years ago you could walk into the recpetion at Molineux and nobody would have a clue what was going on anywhere. Now it's scary. There is something here and that thing I think is 'busy'. There is an air of busy bollocks going on.

Jonny Otto and Jota walk through the reception. I don't say anything I just half grin hiding my teeth. I'm sure I look a right sight. I attempt a little gay wave that I subdue quickly and put my hand in my pocket quick. Boly...his hamstrings are like fucking undersea cables. He looks like an end of level Boss on a computer game. You would go 'fucking hell' I swear. But Jota and Jonny look like killers on a mission. They wouldn't look out of place in a Taratino film. I have Tarantinos private email address. I might send him a mail asking if Jonny and Jota can have a part in his new film or something. They would look great.

I know how Diogo Jota gets through games now. I described him in Volume 1 as having an attitude like a 'Little Wolf' and yet here he is being the Big Bad Wolf. Yaniteds attempt to snap Jota explain many things to me. Yanited have lost the game. They have lost the war possibly too. There is no discipline within this set up to play football. Instead Yanited are 'playing' football.

At Compton Nuno strides out into the press room. He's fast and smiles and waves at us. I do a proper Mom wave and laugh. Nuno. Bloody hell. He's dressed in a tracksuit and is chilled out. He has great teeth. I am still ten feet away from him. Always at a distance. Loads of people I know have met him but I suspect I never will. I am not beautiful enough. I would say stupid things and get ushered away like a deranged lunatic. Back to my bin where I live with a hot Greggs sausage roll in my hand and that face people pull when they give the homeless something.

I'm watching the Yanited match on Now TV and Ollie Skalpshine or whatever his name is stares into the Wolverhampton skies with a face like he's just bongoed half a gramme of Ketamine up his hooter. To be fair Pogba looked like he had partook also. Moutinho keeps taking the ball of his foot. He keeps doing it during most of the match and every time he does it I am laughing my tits off on the chair. At one point the dogs bark. Pogba, Jesus. What strikes me now, is that I'm making connections quickly in my mind and extrapolating my Compton experiences with this display, this dismantling of a very good team by Wolves.

Vinagre was at times unplayable. Neves should have a statue erected right in the midfield the amount of work he put in. But how does one wax about the whole team. I would try to explain the match to Gaz this morning but he says Yanited outplayed us. I look at his stupid vacant face and laugh. He also said we were lucky to win. I laugh some more. There is much jollity by the veg aisle at Tesco. Gaz is being negative again but I recognise it, I've been there lately. It's the disconnect again.

Wolves are busy but they are still engaged for sure. Compton or Shark Mountain as I'm going to call it is a hive of activity. Things look planned and thought about. Things that are alien to me in my disorganised state. Luke Shaw is hilarious isn't he? He makes me laugh out loud several times. Jota is making him look very silly.

Nuno has lashed out a full strength team only a few days before we play Watford in the FA cup semi finals at Wembley. This is a statement he has been making since he came here. Always shape, and hard work, Ideas and movement, communications within the team, making sure we are a team and always to win but not at all costs no, to win our way, the right way.

This is going to be a very weird weekend, I can feel it. Watford are a good team and they beat us up here at Molineux at the start of the season. But we are not that team that got beaten that day. We are much different now. The broader brush strokes of last year has been replaced by detail and layer upon layer of analysis, reaction and indeed solutions to many of the problems we had at the start of the season. Not massive problems but we lacked maybe an extra gear to zip up to when we had teams on the back foot. Who knows. I am excited of course but I'm looking at the season after next. That's the Fosun and Nuno way I suppose. Everything planned and set up.

I watch Olly Bumhole Soulshines press conference after the game. He looks sad and depressed but he keeps trying to get his eyebrows animated like he is pretending that something happened. He looks like a kid that has broken a window at school and he is denying it in the best way he can. I had great excuses for everything when I was a kid. It was the beginnings of a fantastic imagination that kept me out of Prison. Olly looks like that but he lacks the dynamic believable excuses I had. Poor bastard. He will be gone in the summer I will put money on it.

But then again I am a scruffy bastard covered in dogshit and I couldn't organise a bus stop circle jerk. What do I know about how everything will pan out?

Chapter 36

Mexiyamyams, the wrong drugs and the F.A Cup Semi final

I just had a long conversation with a man with no ears. He was throwing a magnet in the canal trying to fish out some treasure that has a value only to our no eared friend. I know him vaguely from somewhere but he has such a poached egg eyed look about him I don't want to hassle him with his past in any way. That of course has no bearing on our club just splurging out some 30 million squid for Raul Jimenez our (currently) 15 goal 'striker'.

Watching our no eared friend dragging the odd steel pailing and shopping trolley from the turgid clay of Wenny cut I try of course to extrapolate some analogy somewhere that links this mangled human being in front of me with us throwing an inconcievable amount of cash out for a bloke when I'm still trying to get my head around Grant Fucking Holt and the rest of the doughnuts Moxey dragged through the golden gates of Molineux to excite the masses. The only thing about Holt that was interesting is that he had bigger man boobs than me. Grant Holt. Jesus Christ. Oh fuck. Sagbo. Remember him?

When I first saw Jimenez I was a little amazed and pissed off. He had great teeth. He seemed lovely. He looked quite normal. He had a nice starter family, beautiful squeeze...he had some nice football too. Thing is he 'looked liked he grew there'. That was the term my mate Roy used to use when we had fitted some component that was a bit fiddly and fettly.

We would stand back and have a few minutes admiring it and kicking it to see if it fell off. At lunch times we would eat our sandwiches on the car park of the factory just behind Monmore Green dog track and feed the 'rots'. Some of them were as big as Cats.

Raul comes from Tepeji in Mexico, it has a lot of similarities with Wolvo by the fact it has basically the same population and shares others...there's not a lot to do there. He soon upped sticks as it was found he could fettle a ball around a pitch with some aplomb. Club America to Madrid, then on to Benfica before rumbling over on a plane to see Nuno and what Nuno had to say.

Jimenez is a Mendes lad I think. Uncle Jorge eh? We haven't heard much about him this season for some reason. Perhaps because those whining wankers at Witton Park are concerned with something else now. But Jorge and Jimmy. He has 'economic rights' dangling off him and some strange financial shenanigans going on which I have no clue about neither do I care. Raul I have watched for a season and to be honest it looked as if he had grown in the side rather than just been lumped in. I know we had some misfires at the start of the season. Cavaleiro and Costa have kind of struggled. Can I say that? Struggled? They haven't found their feet much in this side. There was of course going to be an element of fumbling as they tried to muscle in on the show but with Jota also attempting to derive any joy out of the seasons start it was going to be all uphill.

You see at the start of the season (and this book) I do wax lyrics about the skills of one Rafa Mir who I expected to be that traditional number 9 I wondered if we needed. I expected Rafa to explode onto the scene with his rumbling attacks he showed he could do at Walsall. I still think Rafa could do a job but Raul..

Jimenez controls games up the top. His physicality and his presence are scary for me. Scary because I'm still watching Grant Holts man tits boinging around like two coconuts in a stocking. Now look where we are. Jimenez controls and he dictates. He holds the ball up. He's a lanky git so he can get in the air for that flick on or header. If the ball is lower he will trap, control and move waiting for an onrushing Jota or another Wolves body to slice in and join in with the fun. Is there no way through Raul? Simply move the ball with your feet. I have watched him terrorise defences this season not only with his movement but with his brain. He's not thick this Jimenez lad. He has the Philosophy of Nuno down beautifully. I suspect he wasn't brought in as a pair of legs or as a goalscorer initially...perhaps Nuno requires more from a player than this gung-ho athleticism, perhaps he requires a player to understand his role within the team and to process large blocks of sensory information that overloads some players sometimes.

Of course at the crux of a match when the game could change on the introduction of a new idea or a new movement then he is ready to execute the move and to extrapolate upon it too. Certainly during the season he has grown into the role. Now he has the cut and the jib of what Jota will do, where he will be and what he will do. That is why (I think) they have struck up this strange telepathic ability to know where each other are at the precise moments possibly. I know during the match against Yanited there were moments when it was almost spooky to watch. Plus he can dink a ball in the net himself. Fifteen goals so far and I've seen most of them. Now watching Pogba get robbed by Moutinho last week makes me think 30 million squid is a fucking steal.

My mate Steve rang me up last year and said his removal men had let him down. He was going off his head. Can I help? I've got a van, I'm not doing anything. We could use that and I'm a big strapping bastard, I can carry things. We slaved I ay joking. Well I slaved as Steve has the arm muscles of a fucking boiled whelk. So I got all the heavy shit but I didn't mind. We got it done and dusted and I pissed off home aching but glad I had helped me mucka out. That weekend I was going to Wales for a chill out. Steve come around the next day with a bottle of Moet Champagne and a box of extrememly expensive chocolates in thanks for helping. Wahey, I said to myself. It will make a change from a bottle of Aldi real ale and a stale hobnob. Living life large mate. In Wales I bust the cork out of the Moet and poured it into a half pint beer mug I had nicked from somewhere and away we go.

Here's the difference. That was a 30 squid bottle of plonk. That was a 20 squid box of chocolates I was cramming in my fat gob as I gazed at the glorious mountain scenery around me. I was pissed as a fart within half an hour and people could hear me singing Wolves songs in the forest and whacking the vegetation with a whippy stick I had found. The dogs looking at me like I was losing my mind. That's the difference my friends.

Now Wolves are rocking the fucking Moet and the fresh Belgian chocolate grooves. The feeling I got from the Moet is that yeah, I could get used to quaffing Moet while I relaxed in my mountain abodes. Grant Holt wouldn't even make it onto the shelves of Aldi. Refreshing quality over insipid hops. Belgian Chocolate artistry over half a packet of Hobnobs. It sounds like Raul is Belgian here but trust me I couldn't wax over the insipid luxury of an Enchillada so you get my drift.

Welcome Raul. I hope our madness and stupidity doesn't make you wish you were somewhere else playing footy. In Nuno you have a Philosopher. Here you will grow into an unstoppable player and one festooned with honour. Jimenez is the Moet of players. He tickles the taste buds footballing wise, bubbly, tickles your nose, and he has pedigree and class, quality. The beautiful sod has the looks of an Italian movie star in one of those Fellini films maybe. He has pathos and emotion in him, Da Vinci would have drawn him as a young David possibly. The touches of tempura would have been delicate as not to disturb the deep emotions that drive the whole character of Jimenez.

Which brings me to the FA cup Semi on Sunday. Watford, the Elton Gollums. They have been running riot over the past few weeks doing a number on some big teams with their style of play which is quite similar to ours but for one thing. They only really have one string to their bow. Will they put on a display for their fans? I'm not sure, have Watford sold out their allocation for Wembley? I have a quick look, no they haven't. What's going on there then? What's the zeitgeist with their fans? Don't they want to watch their team? They don't seem much bothered. I like this. It sets the scene for a Raul masterclass, a slice or two of madness from Jota and the team will flourish in the madness of our joy, I can see it now.

You see Wolverhampton love a Cup run and a chance of glory. We don't really talk about it much but the FA cup and a trip to Wembley is a real thing for a lot of Wolverhampton residents and Wolves fans. We see the whole event as another way to show the world that we exist and we live. As soon as we were going to Wembley the ghosts started creeping into my mind. The semi at Hillsborough against Tottenham where I could feel the air being squeezed out of my lungs in the Leppings lane end, losing my shoe and walking back to the train station with one shoe. The Sherpa van final delirious with happiness, singing, shouting as a Burnley fan irate and insane through ineffective punches at my head after we stuffed them in the game. Thinking back now out of five of us that went to those games only two of us are alive now.

That's why I'm going to Wembley. That's why I'm taking my seat down the front and going to watch my team. I know we are beautiful and crazy on the pitch. I know Nuno will have us set up. Wolves isn't the team Watford beat a couple of months ago when Raul was raw and learning. Moutinho was trampled in that game. Now we have Donk. Now we have intent. I'm going to watch our team for the people we have lost because in my minds eye I can see again all the ghosts pressing against the seats willing us on to victory. I can see them as fresh as if it was the 80's all over again. The places we went and the madness we experienced.

So here is me. Ghosts on the one side and coat choices on the other. What's the weather going to be like, will I be too hot? Should I wear my walking boots instead of the Adidas. Should I dress smart or just go in my normal scruff? How much money should I take? The ghosts gather laughing. Who fucking cares. Have some beers, have a chat, sing the songs loud until you can't sing any more. God help our poor minds.

Did you get a ticket? There are many tales of woe here. Attempts to coerce tickets from friends and family. A vicious battle to obtain this script, this odd piece of card embossed with foil prettiness maybe, some element of worth, maybe it insuates to us that it is precious in some way? We have paid a lot of money for it. We hold it like a Willy Wonka Golden ticket. What we don't do is run outside in the street as the movie camera rises on it's cherry picker platform over the roofs and gardens of our neighbourhood as we scream into the sky holding the ticket and waving it in the air like some errant mad gump or an insane escapee. No we don't do this. Instead we hold it like a cursed thing. We are glad to have it but...Wembley. Semi final mate. FA Cup.

What will those minutes be like? In that cavern of a place. We will stand and sing our songs full of gassy lager. Expensive lager with all the alcoholic content of a bitter shandy. It's always 'Lite' something and has a crisp refreshing taste. There is normally some curly blurb advertising about it. Beautiful people drinking it and having fun. The sun will shine I hope. The walk will be something to tell somebody about I daresay, that walk towards the stadium. Everything is shiny again. Everybody has their new

Wolves shirts. I see Jotas name on a lot of them. Jimenez too. The odd Neves. Everybody is smiling and laughing. They are on a day out and are slathering the spectacle down their throats as fast as they can. There are shrieks of excitement from some. But the lads are quietly drunk now, the factory grey skin of them in contrast to their 'outside' working mates who are cherry red with building site windburn and Spring sunlight. They queue and stare at their Adidas shoes, fumble with a ticket. Laugh at something they didn't understand because they were thinking about something else. The seat number, the gate number, the concourse this and that. You see somebody you know and you just gurgle something stupid at them as you press your way through the madness and the darkness too.

Nuno will be thinking now. Pressing flesh and doing crazy high fives with people. I bet he has done his homework on Watford. They took the piss out of us at Molineux. They are somewhere without actually getting there if that makes sense.

I bet he is relishing this chance to do Watford. I think out of all the games he played this season the Watford defeat is one that would rankle the most. It did with me. Today isn't about the Cup and the Wembley day out. It's about revenge. I want to see us break this Watford team. Make them return home with their hands holding their heads as they stare out of the team coach blacked out windows seeing the long lines of traffic and their own battered countenance like a spectral image reflected back. I hope we destroy them I really do.

So the day after Wembley, the semi final of the FA Cup? I'm cutting the grass on the front garden. It's a lot of grass and I have left it maybe a few weeks overdue for a mangle with the Flymo. It's fucking typical isn't it? I'm taking out my rage on the vegetation, wrangling the mower like I'm trying to strangle it. Whipping the electrical lead like a whip, lashing some bastard half to death. What a pretty plant. Mow the fucking thing to death. Chop it's shitty head off. The lead tangles in a Rose bush. I rip the bush out of the soil in a rage. Yes, I'm in a mood. The extension lead is stuck in something. I rip it away and throw it up the garden. I fetch it back. Go to turn the mower on again. It wont come on. Somebody has turned the fucking plug off. Fucking hell. I want to weep so I sit on my bench...in my pocket is yesterdays gold carrier bag I had to hold up in yesterdays 'Fanorama'. I might put it over my head.

'You've missed a bit' Shakey Jake says. He's at the gate, tries to open it. He pulls the gate off it's hinges. I am not smiling or laughing.

Chapter 37
The Eltons, A Semi Final and The Wrong Drugs Again

Arriving at Wembley I manage to make my way into the ground and I fancy a quick slash to be honest just to make everything run ok when I'm in there..."Mikey!". Some Wolves Youth I know is shouting me and grabbing me and we exchange pleasantries. He wants me to come into the cubicle with him...oh ar?

He shuts and bolts the door and takes a small plastic packet out of his Stoney. A bump before the game? Why not, I'm on me holidays ay I? It's a day out, I haven't had a drink...and I'm justifying my drug use can you see? He dips a none too clean front door key that's hanging from a bit of string around his neck. He dips it into the powder at the bottom of the bag. A good bump for sure and I bend down and get it up my nose. He laughs and I laugh and he's off into a throng of similar youth, same trims, same Stoney gear.

I laugh again and wait for the coke to blazzle my head but instead. The bog door is like a curtain all of a sudden. I can't find the lock on it or how to get out. Oh Shit. It seems like an impenetrable fog, a delight of warm visions, tones, noises are now muted and it's like I have headphones on and the Jazz coming through them is biological not soundwaves. Bollocks. Something has gone wrong here.

The lights are wavering, I feel cold and then hot and then laugh out loud while all these people are pissing. It stinks in here. The floor looks like a fucking sea. Somebody says something to me and I walk past them jibbering. Little sod has given me a bump of Ketamin instead of Coke. Now instead of jabbering away at the football I am contemplating the roof of Wembley with a fucking wandering pair of eyes. I must look like Marty Feldman or Chunk out of the Goonies. I have to sit with civilised people at this game. Bollocks. Shit. Am I ever going to see it?

Fuck, I have to behave so I am fighting the K-Hole like a Space Marine. I see the lad eight rows back from me and he is looking at his Adidas in some sort of contemplative Buddha shape. Ketamin makes you insular and inward looking and all I want to do is look outwards at the team. The car breaks down on the way here. I have a bump of Ket. I feel like I'm swelling up and I wish somebody would let me down again. The team are warming up and it looks like we have 200 players doing the YMCA dance. Then the pitch is a Snooker table and all these players are now balls. I find my seat I think. People are telling me things and I don't know what they mean so I shut up and don't say anything. I tell Mari next to me that Gomez or whatever his name is has a head like a pencil rubber but all I say (I think) is, 'Gubbler bubbler mini nunnel balbb gubbler'. Where has Mari gone?

I am laughing at Watfords Goalkeeper on the big screens of Wembley pre match. I am by myself and I am laughing by myself. Gomez or whatever his name is has a head that looks like the rubber on top of a thick kids pencil...sorry a kid with special educational needs...er on the 'spectrum'? I'm sure I have already said this to somebody. Where the fuck is Horace? Gomez is funny and I am laughing at him. He looks like a fire on his face was beaten out...with his own face. I'm not in a good way here folks, dear readers. I don't know what's happening and strangely I don't care either. Ketamine is a Horse tranquilliser. I am wrapped in a warm voluminous duvet with only my face hanging out. I can't feel my hands and I grab my own face to see if I am actually still here. The car broke down on the way here and now this. My fingers look like deep sea anemonies. They might even be somebody elses fingers. Has the match started? People are singing the Jimenez song we nicked off Liverpool who nicked it off River Plate. Is that right? Does Raul always score? Who is Raul? For a minute I am at the Sherpa Van trophy again and watching Robbie Dennison.

The Elton Gollums up the other end are waving their flags like lunatics. We have plastic bags to hold up so I miss most of what's going on when the teams come out. My arms ache and I put them down. When I put my arms up my shirt collar becomes tight around my neck. I found out today I had left the cardboard stiffener in it. It's a new shirt see. No wonder I couldn't breath yesterday. I put the bag down when I start to feel faint and lose the feeling in my hands. My coat is too small. It's Horaces. I am expecting one of the buttons to ping off and embed itself in the bloke in fronts head. He pongs a bit to be honest. Athletic shirts aren't meant for unathletic people. My head has this wrapped in cotton wool feeling. For a minute I think we are in the play offs and we are playing those stripey North Birmingham bastards. A.L.B.I.O.N shit on them shit on them. But it's Watford and I'm trying to work out if Watford is an anagram of West Brom and I mean it's troubling me and for most of the first half that is all I'm thinking about. I'm sure that's Robbie Dennison on the pitch. Fucking hell Nuno why did you bring Robbie back? He must be 80 years old now. Jesus Christ it's Nigel Vaughn! No seriously...but no it's Jota. Jesus Christ on a bike. I laugh and say to Mari 'Schubble hubba dunga runnel splurk' or something. She looks at me like I am deranged and yes. I am.

I look around to see if I know anybody around me but all I see is strangers really. Apart from Mari next to me, and Carlos her son. I only got a ticket through Steve Greens kindness. I ay paid him yet either. All my mates are elsewhere dotted around. We are very colourful for sure. There are Ponchos and Sombreros and all that bollocks. People eating Krispy Kreme doughnuts (85 quid for two) or a Bagel (59 quid for one). I can tell the dude in front of me doesn't know the team. He keeps getting the names wrong and the songs too, then he shuts up shouting for a bit because he is eating a pie and he has to concentrate on that as it cost him 90 quid. I am staring at the bloke behind me of me eating a bagel. His lad is looking at him with plaintive eyes hoping for a bite but the greedy bastard is eating it all himself. A piece of Lettuce is on his lip dangling. I feel sick. Then my foot goes to sleep.

There is football going on...sorry. I said a few pages ago I think, that the FA Cup is nice but we are in 7th place so far in our first season back in the Premier League. We have over attained, we have done fucking brilliantly to be honest. I am so proud of our town and our team that I have become a lot happier over the past few weeks. How beautiful our team are and how fucking magnificent. At the end of the match a few of our players collapsed in exhaustion at their loss after extra time 3 goals to 2. I wanted to run on and pick them up and say stand proud, applaud the Elton Gollums if you have a mind. But be proud of how you fought. Fairytales never come true, you know that. To reach a final where we would have beaten Manchester City and won the FA Cup? Europe next year? The madness of bantering the idiots down the road to death? Oh man. Heaven it would have been.

I don't care what happened during the match. Honestly. I knew the trip would be weird, I felt it in my bones. I had a feeling things would go to shit. It's too soon. You can't have your cake and eat it. It's too bloody soon, you can't ladle this lovely football and this zeitgeist all over us without some comeback. There has to be a Monday morning, just has to be. Otherwise we would just be living on a great big fluffy Gold and Black cloud forever. You know life isn't like that.

But is that time now? We have one of the smallest squads in the Premier League. Our depth (after) rebuilding this club from the bottom up has not been great. We do lack some volume to the squad probably if not in terms of quantity then definitely quality. I notice when other teams make a substitution then it is with a quality player, a star in their own right, game changers. I think at the moment we lack this and the important variable in this moan isn't the investment or the ability of the club staff. It's time, that is the most important variable. We are still very much learning to walk in this League. I thought at first it was a pantomime of a place where expensive players groove the whole thing. But it's much more subtle than that, much more layered. That I think is the moral of this heart break for us. It's still bloody early, we are are still one year ahead of the plan. We aren't supposed to be promoted until the end of this season.

It's a puzzle that takes a thinker to break down and find a way through to Europe via finishing in the ambrosia end of the table high enough to escape the mid table hand biters like Everton and West Ham. We have a young squad of men for sure. They too learn with us what this place is all about. But all of us do not know this place. Us fans included. Wembley wasn't a day out for me, it wasn't a day on the lash or doing key bumps in a pissy London toilet. I just wanted to give some thanks to the team, I wanted to enjoy just watching them play football. There were some surreal moments for sure, Ruddy threw some weird shapes. Boly looked like he didn't know what was going on. I'm naming names and I shouldn't because nobody is to blame. Nobody at all. If anybody was to blame it was us, for daring to dream again after the joy of last year. That dreaming was in full throw for sure. Robert Plant must have had his photo took with everybody yesterday. For a very private man he loves the Wolves fans. I contrast this with Elton John who drove past us after the game in his Rolls Royce with black windows. But Planty...He was dreaming in every photo I've seen. You can tell. It's obvious. Dreaming.

We looked tired for sure. Gone was that zest of the Yanited game, the zippy passes and the fluid gracious movement. This was a lot tamer and

Watford for most of the game were the same. Then they find a cheeky key bump of their own and we are chasing shadows all over the pitch. Doherty the scorer of our first goal looks scared to death again. Raul is tireless he is everywhere...but nowhere at the end. We can't find that extra, that little bit left in the tank. Neither can the Wolves crowd. The atmosphere is muted when it should have been deafening. We probably knew, the fans that do go to a lot of games, that this was just too much to bite off, and we choked. 3-2. Fucking hell. What a demolished team that is. Now the Ket is wearing off a bit and I want to go to sleep maybe. The faces around me are long and sad but the fact I snorted half a teaspoon full of some strange Horse tranquilliser has made me immune to such sadness. Still Wolves ay we? Still a great team. But then I feel like a twat for being a twat.

Me Horace and Ammo are in the restaurant after the game eating. Ammo is sad because we are waiting for the AA man to fix the car. Beaconsfield on the edge of the London sprawl hangs like a piece of snot from the honking great hooter of this capital city. Horace is sad because he never got a foam hand.

I am sad because I'm a fat bastard and my clothes are too tight and I am still eating. There is a man behind us. He comes in with his girlfriend, she is as big as an aircraft carrier. We watch his sadness as she orders enough food to feed a large family and proceeds to cram it in her gob as he just looks at her eating. It must have cost easily 50 quid. Horace counts eight portions of fries on her plate when he goes past on the way to the bogs. I stare at her back, it's wider than my fridge. He doesn't say anything, he just watches her eat. We all watch her eat as the AA man does his car shit and we can begin the long journey back. I think about Nuno while I watch her wrench a Chicken wing around her mouth like an electric toothbrush.

Nuno looks like he is cutting my grass. His hands are everywhere and he is shouting, angry, demanding, controlled, then incensed again at some transgression of his team or the Elton Gollums. I love him I think. I've never seen such passion in a Manager. After Lambert, Jackett, ok Zenga was a lunatic, but we all knew that. Nuno will have things to say and I see this...even at the last gasp, the last dying minutes the backroom staff never ceased to debate, point, record everything that was happening on the pitch. Even a defeat can be useful.

It gives us experience and we use that experience in the future too. Nuno himself chews his moustache, pulls his beard, exhorts and commands until all is lost and you can tell there is no darkness in him at all. There is anger for sure, but not anger at the team or the result. It is anger at himself, he should have seen this or that, he should have applied this or stuck here, there, moved this way brought so and so in. He looked like he had just mown my grass for sure.

Coady was gutted. That is what hurt me the most as he is my favourite player, still. If we could have won the game I would have been happy just for him. Fuck my happiness and joy, it would all be for the team, just them. Instead Conor walks off dejected. But there was really no need at all Mr Coady. You were all magnificent...and Conor, one day you will hold aloft an honour we have won. Then we will sing, then we would dance too.

There will be a thousand and one inquests on social media by fat men with their faces buried in phones with their other hand fondling their genitals. This is the way of the wong for sure. My own mind will not be sullied with that bullshit. I apply a forensic eye to the bigger and more Fosun like picture.

Our Owners would have liked yesterday very much. The whole history of this tournament and the history of our club is very much revered by them and now they are part of the narrative. Fosun will want to lift that Cup trust me. If they weren't keen before this year they will be now for sure. The pomp and the circumstance will get right in their blood. Now they will amend plans and ascertain the tactics and the policies needed to dominate these kinds of games in the future. Now the phones will be ringing, text messages, emails, interactive whiteboards, seminars maybe, learning, building and teaching too. Molineux in the close season will be insane. There will be no let up, no close season, no self congratulations. I am reminded of when Jez Moxey went on holiday during one close season not so long ago. Now, there is pure intent.

We are not angry, but we are sad, but not that sad. It's but one battle lost and the greater war to win. There will be other Cup runs in the future for sure. Probably the road will be as bumpy as Troy Deeleys face but we will get there at some point. The dude with the girlfriend/fridge is paying for her food. He picked at his fries and left most of his burger. His heart wasn't in it. Now he will probably get his dong sucked in his 05 plate Audi with the bass box in the back and the alien head air freshener. He will watch it rock from side to side as she does her thing. He will probably watch us get back in Ammos car now it's been fixed and wonder why we look sad as he gets his car park blow job off a human boulder. We aren't sad mate, we are just pissed off we are too old to smash things up any more.

The day after the whole Wembley thing we are still pissed off of course. We are 'snarky' at work. 'They' laugh at us, you know who they are, the Wittonites, the North Birminghams, the Small Heaths. We mumble under our breath, we throw things. Even the dog just stares at us wondering what's going on. I keep going on Youtube to see what Nuno has to say about the whole show. I do this because he makes me feel better about the whole thing, that there is somebody looking after our delicate football fan brains, massaging them with the right words. I would have loved to have been at the Compton training ground this week listening and learning more about how 'we' do things now. But we are just the smelly fan, we have to deal with this shit ourselves of course. Us and the dog. Often I am reaching out to people who's opinions I trust trying to get them to talk to me about the game. I wouldnt call it a 'post mortem' but something similar. The odd message or conversation with someone who understands this game better than me can have me drooling or crying.

But how beautiful we looked walking down Wembley way. There were thousands of us, all dressed up half pissed for the most part. Crazy with the whole day and what was about to happen. Horace always said Wembley is great if you win, but the long journey back with the cold fingers of your hangover kicking in, a headache from singing so much, your feet hurt, you have spent £200 on a bagel and a doughnut. What terrors those journeys are. Watching England slide past the windows as we travel back to the homeleand.

We of course travel back to 'Wulvo' because that is where we live. Some go back to their own towns and cities and Wolverhampton is simply 'Wolverhampton'. Where do we live again? Wulvo? Nah sorry...Wulverampton. To others it is 'Wolves' but I don't know people who call it that, we don't move in the same circles I'm afraid.

Chapter 38

Southampton and Blood is in the Water

Awake!. With a face like a free range finger banging, like a laughing Snail, like a wife swapping party in a leaky Yurt. In the distance Nuno is packing his flip flops...

Walking out of the Shampton ground after that 3-1 defeat I was happy. In fact I was in quite a jolly mood. Most of us were pissed off of course but it was that round shouldered defeated look that crept around most of the new Wolves shirt clad masses. Even the Shampton Gollums streaming out of the ground looked sad. I tried to hide my happiness for a second, failed. Started smiling again.

'We ay won a game since you deleted ya blog" Some dude says to me. I don't know who he was but he knew me. Three Cops are staring at me too. I'm starting to feel paranoid so pretend to blend in, I fail. One of the Cops takes my photo. I wonder if it's going on Instagram. I hope I haven't got a bogie on my nose. I was a bit sniffly in the ground.

I wasn't sad because so far we have had an amazing season. Top half of the Premier League mate. One of the best young Managers in Europe, a young rapidly learning team who bear the scars of their first year in this madhouse of a league. It was a baptism borne from fire definitely.

"Traore you useless cunt!"

Someone shouts behind me. They have shot their bolt a little early. Adama has the ball and is about to...well he doesn't fall over. Somehow he is back on his feet and he is hurtling towards the byline. He is unstoppable once he works his magic...if he doesn't fall over again. The comment is unleashed towards our player but Traore rights himself and is off again. Boom! He sticks a lovely cross in but there is nobody there and the ball farts across the box like a wet wipe in a lay by and frizzles out for a throw in to them. They take their time fetching the ball. They are ambling now in that way we have seen so many so many times before. Gamesmanship I suppose. But like I said before when you use those tactics during a game then you don't really have anything else to offer.

We didn't really play, I know that. Perhaps that's wrong. We played, but the Gods had other ideas on the outcome today. It was Shamptons turn to embrace the victory and the plaudits. I think the win makes them safe from relegation now but I don't care. The whole place could get bulldozed for me. I have no love for this place.

Errant defending by the whole team allowed Shampton three glorious goals for their fans while we tended to run around in circles doing lovely shapes but really nothing that was alive and dynamic at all. Perhaps it was that wounded team thing, they always fight harder. Relegation blood in the water and Shampton have found a little energy from somewhere to grind a win against us. Every effort we tended to rustle up was negated by a bobble of the ball to a Shampton player. Our attacks were often disjointed and weird. Nobody was in the right place. We weren't in pieces but faryed I think would be a better description.

You can blame certain players definitely. Some were well off the mark in terms of movement and shape and that disjointed rythym seemed to grow more discordant as the game went on. I wanted to do the half time team talk to be honest. Ten minutes with them and I could have moved them a little. Pointed out a few observations. But I'm not the Coach. I am just a frazzled broken doughnut.

Every tactical error was a glaring 500 watt spotlight into how a teams preparation for a game can become unravelled and tattered within seconds of a game starting. They scored in the second minute. My eyes hadn't even had time to focus on the pitch before a Shampton blob of colour lifted the ball over Rui Patricio who punched the turf a bit just to show how pissed off he was and Coady stands open mouthed in shock before his brow wrinkled and he looked like he wanted to punch someone. We are chasing the game again. Fucking hell.

This time of course I couldn't blame the Referee who seemed to have some relationship with the rules of the game but applied them in a very slap dash way and in situations where he should have allowed play to flow he was quite happy to brandish the odd card at a Wolves player after some innocuous challenge or well...for whatever fucking reason. It was a pretty surreal comedy of officialdom to me. Standards of refereeing eh? The Linos had the same problem. The ball is dribbled just out of play by a Shampton player. The Ref blows his whistle. The flag stays down. The Officials look at each other. The players look at the officials. The Officials look at each other and eventually the Ref decides on giving a foul. Even the Shampton players are bemused. Jonny Otto looks like he's ready to burst into tears. I would love to hear what goes on over their microphones and headsets. It's probably like listening to Teletubbies running over the grass excited and confused at something. The Lino looks at the Referee like he's just been found pissing on the new rug. Puppy eyes at the Ref. Please make the decision for me, I'm just a sensitive twat with Soya bean muscles and a trim that looks like he's stuck his head in a Hoover bag. The Ref doesn't have much of a clue himself because he is huffing and puffing trying to keep up with play. Fat bastard.

I lost my voice singing maybe thirty minutes into the game. All that was coming out was feeble croaks. I was fucked to be honest. Mentally fucked...not by this game but from last week at Wembley. I haven't read a thing about the game at all. Not a photograph or a piece of video about that day has entered my conciousness. I don't want to know. I am having a moment of dissonance about it where it floats to the top of my mind before I shove it away. I am trying to forget...and I wasn't even playing. This isn't a semi final hangover, this is a deep malaise. If it's bad for me, how is it for them? The players?

Yes, we do have a squad of highly paid athletes, totally professional footballers but they are human too. They hurt and they get affected. It's not something you can pick up on those funky electronic performance monitors they have to play in during every game. How do you quantify sadness and anger? That feeling of losing a big game? Then having to drag yourself to Shampton to play against a team fighting for their very livelihoods? Our ideas are stronger than theirs...but not today. Our team are pissing off to Marbella for a week of training in the sun. This is a good thing. A time to heal and to repair minds for the final few games. A time to chat and discuss as a group where everything went wrong and how to put it right. In the sun too. That disc in the sky that everyone feels better once they have been bathed in beautiful sunlight.

It's obvious the team are affected by that Wembley loss. You can tell. Even the stoical dickhead that I am was forced to sit at the top of the garden again with my hands holding me head as I looked at my shoes and my bent leg. Supporting your team is very hard. My shoulders ache with that poisonous weight in my head from that day. There hasn't been a single hour when my mind hasn't wandered to that last ten minutes in Wembley wondering and thinking.

They were affected of course, our players. They will continue to be affected by it for a long time. That is the way us human beings are. Our whole world is built on expectations built up from a substrate or foundation of experience...we expected to win at Wembley because of the dream and the ideas, we expected to win this one too, a bounce back instead of capitualtion.

> *"Oh for fucks sake don't put that useless bastard on!"*
> **A woman behind me as Helder Costa comes on for the final minutes of the game.**

I was aggravated by this point as I heard more verbals, more bullshit flowing down the steps of the stand and echoing from the roof. Today I am more relaxed about it, more chilled out. I am standing between Steve Plant and a dude with tattoos on his tattoes who you can tell has been to Wolves games since he was a kid and has probably been to most of them. He doesn't cuss the team, he is cajoling them and kicking every ball himself. I bathe in his Wolvesness.

People are coming to our games to be 'entertained' and this ain't entertaining watching your team get a dicking. Entertainment is a broad term that means different things to different people of course. I don't feel entertained at any match I go to. I am always exhausted by the end of it, emotionally exhausted. These people need their blood and flesh of the great pantomime. They are no different from the people of Rome attending games where they watch people being hacked to death or eaten by wild beasts. It gives them a platform where they can look at their own lives and know 'we are not them'. If they don't get that blood they become rabid and dark. Hence the castigation of players which over the last few weeks has become less whispered and more shouted loudly as these people find our silence giving them room for their own negativity. If you have wrapped your God forsaken lives in that negativity then there is no better place than the anonimity of a souless football stadium to slather your bile against him or him, or them...people that will and cannot ever fight back.

These kinds of people find that denigrating one of our players while they are trying to do their job a rewarding thing. The denigration fosters a feeling that they are above these multi million pound players. That THEY are the Gaffers mate, they are the ones that order how things should be.

When nobody tells them to shut up their voices become louder and now they are the star performer, they are the actor on the great stage. They hog the platform for twats with more bile and invective, more negativity, more dull bullshit. Years ago in the Southbank someone would have nutted them. Now of course spunking 50 squid on a Wolves shirt gives you a free pass to spout bollocks from your seat? Well done, all I do is observe and record. Their lives have nothing to do with me.

There is a reason I don't say anything negative about my team when I am in a ground or even at home. That reason isn't anything to do with my love for Wolves or even the way I tend to suck Nunos dong at every opportunity. It's because I am not aware of all the facts to base any kind of opinion on. I see Ruben Neves a little out of position for a few moments, I see Willy Boly outsmarted a few times, I see a big hole being opened up down our left wing side as Jonny goes for a jog up the pitch to try and bang a few crosses in. I see many things that my poor shitty brain in it's weird way sees is a bit wrong and a bit different to normal but I keep my mouth shut and only open it to croak a song out or offer support. Because that's my job, I'm a supporter not a fan. I'm not a customer at the great Cathedral of Molineux, I'm a fervent believer. I'm a happy clapper not through ignorance but through love.

Also what do I know? When I used to teach Science I had a scrap pice of copper pipe about 10cm long in new money. I used to get the class to measure it with their rulers and write the length down. Be exact as you can I used to say. Be as precise as you can. Write it down and don't show anyone else. I would ask each pupil to bring me their answer on a slip of paper and write the results down on the whiteboard at the front of the class. Most of the time there would be a discrepancy in the results. 9.7cm to probably 10.5 cm. There was a lesson in that for them. The results were often different because well...I'm not going to bore you with a lesson on the scientific method but each pupil had a different 'reality' than the others. Maybe a mangled ruler, maybe they were tired and couldn't concentrate, maybe they had forgotten their glasses and couldn't see the finer MM divisions.

We see the same thing during football matches of course. We all see something different during the match because our realities are all different. I see Jonny leaving a big gap, others see Jonny joining an attack. Both are right in any world but our objective realities are different. It's all relative, all of it.

Jimmy volleys the ball into the stratosphere. Now it's that high it ceases to have anything to do with the game and is in essence a low flying satellite.

At the post match press conference Nuno storms out. He is annoyed and angry. Crap questions, valueless questions from fuckwits who should know better. These people are highly paid Journalists and I hear better debate from my crackhead mates down the canal. Nuno would want to be forensically working out what just happened while the match and the events were still fresh in his mind. While the crime scene was still 'hot'. Instead he has to sit through this bullshit part of the pantomime. The whys and wherefores, the details about it, the nitty gritty. Instead he has to entertain the gaggle of fuckwits with Ipads. Listening to the questions made me as angry as Nuno to be honest. Nuno Espirito Santo has become the conduit for me to understand my club better, he has opened up a way for me to communicate my feelings about what is happening and why it is happening.. He is as precious to me as the team and I have nailed my colours firmly to his mast.

There is a trust I have in him. I am not a member of the herd. I am not one of the pack, and I am not part of your 'Wolves family' either. Nuno to me is the eye of the pyramid. Through him I understand things better, through him I suppose, the ghosts of the past years rolling around the bottom of the leagues have been exorcised.

Conor Coady is defending half the pitch because everyone else are throwing attacking shapes all over the pitch. He is shouting orders but can't do everything. I know Wembley hurt him, I know this game will too. I could weep for him. Watford seem to score everytime they attack. Even I can't see where they are coming from.

If anyone realises the grand Fosun schemes and plans it is him...and if anybody understands 'journalism' it is him too. He is in effect being asked to validate meaningless questions with meaningless answers and join this whole circle jerk of information sharing with if not delight at least some jollity. Mourinho at Chelsea and Yanited was a Master of this. A shrug of the shoulders and some Latinesque mumbling would suffice for these reptiles in the sports press. It validated what they thought of Mourinho and the meaningless shrugging of Joses tiny shoulders would in essence validate their own meaningless questions.

Nuno doesn't do that shit. He is not a Teacher of Journalists. It is not his job to define and focus these stupid questions into some viable and constructive answer. He doesn't fucking care about their jobs, or them getting a few words, quotes in their columns. Nuno is too honest to partake in this airy nonsense with Journalists who's circulatory system is choked with the fat of too many Premier League press room buffets and Greggs sausage rolls.

Nunos display of impatience filled me with confidence. If I was him I would have quite happily picked up a chair and started to whack Journalists around the head until I could grab a big camera tripod and start some serious head mashing fun. I would have locked the door so nobody could get out. Just me and them, before someone forced the door open and I would be triumphant amidst a tangle of bodies in tight trousers, Berghaus coats and desperation.

There will be a point where Nuno refuses to perfrom at these events. I can see it coming. We may see that smiling public relations, affable, happy, nurturing Nuno replaced by the firey Portuguese Philosopher and Warrior. Perhaps Nuno just tuts like I do when I hear our fans cussing the team. But I would put money on Portuguese swear words echoing off the walls of the corridor back to the dressing room. I would say this to Nuno...fuck going to the dressing room, lets get some axes and go back to the Presser.

Over this Summer we will be breaking our transfer record a few times.

There will be players coming in to replace those we have grown to love and to worship. The names going will surprise us. It is how things should be done. With these additions of skillsets we will also see new players from the academy promoted. These are the players I want to see next year. They will be hungry and they will be ready. Nuno has had them for a couple of years now and they will know exactly what to do and how Nuno wants them to play. We will learn and we will be stronger.

A Shampton fan in the stand to our right catches a ball launched into the crowd. He catches it and puts the ball under his seat. He wont throw it back. The rest of the Shampton fans cheer. Fucking Spatulas and Gollums. They keep singing their one song..."When the Saints go marching in". They sing it loudly at times and others it sinks to a meaningless drone of dirge like proportions and then rises to a volume and musicality of a Mongolian Goat skull funeral cello. Dear God get me out of this place.

I came out of the Shampton Stadium among the Gollums of that place quite happy simply because I am looking to the future. Wolves is the only thing I allow myself to think about in terms of futures and 'what will become', it's just the way I am. I am starting to slowly understand what the fuck is happening. It is scary and it is exciting. It is something (I will admit) I was struggling with up until these few defeats. So it took two defeats to work it all out? Well. Nearly.

We can look at these macro level events like these defeats and extrapolate that with measuring a cooper pipe in a classroom. We can debate everything about the defeats and the team as much as we like but everyone will come to a different conclusion. But the pipe will remain at roughly, give or take a few fractions of a mm, 10cm long. I think the whole Wolves project is still on course. Fosun are an arm of the greatest Corporatocracy ever seen in the world. They are driven to succeed through four thousand years of Confucianistic thought and through a hundred years of redefining what China is all about. Success, triumphs, madness and kudos, business, money, profits. I am here to write about it of course, it is going to be crazy as fuck I assure you. Things are going to start to go fucking insane.

"Have you seen the season ticket prices for this year? It's a fucking disgrace and blah blah blah"

Yes. I have seen them. Yes I can't afford it. No of course I will be getting another season ticket. I couldnt afford a season ticket when I first bought one and they were about a hundred squids. Nothings changed, I still can't afford it, but I'm still getting one. I will pay by direct debit this year and spread the love out. Make some cutbacks. Force a little austerity into the whole purchase. I don't know whether or not to.....bloody hell that Raul volley just went past the window of my house. It actually travelled 500 mile up the motorway, fair play Raul...where was I ? Oh yeah, cutbacks. I will cancel my subscription to PornHub straight away of course or I can start giving out hand jobs to people underneath Perry Hall bridge at £5 a pop.

Harry two Jags from the Wergs road will absorb it ok. In fact he will love the price rise as it will give him something else to moan about as he bores the shit out of his 'friends' over Lunch at the Patshull Park Hotal after a few holes of Golf.

Liam from the Lunt will do a load of extra weekends over the Summer in the warehouse where he works picking up plumbing paraphanalia for minimum wage. He wears a High-Vis vest with 'Nuno' written on the back which annoys the fuck out of the shithouse Sandwell Town fans who he works with and the one Villa fan who nobody talks to because, 'He's a bit weird ay he?'. He is always arguing with the Sandwell lot. Always. It's not football banter with those lot. Every word is vehement and hateful. The Nigerians and Kurds who also work there laugh when the banter starts but they don't understand and will never understand either. The Polish understand as hate is layered through them regardless. Yes, Liam will renew again.

Soon this whole period (Wembley excluded) will be a memory. The 'Pilchard' in batter that was described as 'Fish and Chips' in the Shampton city center bar we went in beforehand will also be a bad memory, The bloke who owned the place didn't like us being in there you could tell. The Doorman/Security body didn't look overjoyed to see us in there either. He was shitting himself. We did look rather scowled and not happy even if we were. Knocker said that someone we know looks like a Mr Man and I had tears rolling down my face in laughter. That night I am outside the Tesco One Stop buying some Rizla and I see Gaz Mastic with his dog.

"Lost day we?", Gaz remarked.

"Ar", I reply.

"Ay it", Gaz says.

"Ar", I reply.

Chapter 39

Where we play Brighton and Hove Albion and try to have sex with shop Mannequins

Awake. With a face like a rustly haircut, like a strange car parked on your drive, like a porridge deodorant...in the distance Nuno is looking at bottles of an Amber liquid being unloaded from the Brighton Team bus...

I must have thought about a thousand angles and dangles about what to say about that Brighton match and a bit about Shampton too. It keeps needling away in my head at inopportune times, usually in Tesco One Stop while I'm looking at things to aid my munchies. Thing is dear readers, I was looking at Pringles (which were on offer...quid). I like the odd Pringle while I am watching Nuno press conferences on Youtube. I often spit mouthfuls out in laughter when Nuno gives the assembled Press Lizards the hairy eyeball. I wouldn't like to fight Nuno.

I have watched several TV programmes about Bear Grillies or whatever his name is. Public schoolboy, ex Special Forces and now TV personality and all round bloke who like to jump out of things. Our Bear is a typical Rupert really, he has a voice like a bloke that thinks he's being blokey with other blokes but you can tell it's all bollocks and hot air. Short phrases that are very terse with this passive aggressive grin he puts on. I have no real opinion of what he is but I can draw a paralell with him and the Brighton match I just watched.

Anyway, there's Mr Grillies in some desert environment. He's 'surviving' the environment using his survival skills he learned over the years. It's brilliant, as he is kind of teaching us how to survive the Sahara desert or someother hot shit hole. I will never go there Bear, I will never visit it, neither will 99% of the doughnuts watching your programme. He is drinking his own urine which is a past time that most of his cohorts he hangs around with do at Rugby events and the such like. It's not a bad or scary thing for him to do this. At one point I am sure he is actually gargling his own urine in a joy that seemed out of place.

Brighton and Hove Albion at Molineux. They kind of played and rumbled us on our visit down there a few weeks into our promotional season. I was that angry after that match it took me a few days to calm down. I kept kicking things around. Their fans are weird as fuck. Imagine a walking coat, windproof, water proof, snag proof. Loads of pockets, brown cord trousers, comfy walking boots, a pub lunch...their Instagram accounts are probably full of their shit battyman dogs that they shout at a lot while they are carousing around some Godforsaken green area around their ends. They remind me of a country pub lunch...and posh dogging where they hand out wet wipes.

But Bear Grillies...sorry. I decided to bike up to the Molineux as I had some cash flow problems. I was down to my last five squids. I had to get fit too. My leg felt better since the sun had decided to come out. I cycle up past Wednesfield, past Bentley Bridge shopping center and all the homeless dudes in crap tents. Past the back of Heath Town and up to Broad street Basin, up the ring road and hey presto. It was quicker than the bus. There are a few people I pass in the new Wolves shirt using the cut as a pleasant amble up to the Palace of Gold. I thought about the Shampton game a lot. I was still pissed off so I speede up sometimes in a bit of angry pedalling. Those Shampton Gollum songs haunt me a little.

Of course Southampton caught us at a bad time. This Wolf-Machine is a very delicate instrument, kind of like a Ferrari. Temperamental at times, you need to give it full attention to get the bloody thing running. It has personalities and athletic madness that staggers me. But when it does run (most of the time) it is heaven. A true beautiful experience. So I can say maybe we have had a few misfires over the last week. That's cool, it happens. Ferrari engines eh?

I have reread my last ramblings over the past week (Viva Nuno) trying to see any dichotomy between the two seasons. I read about the trips to Burton and Barnsley and then see the actual distance we have come in such a short time. We are still a year ahead of schedule. I bet there's a FOSUN wallchart somewhere on their Moonbase where Guan Ganglechange and Laurie Gargleypimple or whatever his name is whizz around in their electric control chairs barking orders. I am glad they are in charge because I slam on my brakes and fly over the handlebars eating a bit of gravel and getting my trim in a state. A Heron had flown out of a bush right in front of me. I sit there for a while thinking.

I get to Molineux and chain the bike to the railings in front of the Feathers pub. It's now some university building. Whoever give the go ahead for that sale needs their balls chopping off. The Feathers was a great little pub. There are a lot of new Wolves shirts around the stadium. It's sunny for a change, warm too. It's the end of the season coming when football is no more. I moan about the season around December and January standing outside cold grounds on colder days and I wish the whole sorry fucking football season was over and now...I'm a bit sad. No more footy in a few weeks. No more singing and dancing, no more beautiful football from my team. I feel like a scruffy bastard. Primark shorts (£4), Horaces worn out trainers, an old/new North face t-shirt. I have a flourescent running jacket on that has a few hot rock burns down the front. I've got my lucky monkey pants on that I wore for Wembley and I suspect the power of themn has run out in the same vein the print of that happy little monkey has faded and become like an old photograph of your Grand Parents when they got married just after the war. I could fall in the Southbank I'm that close to it from the Feathers. I look like a right scruffy bastard.

One good thing about being scruffy in these cheap shorts is that I have brown legs from a bit of sun we have received. My broken one looks like an old forgotten Christmas Twiglet. It's bent like fuck, it has dents in it's dents. But looking around at the legs on view today as our beloved fellow fans unleash their legs to the glare of the spring sunshine...I ay done too bad. There are some blue veined nightmare legs about. White as a KKK convention to be honest. Some of these legs look like weird French cheeses. But fucking hell, it's football day thank the Lord.

So...Brighton. What have you got for us today? What delights of the art of football are you going to show us and the world. What stories are you going to tell today? I know they are languishing at the bottom of the Premier League. Things are not going well. There is a smell of relegation about them. A stink of defeat. Just the ticket for us. After the Shampton game we will wax sweet lyrical football. Throw amazing Euro shapes straight from the biggest and best teams. We will be amazed for sure. Nuno will have these wonder players at Wolves synched up tight.

Chris Hughton is the Brighton Coach and I tend not to mind him too much. It must be a nightmare living down there on the South Coast with the pub lunchers and the people who don't understand football. There is no Philosopher about Chris Hughton. Not for the lack of intelligence, I just think he has had to fight so many battles during his Managerial groove that he is tired and worn. He looks it anyway. But it's not all Warnockian blood and bollocks with him at all. He doesn't moan too much and his invective, especially post match, are measured and pessimistic most of the time. It's his club this Brighton thing and he is doing the survival bop for sure. I bet he is forensically totting up the points he can gain and lose. Going through the permutations. I know Hughtons head looks like an Ostriches but this is a lad that's not burying his head in the sand.

But...my friends. Hughton is about to guzzle a two litre bottle of Hughtonade. Yes, a bottle of his own piss. He will gargle it with distaste but hey, anything to survive eh Chris? Anything to keep your head in the Premier League trough. I know this because the game is ten minutes old and I am more interested in the insect that is crawling around in the hair of the dude stood in front of me. Jota insect this one, curling in and out of the strands of hair, darting here and there. They have eleven defensive players and practically every Wolves player in their half trying to find a way through. I can tell it's not going to happen today. We of course are trying our hardest. Raul running the offense, Jota trying to snuggle the ball through to him. Doherty having a pop too. There are that many players in the pitch at the Northbank end I feel that the Southbank has risen a few feet like this is a crazy See-Saw and we are screaming in pain at the football Brighton are offering us. This is Stoic football at it's best. No masterpiece, no ethereal delights, no glee and no joy scrabbling fingernails on a crumbling cliff edge football.

Brightons goalie looks really little. I remark this to Horace who flings back his own bars. 'He looks like Toulouse Lautrec' Horace says.

I am crying, that's too good. I want my coat and my comfy walking shoes, I'm going to live on an island by myself in the pacific and carve a giant statue of Lautrec out of the Volcano. Too good. Horace says he basically writes my books. I would agree. I am going to put his name on the front of this one.

I feel sorry for our little Wolf Diogo Jota. Everytime he makes a run into space he has three or four lunkheads from Brighton flapping around like a drunken Bricklayer in front of him. They are doing everything they can to disrupt the flow of football. It is Barnsley again but we are here in the Premier League. There should be a law against it...but then again if we were in that position the madness to survive and that clawing for points would be the same and we would have laughed at the opposition attempting to play football. The Brighton Gollums are indeed gleeful singing that droning ambivalent 'Aaaaalbion' dirge now and again. I passed a few on the way up the ringroad as they got off their Coach at Faulkland street coach park. They looked like shit Gargolyles unless it was a special Coach they were on. You know...the Club coaches. Brightons two centre backs are labouring shuffling stacks of turds. You could stick them in any of the teams languishing at the bottom of the division. It's just zombie ball from them, clawing fingers between the gaps, mumbling refrains and commands, they look like they have been caught in the act.

Neil Warnock at Cardiff would love these pair of doughnuts with their 50p feet and gnarly scarred foreheads, elbows that look like a Victorian nose. They can jump very high as they must have been doing this since they were kids trying to nut the lightbulbs in the living room because the 50p for the telly had run out and Mom was out drunk and nobody knew how long the corned beef had been in the fridge.

We haven't got a clue about this type of madness to be honest. We play football...look I'm not droning on about how fucking great this Wolves team is but we play football, and it is beautiful football. But we just don't recognise the ugly and the home made tactics any more. We have been spoiled. This Brighton display is the Philosophy of the street corner, the alley and the dark places we never go. We stick the 500th ball into the Brighton box for a Wolves head but the gnarled forehead of the Brighton defence are there...every time.

Diogo has a go of course but it's like trying to thread a fresh turd through a keyhole. It's a messy business and Hughton is staring arms crossed at the gamne, he is motionless, I think he is passed being embarassed by it. But here...a scintillating chance for Diogo from a through ball by Moutinho. A chance? The ball hits a veritable Taggiatelli of band knock kneed Brightonian centre backs and the ball is cleared. Boom. Hundred yards up the pitch.

Raul of course is having the same grief. I'm still watching the insect in the dude in fronts hair. It's a bloody horrible thing, his insect not his trim. Raul is a lovely man, a beautiful man but there is an undercurrent of rage in him I would like to see come out. He has scored a lot of goals for us, he is a member of our team, he sits at the knee of Nuno and listens but at the moment he is too nice, too refined. I want to see him start chewing heads off and getting the rage in him. It's bubbling away, simmering maybe, this mad rage he has. It's like a pot of Chilli on the stove bubbling, smelling gorgeous. Raul has had a few shin rakes and a few elbows. All low level Brighton noise but you can tell he's getting pissed off.

Nuno is stalking the byline and the techinical area. Arms crossed like Hughton. Nuno is licking his moustache again like he does when he's thinking deeply. He of course is seeing things that we cannot. Nuno can rip apart a games defining points in some six hour lecture I can see him doing it. He will have overhead transparencies and maybe a funky powerpoint display. But now he stalks and he is saying 'fuck this Brighton' in his head.

He knows.

Nuno has that Olympian look a visage that is almost stone like until some incident unleashes a windmilling of arms, a look to God above, he grabs one of the Coaching team and vehemently unleashes some of his madness at them while the minion nods and tries to get away from the power of the Nuno madness. He looks at Hughton who having been named the epiutome of the Stoic mirrors Nuno. Arms crossed, brow furrowed and yes, if this is what it takes to survive then pass me that piss, I don't even care if it's mine.

The Brighton Gollums in the lower Steve Bull stand are ecstatic. They love it simply because they do not understand football like we understand it. They do not understand Nunoism either. All they understand is piss gargling. Their solemn exhortations of 'Albion' are starting to remind me of that other vapid and funeral like crowd atmosphere at Shampton.

Moutinho and Neves are struggling not with the moment but with this liturgy of Houghtons tactics. Brighton are a Mannequin of footballing intent. The dummy looks great in the shop window in Dudley street. Skimpy top, little tight bum, long legs. Her hand is turned up like she's asking for your bank card again. She promises so much doesn't she? But smash that TopShop window and steal her away, run towards the Molineux with her under your arm, get her home. Put some Barry White on the stereo. His deep tones throb across the living room from the stereogram. Quickly spill half a pack of Pringles onto a clean plate, maybe some of that Tesco One Stop crisp dip with the four flavours that all taste the same. You hum along to Fat Baz while you flick some filth off the table with a non too clean tea towel. You stick a couple of ready meals in the microwave...Thai Chicken curry. You spoil these bitches mate. You watch them revolve around for a bit before you go back into the living room where Barry is gargling his fat arse through another one of his hits...they all sound the same to me.

You throw a couple of Naan breads on the radiator to warm up a bit while the microwave revolves in the sick yellow light.You can hear crunching...perhaps she is starting on the Pringles...sour cream cheese and onion of course, what else? But the crunching is probably broken glass outside and you notice she hasn't eaten a single Pringle and the dip now has a strange skin on it from the heat from the central heating. Her eyes stare at the photo of Steve Bull ion the wall. Those sightless eyes...

You sidle up to her and notice her wig has slipped a bit so you gaffa tape it back on. You touch her face delicately and loving as Baz grumbles to some sort of azimuth of groaning soul delight. You kiss her and leave a bit of Pringle on her hard lip....that crunching is still going on and you notice the Dog has half chewed her fibreglass foot off. Fucking hell. The dog runs off with it...but the heat of the moment, shades of Eddie Hitlewrs lost finger, the love....No matter about her delicate foot. You find an old sock to put over the frayed and battered fibreglass of her stump. You stick an investigative hand up her top and whisper old Wolves songs to her. Those rock hard titties are well.....rock hard to be honest. It's like groping a traffic bollard or trying to order a pint in the Hogshead pub on a match day.

Your fingers caress and rock hard thigh. Light touches mate, take it easy. You are an artist. You stick a tongue in her ear and nearly choke on a mouthful of shop dust. As you splutter you probe the Delta of Venus trying to get in her knickers. We expect paradise but receive nothing. The delta is as dry as Colin Wankers eyes and as empty as Stuart Atwells 'Congratulations on your new job' card from his old workmates.

Yes my beautiful midfield, you will have no joy today with this mannequin of football on offer from Brighton. It's a fibreglass fanny of a game. This game has now become passionless and less art more work. More drudgery. But we never stop trying. We are the Tortoise trying to shag an old German helmet but thank the Lord we never stop trying, never stop punishing those Brightonian gollums with our madness of football. Even Willy Boly is having a go at dribbling the ball into some space to see if his own enormous Barry White football grooves can crack open half a foot to get a chance in or to let Raul in for a dig. But this rock hard flesh will not yield.

The Brighton Gollums cheer their world cup cheers at the final whistle. I laugh out loud. It is 0-0 and they have a point at least to try and save them. They have guzzled much piss while we have probebd those rock hard thighs for life and found only a harsh unloved desert of Brightons tactics.

The cost for Brighton and Hove Albion? They have gargled and won a point for sure but they leave their self respect in the dust. There is no dream that Chris Hughton can weave the team and the fans into. This is survival economics a kind of footballing austerity. It is a place where

Hughton has basically stated that there is no love/ideas or battle in this Brighton team. They have embraced the gargling for sure and they will not survive next year in the Premier League if they do scrabble to safety.

Horace said that this Brighton team are a Championship side. I would agree with that. If they do tumble out of this Premier League trough and back down a division I will not shed a tear of course. No Sir, good fucking riddance. They have nearly spoiled this beautiful day for me.

I go back to my bike outside the Feathers. I am surprised nobody has tried to nick it to be honest, it all looks in one piece any way. Even the tires are still up. Amazing. I notice, talking to a few people on the way out that generally those Wolves fans who I saw when we were back in the doldrums and the old 4th division are happy, smiling. But those freshies who have just come back are not and there is some moaning. We were playing fucking Burton a few years ago. Jesusn Christ the Wolf-Machine is starting to rumble for sure. I see it and I believe we have not seen the best of this side yet.

But Nuno. What does he think? Who knows? We will only get to understand what this man is about through his ideas and his aspirations for his team, through the choices on the team sheet. Without words from Nuno there is an expanse, a gap where we fill in the blanks with what we think he should do or say. Without words there is a void which we may formulate a Nuno and what we think he should be. We have to fill that void with words in order to formulate some identity to Nuno and to be honest I think we don't have to that with our team. They speak for themselves and they speak with the language of Nuno.

Now of course at Wolves, the football is the personality and the identity. The football we play explains everything about what Nuno is and who he is. We don't need the gossip and the bullshit of personalities in the holistic sense. The Premier League is an abstract place at the best of times what with social media and the razzamatazz of glory and sorrow even.

No now the team and all it's dynamics are also ours as well. Nuno has woven us both together because he knows within his heart the team are nothing without us. He has seen this through the grounds we have travelled to this season. He has observed the caverns of the modern Premier League ground. He has seen and he has understood. I think Nuno has given the Wolves back to us and at the moment it is the only hypothesis I have as to why Nuno is loved by us.

I have been given a nod by several people that we are looking at a few players of a quality that leaves my mouth dryer than Ghandis flip flop or a mouthful of Mo Salads hair. These players are of a quality and pedigree that I would easily wax as outstanding. These players are at big clubs either as part of the team or on the fringes as was Jota and Neves, Boly, Otto, Vinagre. As I cycle back home my mind is all on this trying to extrapolate rumour with how these players would perform in a team that has already put most of the top six Premier League sides to the knife. We are talking about Europe....well others are. We get 7th and we play in the Europa League next season but I am not thinking of that and I am not singing about it either. What will come will come. Where we will be in a few years time who knows. Where we go is an ethereal mad dream...but where we have come from is a concrete reality. We were playing Championship football last year and now this...

Later that night I am reading old newspaper reports about a Mannequin hand that has been found in a Wednesfield canal...

Chapter 40

Where we play the Arse at Molineux and see the fat bloke from Arsenal TV

We have to walk past and around most of the ground today trying to source a Watford ticket for Knocka. I rarely put my head around these places like the Billy Wright stand and the Northbank. It's usually me falling into the Southbank with the rest of the inebriated and half stoned lunatics I call my bredrins. It's a night match but it's not a cold night match. Nobody is in thick coats any more. The hustle and bustle around here is mad. We go to see Steve Green in the WV1 bar in the North Bank. There are many people in there and it always makes me feel claustrophobic but Steve is a beautiful man and he makes me smile a lot with his madness. He does a deal with a spare ticket and everything is done. I can get out of here and we amble around the corner of the Steve Bull and one of us sees that fat dude from Arsenela TV. It's a fan driven TV channel on youtube and people watch it a lot apparently. I don't I'm afraid. I don't care about other fans waxing about their teams. These fan things are quite dynamic and creative and I support it toatlly. It's great. I remember Gary Fucking Newbon mate. Ask ya Dad about him.

Talking, writing, making projects about your team is brilliant. It beats clocking into work in Bilston every morning and before you get all irate I know some people love their jobs and it defines what they are but no job has ever defined what I was about. So yes, write your columns and do your podcasts. Fair play to ya.

Young Liam with us is all about memetic football grooves and who's doing what in football. He loves football of all kinds. He has that open mind about other fans I think. It's a young man thing. Thirty years ago I would have been throwing bottles at Arsenal telly bloke but now I just scowl and get angsty because I'm surrounded by Arsenal fans all Arsenal doing Arsenal things like simply walking on my turf, my area and my ends. Molineux is mine mate and I don't like you standing there looking at it with your Arsenal head. But Liam wanted a photo with him and he obliged as he was polite which was positive....for him. But his countenance looked sad like he knew something bad was going to happen and for once it wasn't me that was going to happen to him.

Gulag Emorycloth or whatever his name is, is the Arsenal Manager. He's not daft old Emory Cloth. He like his teams to play nice football that often is played in the opposition half unlike Chris fucking Hughtons. So it should be a surprisingly excellent game. Because there is nothing the Wolves like more than a team who likes to play football. Because we often play football better and that ends up with us winning, which is great all round really. There are players in his team I have never heard of and some that I have heard of but forgotten and there are some I have heard of but don't like so I'm not writing their names down in my book.

I've watched some Arsenal matches on the Intertube and can honestly say they look like they know what they are doing but dont particulary like what they know what they are doing. They will expand their play of course and start to bobble and steeze their way around the pitch like sexy expensive footballers they are. There will be moments when we are under the cosh a bit. Where our Championship stains haven't quite come out in the wash. I wouldn't call it 'inexperience' but would call it 'momentary lapses in concentration. Metal Azol I think his name is becomes quite prevalent in this early Arsenal bobbling of the ball. Metal Azol looks like the claymation character Morph and this amuses me especially when he comes up the Southbank end and I can watch him close up. Metal Ozil would look great with a hunchback, he would make tens of pounds doing pantomimes and weird porn films.

There are a few nightmare expensive trims in this Arsenal side. 'Yeah man everybody who is anybody is having this trim, Raheem Starving was in here the other week and that Harry Kane bloke...yeah I just shave half your fucking hair off and gel the rest to your head, it's slick yeah, powy trim bruv'. You know the kind. So while they are knocking the ball around us for a bit I am laughing at their trims most of the time. I look around at Horace and he is biting his nails again. Every game for him is a Cup Final and here I am laughing at haircuts. I am so shit, I don't deserve this.

Hang on, Arsenal break and one of their players Harvey Micturation or something has blasted at shot at Rui Patricio our goalie which flew well over the bar. Arsenal are throwing some slick shapes here for sure but man, I've watched Wolves for years and this Wolves side are like Arsenal. They don't care. Not in the same thing as Arsenal of course. Arsenal look half baked to me. Looks great on the packet photo but out of the packet they look a bit pale and cack. Wolves don't care about a different thing. How the opposition play of course. We aren't bothered. This is where Compton looms large at Molineux. Hard work, shape of the team, how they play and fucking hard work preparing for a game. This is the eye of the pyramid, the actual game. We watch and we are amazed but those hours at Compton produce this display. We are having a nibble back now and Arsenal don't look comfortable at all to be honest.

Jonny is now getting his head into all sorts of mischief. I don't know how the fuck he gets into a position but one minute he's defending a move on the edge of our box and the next he's on some diagonal madness from midfield getting his shoulders into some of their defensive midfield, jinking a run here and there. It's mad, I love Jonny Otto, he would set fire to you in a country lane and laugh as he drove off. Madman, I love him.

Matt Doherty is slinky and he slinks a pass to Moutinho who puts a curler in towards goal. It's a chance for sure. When Matt Doherty plays well the Wolves play well. It flies wide and Moutinho holds his face and then he's good to go again. Jay Leno the Arsenal goalie throws himself theatrically towards the ball even though everybody and Bills Mom knows the ball is going wide. It will make a great photograph Jay for when you are sorting through your memorabilia in a few years time sussing out what to put on Ebay.

Wolves are getting that hypnotic rythym going again. The Wolf Metronome that goes, pass, pass, pass, pass, pass, and pass. We watch mesemerised. It's like a snake gently waving it's head from side to side at it's prey slowly becoming more and more influenced by that movement. The Arsenal rythym has now changed on about the 20th minute of the game onwards. They are becoming hypnotised by our moving. Now their rythym has gone, destroyed by ours. We threaten and we cajole their players into the odd mistake, the odd late foot, the errant tackle, the grab of a shirt. Their moaning at the Referee is becoming more vocal. They are in the early stages of capitulation and they don't even know it yet. But I do. I've seen it.

Jonny is there again. He is through nearly, I crane my neck to see one of the Arse players chop him down. Jonny crashes to the floor the Ref blows. I laugh. This is my team. They are going in for the kill. I see Neves take the ball and I laugh again. One nil this is going to be. Jay Leno the Arsenal goalie is too far too his left, he is leaving a gaping hole in the goalmouth. If I see it then Ruben Neves sees it. Man, I could drive my van into that hole. I start flicking the Vs at the Arsenal support even before Ruben Neves licks the ball into said gaping hole and I get a phone in the back of the head and a knee in the chin during the limbs phase of the whole celebration. We are going to put these sorry bastards to the sword today. We love it when teams play football. Brilliant. Arsenal fans are glum and sad. They need to win this game to get close and to stay in those Champions League slots. We will go 7th and Europa league. But I am not thinking about that at all. I just watch the Wolves one game at a time. One foot in front of the other and with enough steps you get where you want to be. I mean who, on a walking holiday talks about how many miles they have left? Is that a good analogy? I don't know but it's the only one I have. I don't think about European football, that's the truth. Not yet.

Ryan Bennett is throwing some lovely shapes too. Interplay. The names I could just type and it would be like a DNA helix of Wolverhampton Wanderers evolution under Nuno. Ryan Bennett was pilloried at Norwich by the Carrot Gollums but here? Under Nuno? What a master stroke his enrollment was. He keeps throwing these mad long balls into Arsenals box to try and get the ball on Bolys head. Boly will flick on for someone else or have a pop himself. But Benno is another shape elsewhere when he passes a slick crossfield ball to someone I cant see because my spectacles are shit. It was as good as anything Jason Beckham or whatever his name is has done. 45 yards if it was a centimeter mate. Boink it went right to...ok I think it was Dohertys foot...coukd have been Jota, anyway. Bloody hell Ryan Bennett, fair play.

Someone remarks that Jota will be a 100 million pound player soon. I can't argue with that. But the sum is so abstract and insane I can't handle thoughts that expensive. So I think about Ryan Bennett some more. I like him, he's great to watch. I love watching our defence as much as our attack. Most the time they just pluck a ball off an Arsenal foot with barely an effort. I wonder if that's a thing at Compton, nicking the ball with no fuss. There is physicality to be sure but most of the time our defence is bloody refined and gorgeous.

But hey! Here's Jonny Otto the Liberian Strangler being beautiful with

Moutinho as we inch closer and closer to the Arsenal box. It's a sight this is. Jonny is mad, I love him. He dinks, shifts, passes and at one point both his legs are in the air and he knocks a cross into the box. Matt Doherty back to keeper lets the ball gently nods over the grasping ineffectual attempts of Jay Leno to get his hands on it. 2-0 mate. Crowd goes wild. I'm watching Rui start to run about and jump in joy. I wish the players would run down the pitch and give him some goal loves and Coady head slaps just to see if Ruis hair actually moves.

I mean come on. We are 2-0 up in the first half against top six side Arsenal. We don't look in any stress at all. I am remembering when their 'Youth team' came to Molineux a few years ago and gave us a humerous arse dicking. Dear Lord above. I don't hate Arsenal for that but fuck them. I hope they are enjoying this reverse role, as to be sure it's happening and these North London knobheads are having a right nibble at each other on the pitch. That's good. When they start shouting at each other it's a positive sign.

This makes me watch Wolves a little closer. We don't seem to talk much at all. It's an observation for sure but watch them. It looks like they have been that well drilled that they know intimately, each of our players, exactly what role they are playing and how to play it. We don't need to shout at player B or C to cover so and so because it's already being done. That's when you see players point to certain areas that need cover. They point to direct a team mate but the team mate is already on his way there. It's a done thing. So there is much pointing but no shouting. Apart from

Conor Coady of course who needs to let everything out because that's just how beautiful he plays.

But look here's Jota. He is throwing his own shapes again and he is powering his way towards goal. Who started the move? I'm not sure, was it an Arsenal mistake? The ball chunders and Jota thunders and I am celebrating Jota run by shouting and screaming like we have scored. Which Jota does after avoiding that Micturation blokes challenge and whacking the ball into the net under the pantomime attempted save from Jay Leno. 3-0 mate. Laughing? Of course I'm laughing. I grab strangers and friends to celebrate. I am laughing and shouting because that is what we do. They have come to Molineux these world class fottballers to give us joy and happiness. They have delivered us so many emotions that today is just icing on the cake. A delicious array of football the like we haven't seen since the world was pretty much black and white.

You know the score from now on of course. Adama comes on and Cavaleiro too. Immensely funny when you would expect Nuno to put on some defensive minded players to allay an Arsenal fightback. But no, Nuno puts on a couple of attacking lunatics like Cav and Adama. Brilliant tactic if not from a footballing perspective from a philosophical one. It was a statement wasn't it? I am happy, it was crazy and it was fulfilling. These days in the sun are always the best for me. On the way back to the car I am behind an Arsenal fan whos GPS on his phone isn't working properly. They don't know their way to the station. They are lost. A bit like their team.

Chapter 41
It's revenge time at Watford and the slap happy Elton Gollums have lost the war of ideas

We have 'legends' at this club at the moment. Those legends are Moutinho and Raul Jimenez. They are Doherty and Coady, Bennett and Jonny Otto, they are Jota and Ruben Neves. We can mention the rest of the team too. We are the outsiders, always have been. We have always been the ant in the afterbirth when it comes to anything Wolverhampton is famous for. This is the way it has always been. Of course to fans from outside the City, who live and work somewhere else this fly in the ointment, mentality we have will always be the driving force for anything we do. That is why I suspect that Nuno has done so well so far because he is like us. Fair enough he comes from a beautiful paradise of an island in the sun. But his inner self I think tends to reflect the 'Wulvo' mentality better than anybody that has anything to do with Wolverhampton Wanderers.

But we have a 'chasing pack' thing going on now. We want 7th place and some Euro footy thanks very much. I think everybody else does too including the Elton Gollums although if they win...hold on. Hahahahahahahahaha...against Manchester City they will get a Europa League place? Something like that. I'm not well versed in how you get into Europe when my head is still watching Burton play against us...and us losing. But yeah Nuno...

He strikes a chord with us. We are (I suppose) all outlaws and superheroes, legends and superlegends in our own heads. But we also know our fragility and our weaknesses, in fact they probably drive us more than we admit. Watford FC are reflective of our fragility as a team. When we seemed to crumble in the face of that Watford performance at Wembley I had long deep thoughts to myself over why it had happened even if it wasn't important and the time I sensed a problem within the team. I didn't know what that problem was.

Wembley was a good day out but I didn't look forward to it and in no way was I confident on winning it either. Something was not right about getting Watford in the draw. We are too similar at times, in our tactics and in our play. I could see that there was an element of Warnockism blended into that Nuno like attacking front three of the Watford team. There was a madness there I didn't understand at all. Still don't. Why are the Watford team playing with such desire and skill. Why do they bother? It's Watford.

I am bitter about the whole day but bitter not for me but for all those Wolves fans having a day out at Wembley. Now I want some revenge and that's all I'm thinking about sitting on the train to Euston on the way to Watford. There are few other fans on here as we are on a late train. The carriage is devoid of life really especially as me and Horace are waxing lyrics of violence and death, football and business, art and crafts. Our conversation is sometimes loud and often vulgar (OK only on my part). The occupants slowly start to dribble from the carriage before there is only me and Horace together with some woman who is waxing lies on her all singing and dancing laptop on the seats opposite us. How do I know she was waxing lies? She was too smart. The dress cut just so, the ankle bracelet, the Hooray Harriet pony tail, the fingernails. It all screamed fake. I was quite happy to sink into the vulgar football fan meme. The light in these carriages always seems yellow and it puts a strange tinge on the people in it too.

Yes, I want some revenge thanks. Watford are scrapping points for that 7th place to give them a chance for Euro glory when they don't beat Manchester City in the final of the FA Cup in a couple of weeks.

People want me to go in strong on the visage and appearance of Troy Deeney or Deeley whatever his name is. I'm not of course. It's not about the Andrew Greys of the Watford team now or the rest of the horrible bastards. It's not even about Watford now really if I'm honest. It's just about grinding on through the campaign and getting to the end of it so that there is a pause of sorts. A cease fire for a little while where we can take a stock check or two, maybe a bloody holiday. I just want Watford to be gone out of my face for a bit.

It's not Villa level stuff of course. You have to admire something about the Elton Gollums. They love waving their fucking flags. I bet Elton himself is here on his Throne waving his pale chubby hand at his syncophants, his flesh is the colour of wallpaper paste. His teeth are like bleached whale bones on a deserted Arctic beach. Watford looks pale too as we exit the train station. There doesn't seem like anything to do here. It looks like every town I have visited this season. Same shops, same people, same shit different team. It's all Stone Island and dodgy looks, youth light on their feet and angry about something. I don't want to be angry and inside my head I am in a happy place. I know today we are going to stuff Watford and exit this place to much merriment. The last time I was here was years ago and it doesn't look to have changed much to be honest. There is fighting and there is angst. I laugh. I am technically disabled ya know. The only difference between me and a bloke in a lekky chair scooter is that I don't claim for it. Let people, young people scrap. I'm past that bollocks now. I am a writer you know. I should be jumping around recording all the aggro for posterity but I can't be arsed. I just hope Wolves lads are making a good account of themselves.

I can see Nuno wanting something out of this game. Of course he sees it as 'just another game' but he knows man. He wants this, I bet the team want it too. Wembley was just a taste of what is to come. Nuno has his eyes on the dessert course and Watford of course are the garlic bread of this campaign.

Do I have grievances against Watford? No not really. They turned us over at Molineux for sure and they did a job on us at Wembley too. But apart from that I can't seem to rustle up any real feelings about them. Walking to the ground in the Watford dystopia I'm still feeling the same vacuous void of no-mind a kind of Zen football fan feeling. There are reports of people being jumped by groups of Watford fans, there are Police with their full complement of street dancing armour on. They are not smiling and I wonder to myself how their briefing went this morning. Probably very well in terms of their Commander waxing fat lyrics about potential trouble etc. But on my account I still have that Zen thing going on and to be honest the filters are all up.

Nuno will want something. He again is in the technical area pacing up and down as the teams huddle and have a final chat on the pitch. Coady is yamming about something for sure. The huddle game is won by Watford who continue to chat after we break ours. I wonder what these people say to each other in that huddle thing. Perhaps it's a chat about how Wolves need revenge after Wembley but I doubt it. We don't do emotions any more. Long gone is the time when the only way we could accelerate our ability on the pitch with grand statements and propoganda over revenge and all that bollocks.

Now it is all empirical. We want to do them because they are 'A Side' or the 'opponent' I suppose. Just another stepping stone to bigger prizes we don't want to think about yet, or refuse to think about. That's the zeitgeist I am getting as I say hello to people and Horace is just staring at the opposition fans with that serial killer look that we have dragged into these beautiful times from the late 70's and early 80's. Their fans are a strange bunch, they seem to enjoy being here and getting into the whole Elton Gollum thing. There is even a writ large Elton lyric on the back of one of the stands but I don't know what song it is because I don't listen to the wailing git after I watched The Who's 'Tommy' and the bald headed little prick ruined 'Pinball Wizard' for me.

Raul looks a little angsty though as he warms up a little. My experience of Mexicans is racing downhill skateboards against them and I noticed they tend to go on a slow burn where they let their ability smoulder like a mine fire. Raul looks that way to me, smouldering and glowing. Patricio runs around grabbing at the floor like it's the first day of his community service litter duty. He is a beautiful man, great harsh trim, decent trimmed beard. I see Pereya or whatever his name is, Watford striker. It looks like he has blue hair. It looks like a fucking shark fin on his head. He's a rangey bugger this bloke. I might like him at Wolves but he seems a bit surly and miserable to me. Jota is staring at him for some reason. Wonder what went on there?

Coady is clapping his hands together in the seconds before the whistle to begin. I can hear him up here and I'm stood quite close to two Coppers who keep staring at me. They are fat buggers these old bill. Their stab proofs are that tight they would probably explode if you did try to stab them. Pop, like a novelty birthday balloon you find tangled in hedgerows down the cut.

The whistle goes and we are off. Watford begin by doing what they always tend to do. They attack. They are at home. Roy Deeley or whatever his name is has been suspended for this game after elbowing some other doughnut in the chin during a match. Watford Gollums say it was not on purpose. I watch the video on YouLube and yeah, he duffed him for sure. Always happens when a player is losing his shine and his pace like Roy has. Will they miss him? I'm not sure, he is certainly the Watford lunatic, the loose cannon, the one who makes things happen. He's on the cusp of insanity this Deeley bloke for sure. After football he will have nothing at all. He will probably be arrested in a 50k car in a few years time covered in Cocaine with a rubber doll in the boot of his Audi and the air freshener Alien head swinging to and fro as the Cop asks him if he is ok because he is weeping...what is it with Alien head air fresheners. I hope they Taser Deeley or whatever his name is when they drag him out of his motor.

That Watford groove is the same as ours practically. Full backs push up to support a three pronged attack (I think). All of a sudden they start to attack Jonny Otto on my left and get tangled up in him a few times. Jonny likes to be the Ninja but often a late foot or a hand on the shoulder and a Watford player will collapse in agony as Jonny looks confused about the free kick. Watford are clever, but like I have said before, if you resort to tactics like these early on then it's obvious to me at least that you have kind of lost the plot. This race for 7th place and Euro fun has obviously got in their heads and they don't want to show us what football they have to show us. That's a shame. But it's only five minutes in and I know we are going to win it so I want to go home now.

"Si Senor...give the ball to Raul and he will score"

Raul is doing the Mexican mosh madness whenever he gets the ball. He is everywhere, has been all season. I got into a sweat about the 30 million squid FOSUN shelled out. Like it was my money...I suppose some of it was. But what quality Raul is. The power in him has been slowly growing all season and he looks like he is beginning to understand what the fuck is going on in this League. Watford are all grabby arms when he gets the ball at his feet. They love him too obviously. He lets a ball just glance off the outside of his knee, it's a subtle jink of the ankle and he is off and lays off to Moutinho and Raul has turned and is in space. He bobbles the ball, it's a chance but gone. Watford tend to fly around him when he gets the ball.

Jota too is a handful. His speed after his early season injury has increased, now of course he's a riot...a one man riot of course. When he gets the ball opposition teams tend to freeze a little for one moment, a split second. Jota never takes his eye off the ball as he runs and dribbles the ball waiting for some Wolves player to catch up. Jonny Otto is getting a sort of connection with Jota and Jota is making a connection with Raul who is sort of coming to an agreement of sorts with Doherty so there is a line of four players...Doherty-Raul-Jota-Jonny Otto that fling themselves into the mix. When they do of course shit happens, mad shit. Chances and chaos in the box and I'm jumping up and down every time they do it. That Zen mood is gone and is replaced by madness.

Watford are rumbling though for sure but again the odd elbow and foul are Championship hangovers or something. No need. Both teams are here to play football surely? Their Coach has a bloody tight suit on. You can see the veins on his spindly arms through it. Nuno would do Garcia in a fight for sure. I'm thinking abouit Gaz Mastic while the match goes on it's way. I went to see him this week and his Missus was still there on the settee watching some daytime TV on a million squigsall telly that took up most of the wall in front of her. She never even looks up as I walk in. She has a covering on dust on her and for a moment I'm thinking she hasn't moved from the last time I was here, that might be the same blob of congealed gravy on her top too. I don't want to say much about Gaz in case he hassles me for another four tins of Carling lager for royalties. But Gaz said some funny things about Watford that I can't repeat and I'm giggling to myself as Pereya moans about something Willy Boly has done to him. He keeps pointing at his foot. Fucking Shark fin head.

Three youngbloods in the Watford stand to our left are being ejected from the ground for abusing Wolves fans. I mean what can they say that would annoy us? But the Steward Somalians are adamant they go. There is much abuse from these youngs via the international language of signs that I laugh and I am quite proud of them in a way. At least they feel something about the day even if it is negative. Feeling and emotion in grounds. Remember that? But they are off and out of it. No football for you cheeky scamps but you can sidle into Nandos or whatever and wax ejection lyrics into your phones on your Instagram accounts while you eat shit chicken and wait for the game to finish.

Ben Foster the Albionite is in a flappy mood today. He hates the Wolves you can tell. Ben Foster has a head like a fucking Olmek (Google it now) and has all the physicalitty of one too. He is ponderous getting to lofted balls. Wily Boly is scaring the shit out of him every time Boly runs up the pitch to take part in a corner or a Benno lofted throw in. At the moment I am just sad for Foster. Those stripey bastards down the road have obviously curdled his love for Wolves. Strange that he pissed off from them as soon as he could when the BoingBoings got relelgated. But they still love him, mad times.

Talking about mad I see Mad Terry in front of me as I look around during a break in play. Terry is from Shropshire now after he sold up and left us for greener places. I watched Terry walking across a scrapyard once carrying a whole engine. Strong as an Ox always wears a baseball cap because when he was a youth he got attacked by hammer wielding madmen over something and when it rains the dents on his head fill with water and gives him a headache. Terry has hands like comfy chairs and even his scars have scars. But I don't want to chat to him because he kisses my head and drools on me. His cottage is worth 350K and his outfit probably cost £4. The last time I saw him he was going on about having plastic surgery to his much mangled face. I am always bothered about having plastic surgery. I mean what happens when you die and you are standing in front of God while they fetch your halo and wings and God says..."Whoah hang about, this isnt Mikey Metalenvelope this is an imposter, I don't recognise him!" and before you know it I'm being escorted out by Somalian Steward Angels flicking the V's at Saint Peter as I'm bundled past.

Bloody hell. Conor Coady just flung himself in the way of a Watford poke of the ball. Rui dives at nothing it was that pokey. Nuno is going mental in the technical area then he turns around in a huff and moans at one of the Coaching staff who don't say a dicky bird. Nuno doesn't want anybody to chat with when he is ranting he just needs a receptacle to pour his annoyance at. Coady is also shouting again, he claps his hands three times to instill some discipline in the players in front of him but maybe they know they shouldn't have let Watford in that close but it's hard as fuck. The Elton Gollums move the ball like Arsenal did for sure. They are a good side, but that madness they have actually does them harm because the chance is lost through some terrible forward movement. Every Watford Gollum was three yards in front of the play. Everybody was early. Nobody there. It's all flaling arms and sharkfin heads and that little blonde haired horrible Elton Gollum is everywhere...but I know he will have the second half off. He's a bit of an idle git for me. Doherty is trying to drag the shape of them wider I think. Two of the Watford front three like to narrow up in front of goal and Matt keeps pushing the little Hitler Youth kid wide. Matt Doherty is great. In fact I want to vote for player of the season too.

John Bray from the BBC is standing in the row behind me so I am behaving. No key bumps after Wembley. No alcohol. No throwing things at the Watford Gollums. I turn around and say hello in my 'posh voice'. The last time I met him during Steve Plants book launch John remarked he had been playing Golf at Patshull Park and I told him the story of when we used to poach Trout from there and cook them up in the woods with a 'Camping Gaz' stove. I don't think he was impressed so I didn't tell him about wandering the rows of Strawberries at Bradshaws fruit farm eating our body weight in Strawberries and paying for 50p worth back at the shop. I'm such a twat. I will always be a twat. You can't take me anywhere. I remember seeing Ali Roberts at Bradshaws once and he told us to fuck off.

But Coady is alive to it thank fuck. He reminds me of Stearman the way he flings himself around blocking stuff. Amazing. I voted Ryan Bennett for player of the season. Don't moan to me about it. I know everybody has hard ons for our sexy players and that's the thing. But Bennett for me has done strides during this season. Learned stuff, took defeats or cock ups on the chin. Carried on and learned. That Chelsea tackle, I still haven't got over his goal at Bristol City. Yes, he got my vote. I'm not telling anybody though because they will start telling me who they voted for and why and it's boring. Every player should get a trophy for me. They have been brilliant this season all of them. I suppose it's the way that one player has to be singled out but nah mate. Get them all a big trophy and they can share it all year one month each or something. On the sideboard with the rest of the tat they will sell when money gets tight and memories go a little faded. Nuno is going apeshit again at something and is having a go at the assistant Referee now who slowly side steps away from him keeping his eyes on the pitch.

Jimenez goes down under a well leggy challenge just on the edge of the box and it's time for Moutinho to step up. The ground shakes a bit as Boly runs up to get his nut on the cross. Moutinho wangs in a bloody right curler of a thing but Boly escapes the contact and it's cleared to Neves...'Shoooooooooooot' we all shout again and Neves obliges but Flappy Foster is there with some kind of save and the chance is gone. I wouldn't mind seeing Coady go up for a couple of these chances you know. I bet he would plant his nut on a few.

But hang on...Jota is alive again. He's busting these Gollum avoiding shapes again. By God how I love watching him move forward. It's scary at times. You never know what is going to happen. It's mental. Dendoncker collects the ball and puts it right on Rauls foot and he pokes towards goal but it's cleared off the line I think. I was in celebration mode for a second. Bloody hell that was close. Back up the field and Andre Gray has a poke at goal. Again...it's that little sod Hughes of the Eltons. Sharkfin head throws a cross in and Hughes doughnuts the ball over the bar from close in. I laugh. It's not going to be their day is it? Hughes doesn't look happy and Sharkfin head pulls a face and waves his hand dismissevely at him. I laugh again and go to abuse him with some choice invective then remember John Bray is behind me so shut up and put on my concentrated writer face.

But it happens. It's bongo ball time in the Eltons box as the ball flies around like a pinball. Jota collects in space and plonks a lovely ball on Rauls beautiful head and bonk. It's in. Crowd goes wild. I forget John Bray is behind me and wax a few unheard filthy abuse at the Watford fans and try to see the celebrations but there are arms and legs everywhere here and I'm trying to hold my glasses aloft for safety. They are so battered it's stupid. There is more glue holding them together than cheap plastic. 0-1 and it's on mate. I can tell the Elton Gollums don't like it as a few are being chucked out. I laugh some more.

There is no way I'm heading to the concourse for refreshments. It's that small it's like a cattle car down there and I don't think they are flogging alcohol either which makes it pointless. So I stay upstairs and cobble together some conversational lyrics for the previous display. We look OK to be honest. I'm not concerned by anything, this is a football match with two teams going at it. If we win we get a four point gap on the Eltons and that chance we aren't talking about of the Europa league. Everybody in the stand is talking about it but I keep my mouth shut. I can't afford the bus fare to town to watch the match. I laugh. I will get there somehow, get a loan or something, sell some stuff, go out and flog some of these books in the shopping trolley I 'borrowed' from Poundland and walk around the Molineux in the summer hawking them like a Gyppo selling pegs. Europe eh?

Ryan Bennett obviously felt the scores needed evening up and delightfully weighted a lovely ball into his own box for an Elton to smack in the equaliser. Fucking hell, that didn't last long. Bennett of course has rarely put a foot wrong all season for me so I'm going to give him this one. Dropping clangers is part and parcel of the game. You can't concentrate for 90 minutes of football this fast paces, you just can't do it, it's inhuman. Are we not entwined with frailties as human beings. Our own cock ups are done in front of few people of course but Ryans is on worldwide telly. But I say this Ryan Bennett. 'Dow worry ahk'. Simple. Forge on for a winner, shit happens, forget it for now and leave it until you're sitting in the garden in the summer staring at the distant horizon. Until then mate...it's still football time. It was that sod Gray that scored too. He loves sticking them past the Wolves that lad. Former Academy lad too, do we annoy them that much when we tell them to go that all their careers are based on busting a few goals past us? I dunno.

Jose Holyballs or something has just elbowed Jota in the face. They like doing that these Eltons for sure. Don't they know who Jota is? Diogo couldn't give a shit how many times you elbow him. He doesn't care, he's not bothered. It hurts and he gets up. He must be made of Titanium this lad. The Referee blows his whistle and Jose HolyBollocks gets a yellow. He should have gone off. Watford are a bit dirty now. They feel the game is slipping away.

We attack and we play. The second half is really just Wolves getting into their stride. I mean we never really change our shape and as I've said before it's relentless for the opposition. Moutinho curls a beauty of a shot in with his Holy Foot of Glory but it's just over or wide, I can't tell from here because I had a doughnut next to me waving his arms...but a couple of minutes later it's all over really.

Neves is being Neves again. He collects the ball in his own half and Watford are semi deep not knowing whether to push out or drop deep. Their line wavers but Ruben Neves through the tangle of Wolves and Watford legs sees a flash of movement. It can only be one thing. The Jota in his natural environment doing one of those slinky runs into space and he runs and he runs as the ball arcs forty yards over every Elton head. Horace counts six Watford players that pass just cut out of the game. Foster the Elton Goalkeeper is flapping before he has to flap. It's a Pre-Flap of course because there is no way he is going to get his hands on a Neves ball, no fucking way because even where I am standing I see the spin Neves has put on it. Kind of a back spin I think. But the ball is now alive with the Holy love of Neves and as much as Ben Foster flaps like one of those flappy pompaloon things outside of Carpet warehouses it's not going to happen mate. His big Olmek head isn't up to this slice of magic, and magic, that's what that pass was. The ignorant and the Heretics will say it was a cross but we know better, we know who Neves is and Jota does too. Becuase Jota stick a leg out and side foots it past Ben Foster who is doing a brilliant impression of batting away a beer garden wasp. Hilarious. 1-2. It's like that at full time which means we have won. I am laughing as I grab onto John Bray behind me for some Mikey Goal love. I am glad to see him laughing too and we are all laughing because we are Wolves and we are living in Nunos dream.

I read later that Ben Foster said the wind blew the ball off course a bit and made him flap....yes Ben, it was the wind of change that was blowing that day.

Outside the stand and in the street the sky is brassy and has that colour London always has in the summer. The air is as still as Ben Foster for that last goal and the Eltons are filing out to go back whereever they come from. Around us there are a few scuffles and choice naughty words but I don't care. I just wanted to get in, get three points, get out. Which means a rambling walk back to the station behind a load of lads from Wolves who really don't care that they are in the middle of a crowd of Eltons. They sing and we laugh. Ryan Leister collars me and bellows in my face 'Revenge' and he is right. Ryan is a beautiful man and this is a beautiful day. Thank you.

We only have Liverpool to play now. Last game of the season and the Scousers have been playing see-saws at the top of the Premier League for a while now. I'm not bothered who gets the title this year, there has only been one winner for me and that's Wolves. We have certainly smashed the doors down in the cosy club and put our dirty boots on the top table. I am much reminded of the scene in the Blues Brothers film with Dan Ackroyd and the late John Belushi. Of course they didn't fit in, their suits were a little smelly, they were a bit smelly too. We tend to eat and talk at the same time.

We have had some great days away but now those days are in the past. It's just History now, faded pages of memories. In the future of course some people will write books about these days just gone and fill in some of the gaps and that's good, that's positive, we love reading about Wolves.

I think we have played most of our games this year, this season, with one foot still in the Championship. We still have the backbone of the team we were promoted with. Matt Doherty was playing league one football not so long ago. We have new members of the team that have dovetailed in beautifully with the rest of the squad. Moutinho is a revelation. His play is sublime and beautiful at times, others he is not afraid of getting his face in opposition players to get the ball back. He is perghaps the best player I have seen in a Wolves shirt. He amazes me. Yes, he deservedly got the 'Player of the season' award this year. Fair play to him.

Raul Jimenez has also shone. His play is outstanding, he will have a great future here if he stays. I hope he does. There is some stability in having a Philosophy to play for. Some meaning, some target apart from points hauls and climbing up the table. Yes we have over achieved and we have stormed the posh restaurant for sure. But those with a keen eye will tell that we have done far more in a short time than any of us felt was possible. This is the dangerous time now, this is when things can get very hairy indeed.

But how can it get weird? This team even if they are taking the piss regulary out of those teams that have been here longer than us is funny. I have laughed much. But then I stop laughing. Zeitgeist. I know I tend to use that word a lot when I write because that's what I tend to do when I look at sport and things connected with it. What is a Zeitgeist? Zeitgeist is translated as "spirit of the age" or "spirit of the times". It refers to an invisible agent or force dominating the characteristics of a given epoch in World history. Well...I guess that our World is pretty much Wolves and I see the the Zeitgeist as being entwined throughout the club over the past two years. But this feeling, this spirit is a very delicate thing. You can tell that Nuno knows this himself. He will not give a moment of thought to whatever success we may have in the future. He doesn't look to it, he doesn't plan any European adventure and I don't even think he planned this return to the Premier League either. Nuno is all about nurturing and building. We are early here at this posh restaurant of course. This should have been our promotion season and instead we are in 7th place in the Premier League after our win yesterday at Fulham. Trust me too I haven't got a Liverpool ticket either so I can't wax about that match. Shit ay I? Horace said he wasn't going because if Manchester City fluff up and the piss drinking Gollums of Brighton and win and Liverpool lift the title in front of him he couldn't hack it. I appreciate that of course. But at the end of the day if they did win the Premier League title they would still be Liverpool. Still be weighted down with their 'history'. Probably still get offended by something. But yeah, Horace would have gone apeshit, maybe apoplectic with rage. Good job he didn't go.

It wouldn't have bothered me much. I would have given the Liverpool team and their supporters absolute pelters of laughter and flicking the V's. That would have been the day out for me, and of course watching our team play it's last game of the season. Reg Marney or something scored their two goals against our none. But the feedback I got off people travelling back was positive and happy. We just need that extra forensic pass or chance. Maybe that smidgeon of extra quality. Nuno and Fosun don't have to buy big in the Summer...but they will. They won't be content mate, not a bit. They want a 'taste'.

I'm cool, I've seen loads of games this season. I have been greedy for the football we play and I have wanted more and more of it. But I knew it was bad for me. I know the zeitgeist is delicate. I don't want to wear that feeling out. I don't want to be greedy. We are delicate as fuck. Fosun our Chinese Overlords have money to spend and people in mind to splurge that cash on. I see this, it's the same policy used by the Manchester Citys and Liverpools and Tottenhams. It looks like it works too as these teams bobble around the posh end of the League. I understand Fosun wanting it. I understand completely. But...the zeitgeist?

I watch and I observe and that is my skillbase. I record also, I write down things I have seen so I can look at them later and come to some sort of hypothesis as to our success. So I don't see this player or that player as having any other role apart from 'being a member of the team'. I watched the players roll into Compton after a hard training session a couple of months ago. Of course as a supporter and a fan I should have been gurning my tits off and trying not to piss myself that I was so close to them, an arms length.

Maybe if Rico the Security dude wasn't so close I could have run up to Nuno and grabbed him, maybe kissed his forehead and waxed a few love bars before Rico threw me out and banned me from ever going to Compton again. But I am an observer first and foremost so I just screwed my excitement up and threw it away for a while and I watched.

This team enjoys playing together. You can see it. The subtle communications between the players as they rolled in sweaty and knackered was an epiphany for me. These players are a T.E.A.M. No doubt my friends, no fucking doubt at all. Never look at the 'Interpersonal communications' but the 'Intrapersonal'. How they walk how they look when they are by themselves carrying a bag of balls or smiling at the Receptionist. They are a team and are as delicate as a rare Amazonian Orchid really. That delicate zeitgeist or spirit is a very precious thing and one that Nuno understands perfectly.

What is Nunoism? It's the protection of Fraternity of the brotherhood these players have at the moment, it's the relationship he has with them and the trust as well. It is delicate and it is rare. We can look to Colin Wanker I suppose for an idea of what that comradeship actually provokes. Cardiff shouldn't have been promoted last season really. They had a bunch of nutters and freaks in their team that would (if they were in another side) would have been anonymous journeymen. The day labourers of football. But Warnock instilled such a madness within the club that yes, they overachieved massively.

Promotion, even taking us to the wire in games we played against them last season...and a few dodgy moments when we played them this season too. That madness Warnock gave his team bonded them in their dysfunctionality. As mad as Warnock is that philosophy permeated the Cardiff team so that every game they played was a battle, a war. He whipped them into a frenzy with his insanity and it got them a season in the Premier League. I intimated that you can't actually keep that level of insanity up and that has been borne out with their relegation yesterday. But fucking hell they had a pop didn't they?

Ethos I suppose as well as Zeitgeist had a part to play this season. Now how do you build on it? What is the future now?

Fosun understand commerce and economy. Their business model is based on investment and a business acumen that is as deep as a bottomless lake. They will want to insert high value players into this team. They will want to take advantage of Wolves success by committing vast sums to a further push up the table, to not only barge into the restaurant but to get the biggest and best table in it. That is I'm afraid to say...short sighted. Now is the time for reflection and analysis...

Fosun should spend this Summer thinking about the metaphysical and spiritual aspects of this seasons success as well as the empirical and the quantitative. Player purchases, those quality players that change games will be at the forefront of the Fosun massives mind. Because that's how the Chinese do business. Investment for them is just another weapon in the armoury and they want good weapons. But Nunoism is different. Nunoism is about a slow patient build up where each variable in the whole Fosun-Wolves experiment is carefully nurtured and protected until it becomes a well oiled part of the whole machine. Nunoism is where the metaphysical dynamics between everybody in the Wolves set up from the Molineux cleaners straight up to the board of Directors is carefully and intelligently cared for. It's really a massive Chess game that Nuno plays and will play in the future.

Nuno already has the fans on his side. He has given us such joy and happiness I can't express it. He has given us hope and a taste of glory. Europe? Well...it will still be there in a few years time, it's not going anywhere for sure. We may even be playing some European footy next season depending on results next week but I don't care to be honest. If Nuno uses the Europa League as a dress rehearsal from the Champions League I will be quite happy. If we get dumped out early on (which I doubt) I will also be quite happy too. Because it's early days my friends, very early. We haven't really been stress tested yet. By stress tested I mean, we haven't had obstacles thrown in our way like other clubs have in terms of petualnt overpaid professionals who can't be arsed to play (Pogba et al), we have had a fairly placid press too, especially the local press. But that can change in a blink. This is the maze we have to find our way through before we drink the ambrosia of nights in European capitals moaning about the price of the hookers and the awful quality of the Cocaine we just purchased from some dodgy as fuck Turkish dude we met in a bar.

Early days my friends, very early but in Nuno we trust. This club isn't really about Fosun-dollar and the glamour of the Premier League. It's about hard work, always hard work, and patience and nurturing. It's about taking things one step at a time and always remembering where we have just come from and where at some point in the far future we may end up again. It's about passion and love but here's a word too, loyalty to the Coach and the team. There are going to be troughs in the future where we think it will all go to bollocks. This is what happens of course, it's the way of the world. But how well prepared are we for these times? It's OK wearing a Raul wrestling mask and gurning your tits off at a game after five pints of weird expensive beer...but what happens when things are a bit shit? Are we strong enough? Are we prepared?

Way back in the past of course when I was watching drops of crimson blood splatter on the art sculpture thing right in front of the University art block these subjects never troubled me. Was it 1978? 1977? I'm not even sure any more. Football isn't what it used to be I know that. Stepping over the odd unconcious body was the norm in those days. But now? Much different my friends. When I was a kid I used to climb over the wall of the Molineux at night and go and sit in the Southbank sharing a cigarette with a mate as we huddled in the dark. There wasn't a match on. We just felt safer in there rather than being on the outside with the mad Rastas with machetes or the Pakistani clans having a battle or three with swords. It was good to avoid the Skinheads too. I had a kicking off a group once where I didn't even touch the floor for a few minutes.

The Molineux was always a safe space for me. A place where you could just sit and have a bit of peace from the madness around at that time. It was crazy and sad in many ways. I still think the same now. I only feel at home when I am stood in the ground somewhere, and I don't really care where either. We used to do funny commentarys that had Derek Dougan or Parkin or Waggy doing mad shapes. In those commentarys we would always win the game. That was the way it was. Football has changed, Molineux is going to have big changes again, the team will go through changes too but I suppose we will always be the same. Us fans carry the club on our shoulders and it is a weight of history and sometimes that weight gets a little heavy and we tend to complain. That's cool, that's positive in a way.

But in the future, regardless of that weight we have to be strong. We have a chance now to concrete our intent firmly on the landscape of world football. This means we have to adapt too, we have to embrace the changes that are to come but we must never forget who we are. We must never forget where we have come from. While we sun ourselves on holiday and do all the summer things we do without football Wolves will be a hive of activity and madness. I salute them. See you next season hopefully. Watch what yam doing and be nice to each other. X.....China? I wonder if Tatter or Hatherton Wolves are doing a Coach?

Thankyous and Fuckyous

I give mighty thanks to Horace. I've never met a bigger Wolves fan than him and that's the truth. This book is also his book. Thanks to his constant urging and consoling this book got written. I mean the twat thinks he writes these things anyway but he's nowhere when I'm trying to type the fucking pages up hahahahaha. I'm not a Writer really, it's all a big con. I don't know what I'm doing at all. Thanks to his driving through the rain and his humour I got through it all. It was like a War. Thank You Horace, you are a fucking diamond and I am proud to call you my Brother. Thank you to Julz too who I daresay cocked the odd eyebrow at mine and Horaces antics.

Thank you Knocker Powell you massive Giraffe legged bastard. He fed me a lot last year when I had nothing but more importantly he listened to me moan constantly when he visited me laid up with my leg in plaster. To Richie Lamine, dude you are massive and a fully fledged lunatic. I am proud to call you my friend. Declan and Tat, two insane people from way back in the day, they make me happy when I see them because they have always been there in the Southbank.

Thank you to Steve Gordos, David Instone and Tim Nash some of the best writers about Wolves the Express and Star has ever had. They are sadly missed.

I would say thank you to Charlie the Bank Robber, Bouncy Dave, Gaz Mastic, Nine Volt Bob, Kate Wright and her beautiful husband Neil. Wayne and Anita Millard who always remind me that Wolves fans are fucking great for the most part and I always laugh when I chat with them. Thank you to Ryan Leister from the Birmingham Mail, he always amazes me with his great fucking teeth and his madness but also with his opinions on football which are forensic sometimes. Thank you to Pat and Ian my Podcast dudes. We had a right laugh doing them, the dog farts and the biscuits, Ian going off on one about Eddie Howe, you are both treasures.

   Big up to Simon Saysyeow for that mad night during Steve Plants book launch, they really shouldn't have let us in to these lovely events. Thanks to Danny Whale and Ryan who sit in my row in the Southbank. They always roll in wrecked to fuck and I don't know anybody with as much passion for life as them pair. Thanks to Steve Plant and Pottsy. You pair make me giggle like fuck sometimes. We have been through some times trying to navigate through Social Media and Steve helped a hell of a lot by being an ear to some of my moaning about it. Thank you to Downer, we shared some painkilling gas last season and you helped me laugh at a very painful time, this season you have done the same and I salute you Brother.

    Thank you to Dickla from Gornal who gave me so much love in the Southbank I wanted to move in with him and make him Bacon Sandwiches on a Sunday.

   Thank you Steve Green a bloke that fucking idle he had wheels fitted to his chair so he can just roll around instead of walking like the rest of us.

Steve you always make me loff, bless your heart and your family. That Nurse still makes me erupt in laughter.

Thanks to 'Colin Wanker' AKA Neil Warnock the Cardiff Coach, your miserable face has inspired me all season to wax lyrics that kind of strayed away from Football all together. You will be sadly missed next season and the Premier League will be a much duller place.

Thank you to Conor Coady who has made me laugh so much with his lyrics of hilarity. I love him to bits...notwithstanding his football which is a perfect example of what Nunoism actually is.

Thank you to all the supporters from other Premier League clubs who we had a laugh with. At least you understand a few points. I hate you all, thank you for being there.

There are probably people I have forgotten and some people I have purposely forgot too but I suppose you all played a part in the crazy times we had.

So yeah. Fuck you the ex Wolverhampton Liberal Democrat Councillor who decided to write a long Amazon review of my first book and did nothing but moan about it. You decrepid little bitter twat. I had a look at your photo Horace sent me and you have the head of a fucking stairlift chair cushion. Your hair looks like Kim Jong Il's Nans, you look like you make little doors for Trees and pretend Elves live in them. Your Dog hates you and tries to run away. You probably drive a Renault. Honestly, your face, it's that fat I could run a Chip shop on the grease your head holds.

Nobody likes you. Horace told me. Fuck you, this book isn't for you, don't buy it.

I was teaching at a Wolvo Secondary School when your political party introduced tuition fees and had to tell my pupils you bastards have saddled them with a lifetime of debt for wanting to better themselves. I hope you are happy with yourself you shithead. I'm an idiot, I tell people that all the time, how the fuck I wrote a book in the first place is beyond me. I was amazed. Instead of giving some positive feedback you just moaned like a fat bloke in a traffic jam. Fuck Horace for 'liking' and finding your Amazon moaning 'Helpful' as well.

Fuck the rest of the West Midland teams. I know some of you are scrapping away in the playoffs to get promotion. If there is a God I hope you all lose. I'd rather have Dirty Leeds up here with us. At least it's a good day out and their fans understand football.

Fuck Watford. Not for spoiling any days by beating us but because their Coaches suit was that tight it gave me a headache...and he had winklepickers on....and your Town center is a shitpit.

Fuck the Copper at Newcastle for the bit of lip he gave me as I was hobbling to the bogs for a slash. I may be a 'wanker' or like he said 'wan'nah'. Your beard was shit and your Missus sends dirty photos to strangers on Facebook. Fuck South Yorkshire Police as well, what a horrible bunch of people. Fuck the Oxfordshire Police...it's all about A Series engines mate.

Fuck Horace for nearly breaking my arm in an armlock, punching me in my wounded Chemo ravaged Liver, pulling my nose that many times it's getting bigger and uglier. He was moaning about not being given 'Carer of the year' when I broke my leg. I reminded him of when he though it was hilarious when he tipped me out of my wheelchair onto the cold wet road of Bright Street in Reans...and he was going to let go of me down a hill...and he combed my hair like an Emo. He's evil mate trust me.

Fuck all those people who have suddenly decided to follow Wolves especially the one in the infamous photo where they are wearing a Manchester United shirt. We know who you all are don't forget. We have never seen you before this season.

Fuck anybody that supports a team not from their Town. It's disgusting and wrong, not what football is about for me. You ought to give your heads a wobble, especially that horrible woman on the train to Old Trafford.

Fuck all those people with anonymous Social Media accounts who feel their bitterness and misery is great to share with others. What was funnier is that I know people at Twitter and within a few hours of you having a pop at me I had photos of where you live and work as well as all your Facebook accounts. Brilliant. I was half tempted to come around and fill you all in oldschool like, but looking at your Holiday photos and families...well, you have enough misery living with your troll like wives and girlfriends without me adding to it....and your kids are ugly...and your Dog hates you.

Fuck Aston Villa again. Fuck North Birmingham too. Fuck all the London teams especially Tottenham.

Printed in Great Britain
by Amazon